By Scott Bevan & Kent Earle

Published by Easton Studio Press

ISBN-10: 0-9743806-9-5
ISBN-13: 978-0974380698

Books are available at special discounts when purchased in bulk for premiums and sales promotions, as well as for fund-raising or educational uses. Special editions or book excerpts can be created to customer specifications. For details and further information, contact:

Special Sales Director
Easton Studio Press
P.O. Box 3131
Westport, CT 06880
(203) 454-4454

www.eastonsp.com

Manufactured in Canada
First Printing: April 2008

10 9 8 7 6 5 4 3 2 1

I am White Ninja
and you
are my
pickle
side kick

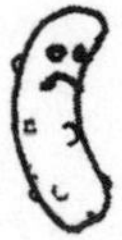

WHITE NINJA

By Scott Bevan & Kent Earle

This book is dedicated to Carlos
Santana and his wicked licks.
It is also dedicated to lanyards.

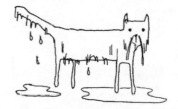

ABOUT THE COMIC...

White Ninja Comics are not for the weak of mind. They are a brilliant satirical commentary on controversial worldly issues.

They can be enjoyed on many levels. Scholars, Philosophers, and the like, who possess the intellect to analyze and break down the comics to their hidden, and often devious, roots, will enjoy White Ninja to its fullest degree. Others, like you and I, however, can still enjoy the comics for their light-hearted surface humor and funny drawings.

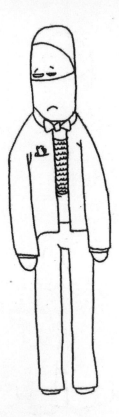

ABOUT THE AUTHORS...

Scott Bevan and Kent Earle are awesome to the max, though Scott is slightly more awesome. For example, once Kent caught the biggest fish ever, so Scott threw it back in the water and tried to stab it with a harpoon. And once, Kent got a huge steak at a restaurant and he couldn't finish it all. Enough said. And another time, for Kent's birthday, Scott bought him a t-shirt with a babe in an animal skin bikini, petting a wolf on a mountain cliff, framed by the yellow moonlight. Anyway, the moral of this story is that Scott and Kent are terrific.

INTRODUCTION TO THE COMIC

Do not read these hilarious comics without first studying this very important introduction!

Unlike most duos in the comic-making business, which have an author and an illustrator, Scott Bevan and Kent Earle take part in both the writing and drawing of White Ninja. Kent draws White Ninja only from the shoulders up, minus the eyes. Scott draws the eyes. He especially enjoys drawing eyes with long eyelashes. After a long day of drawing heads and shoulders and eyes, the two writer/illustrators hit the sack (separate sacks in separate homes) for a good night's sleep whilst the comics are completed throughout the night by elves.

In the morning the two comrades awake to find that the drawings made by the elves, as usual, are visually stunning, but not very funny. Here begins the real work – the work of making a sequence of unrelated images into a coherent, hilarious cartoon masterpiece. They start by erasing any text that the elves have written because it is always about stupid elf stuff. Then, they come up with a scenario that suits the first panel of the comic. For example "White Ninja has poor circulation." Next, they must think like White Ninja himself: "If I was a crime-fighting super-hero, how could I use my poor blood circulation to defeat my enemies?" It should be mentioned, here, that White Ninja's enemies vary from one week to the next – monsters, natural disasters, corrupt business tycoons/raccoons – White Ninja has seen them all. In the case of the poor circulation comic, his enemy might be something more internal, such as cold hands and feet. Possibly cellulite. Within the boundaries of the three/six panel drawings by the elves, White Ninja will invariably solve, destroy, or come to a mutual understanding with the current foe. Voila! No more cellulite.

You are now ready to proceed.

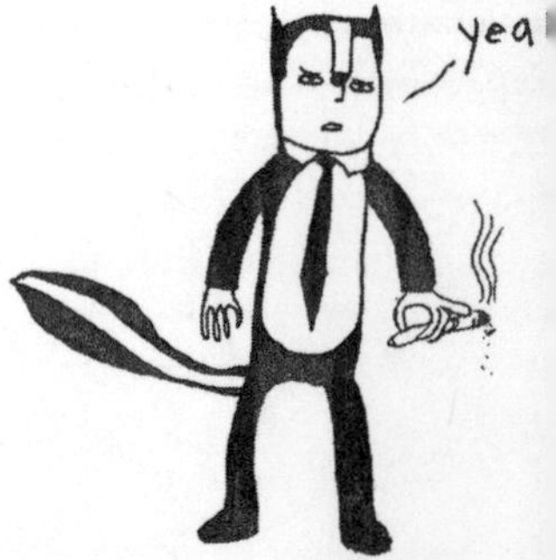
yea

White Ninja and the severed head

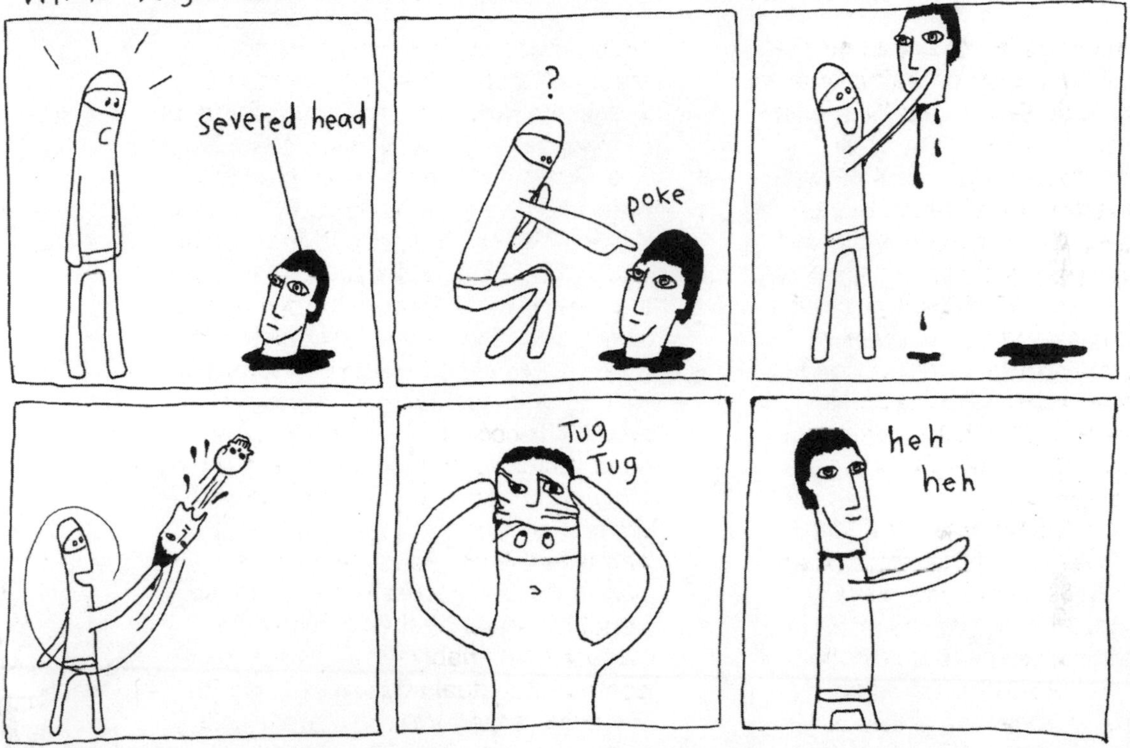
severed head
?
poke
Tug
Tug
heh
heh

White Ninja and the fridge of Blood

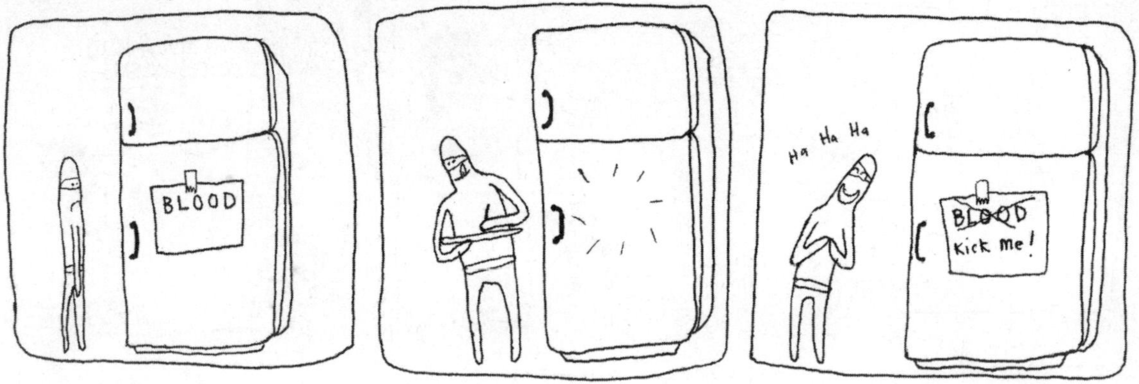
BLOOD
Ha Ha Ha
BLOOD
Kick me!

White ninja in: Catfetish

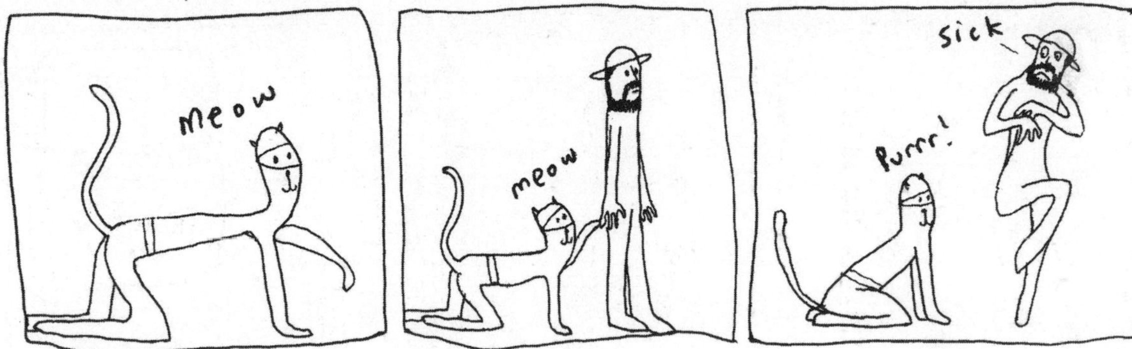
meow
meow
Sick
Purrr!

White Ninja and the little boy that died

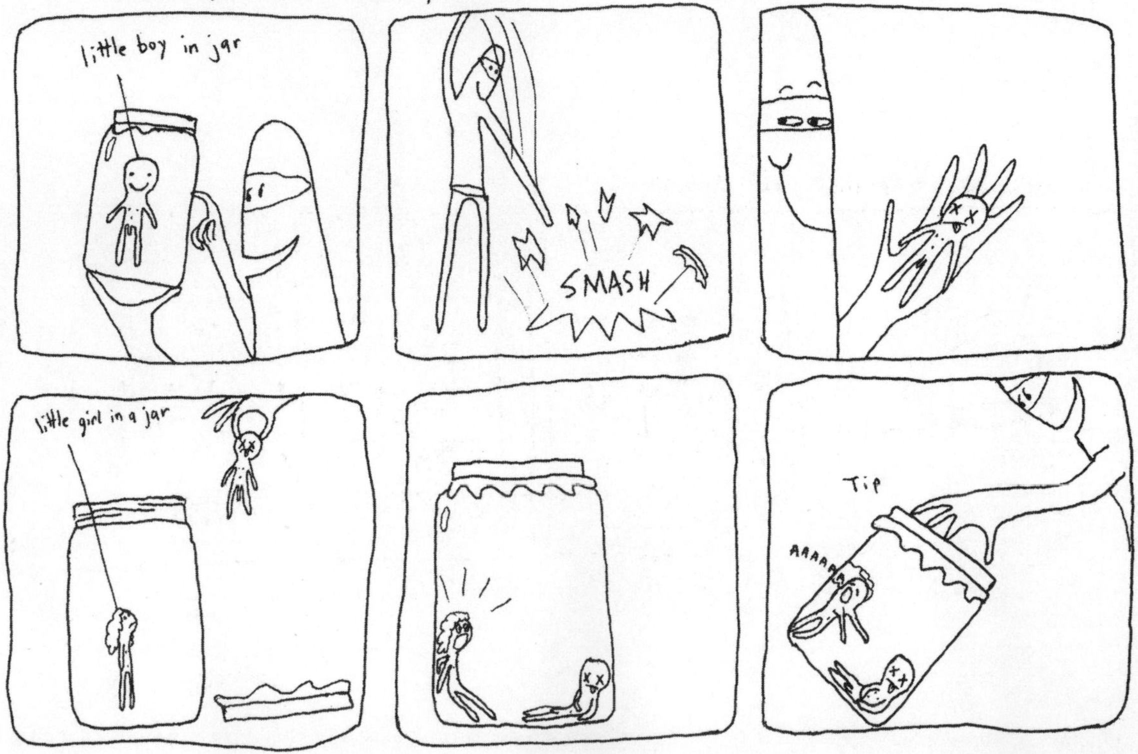

little boy in jar
SMASH
little girl in a jar
Tip
AAAAAAA

White Ninja and the bucket of eyes

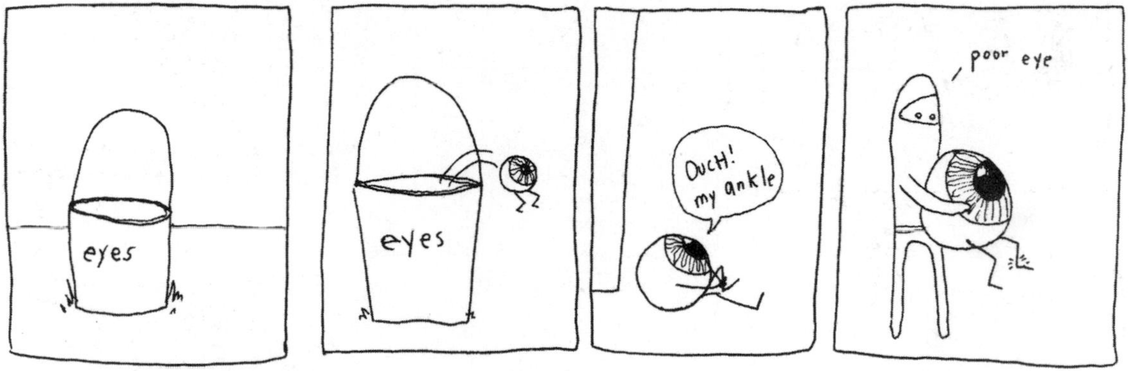
eyes
eyes
OUCH! my ankle
poor eye

White Ninja has a tail ?

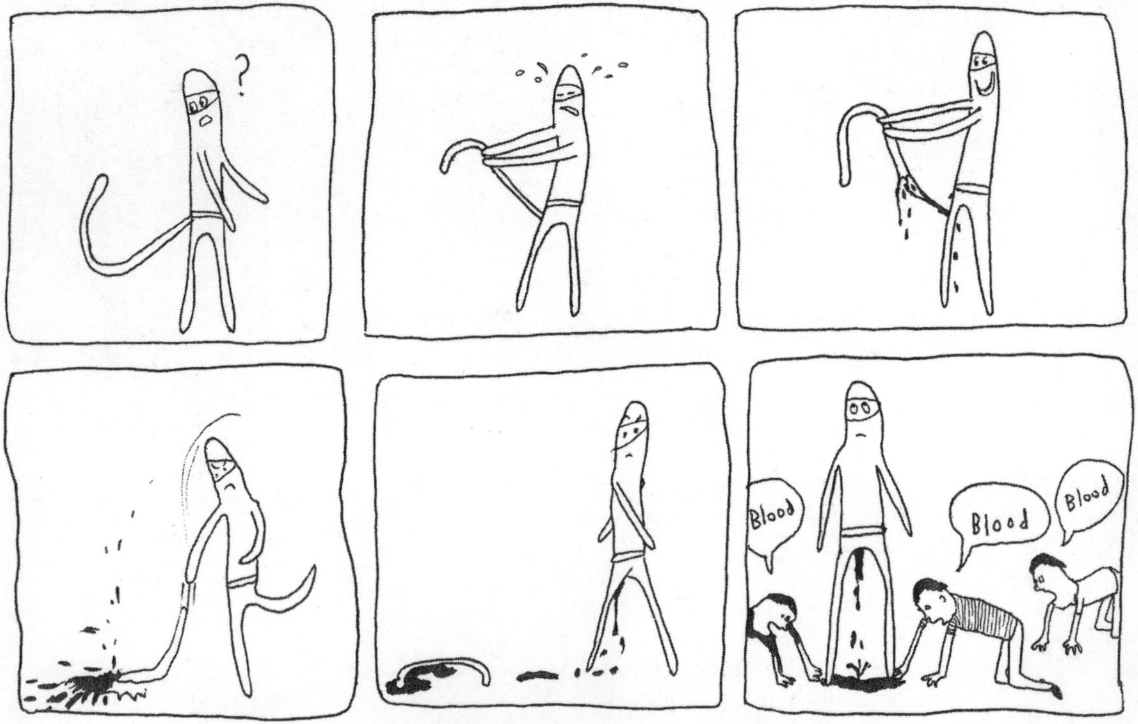

?
Blood
Blood
Blood

White Ninja and the growling pirate

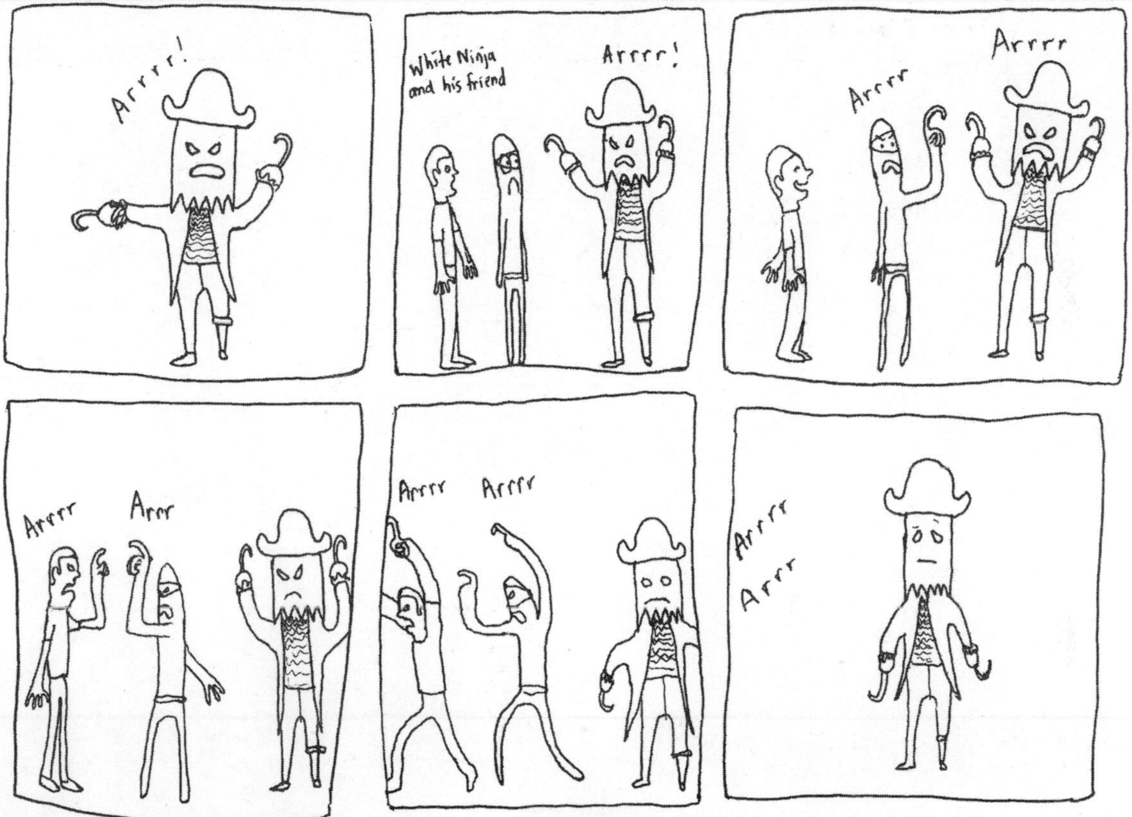
Arrrr!
White Ninja
and his friend
Arrrr!
Arrrr
Arrrr
Arrrr
Arrr
Arrrr
Arrrr
Arrrr
Arrr

White Ninja Training

White Ninja goes ice fishing

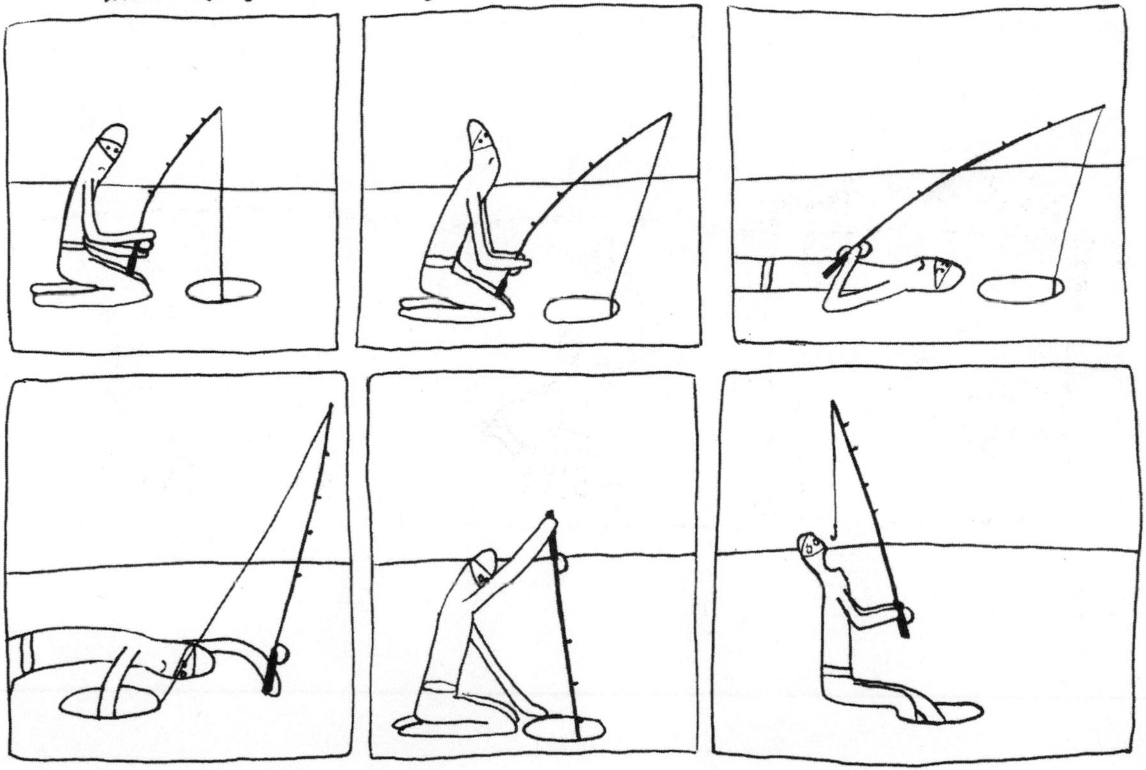

White Ninja is getting Flabby

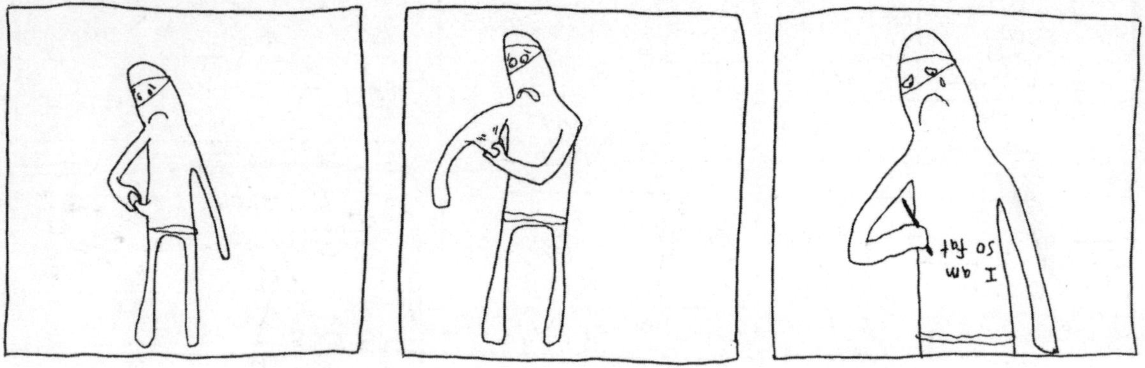
I am so fat

White Ninja to the rescue

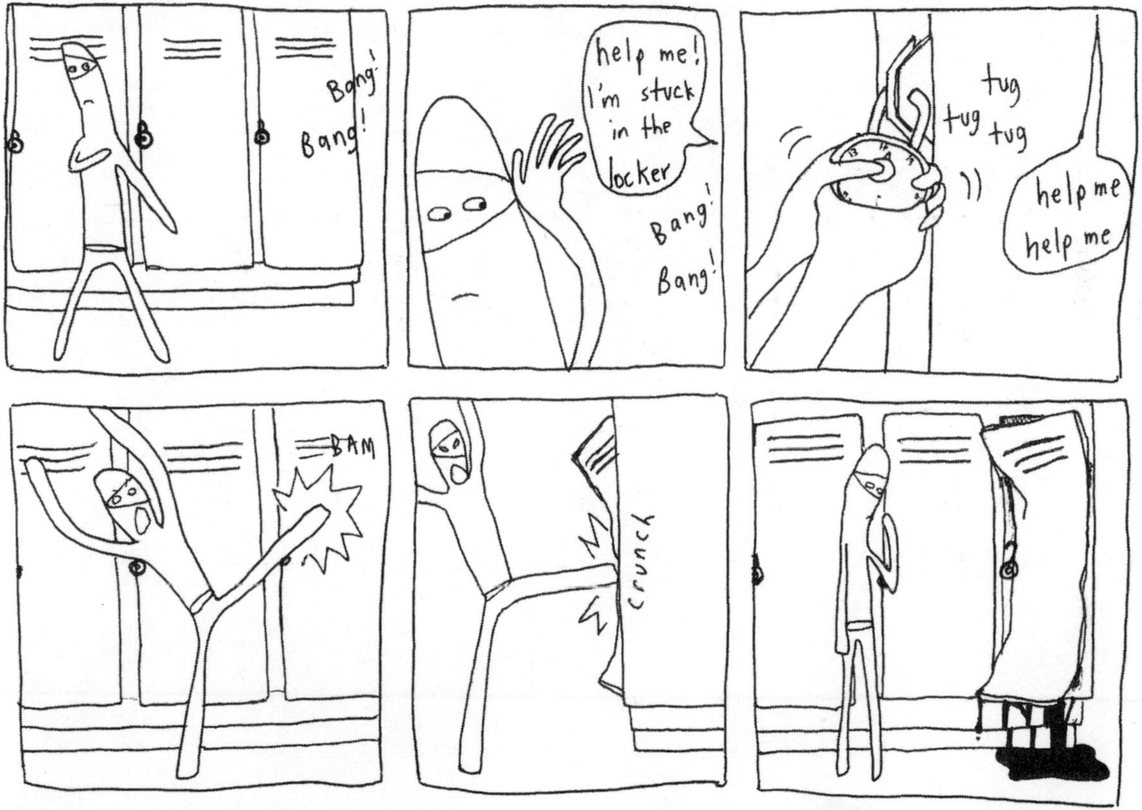
Bang!
Bang!
help me! I'm stuck in the locker
Bang!
Bang!
tug
tug
tug
help me
help me
BAM
crunck

White Ninja in: Bone Bike

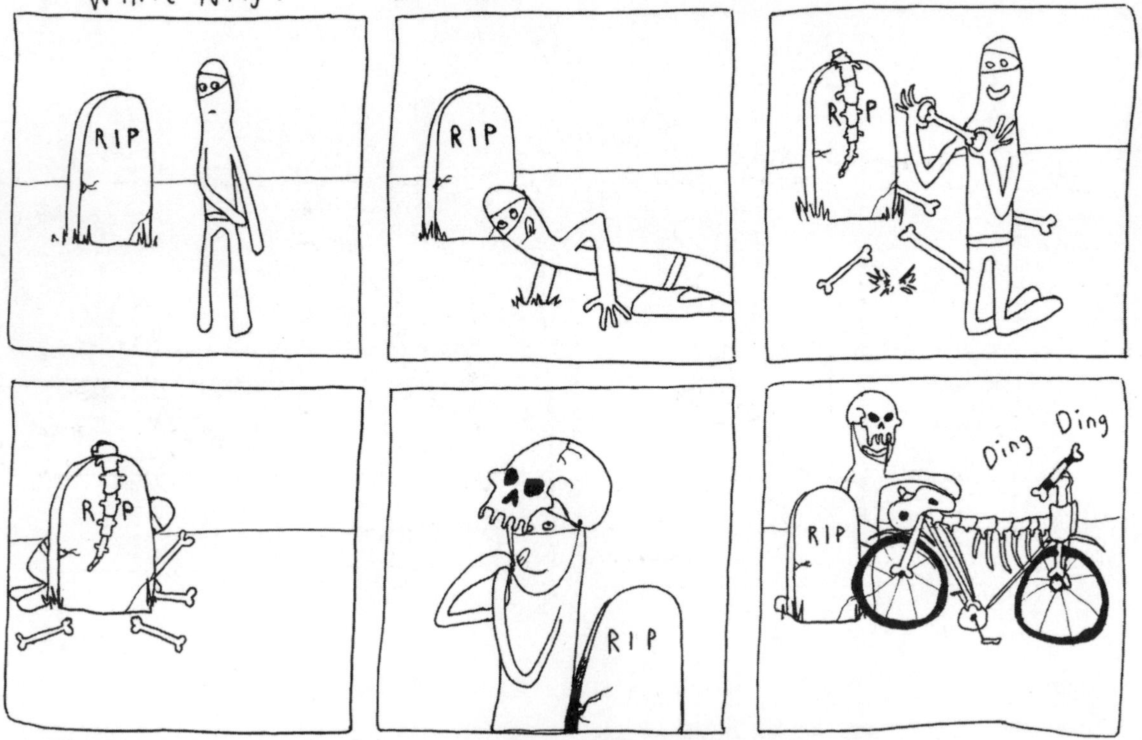

RIP
RIP
RIP
RIP
RIP
RIP
Ding Ding

White Basketball Ninja

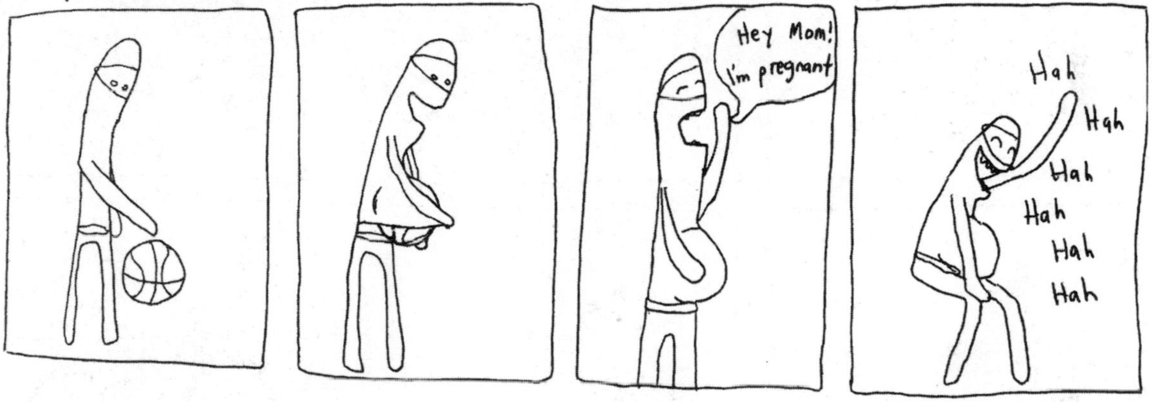
Hey Mom! I'm pregnant
Hah Hah Hah Hah Hah Hah

Is white Ninja a Unicorn?

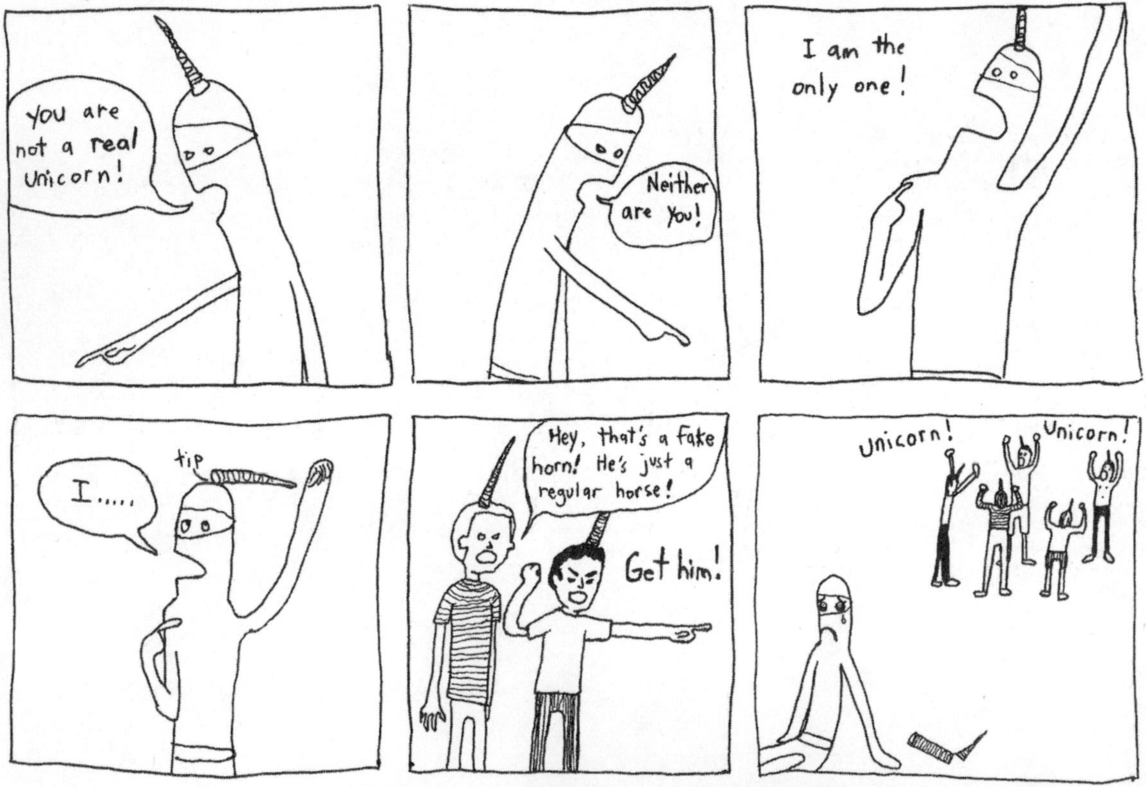
you are not a real Unicorn!
Neither are you!
I am the only one!
tip
I.....
Hey, that's a fake horn! He's just a regular horse!
Get him!
Unicorn!
Unicorn!

White Ninja waits for the bus

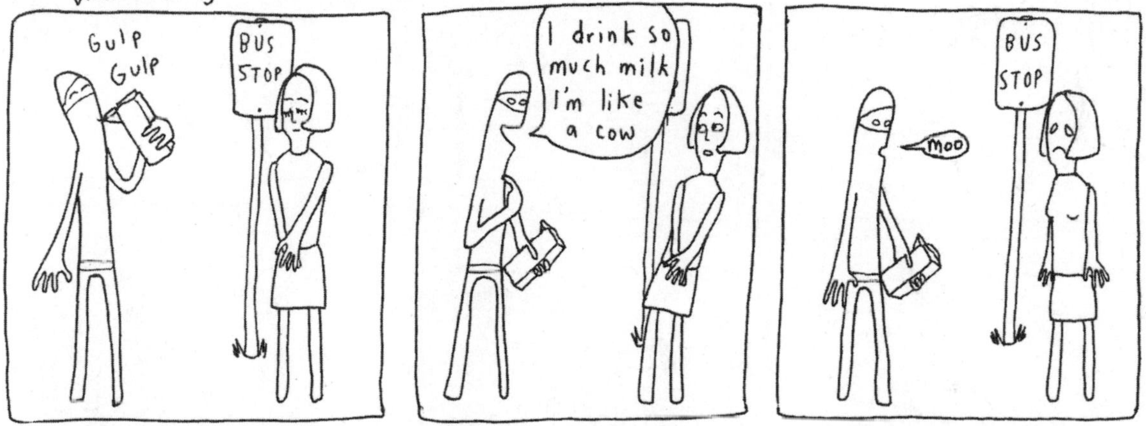
Gulp
Gulp
BUS STOP
I drink so much milk I'm like a cow
BUS STOP
MOO

White Ninja's sick friend

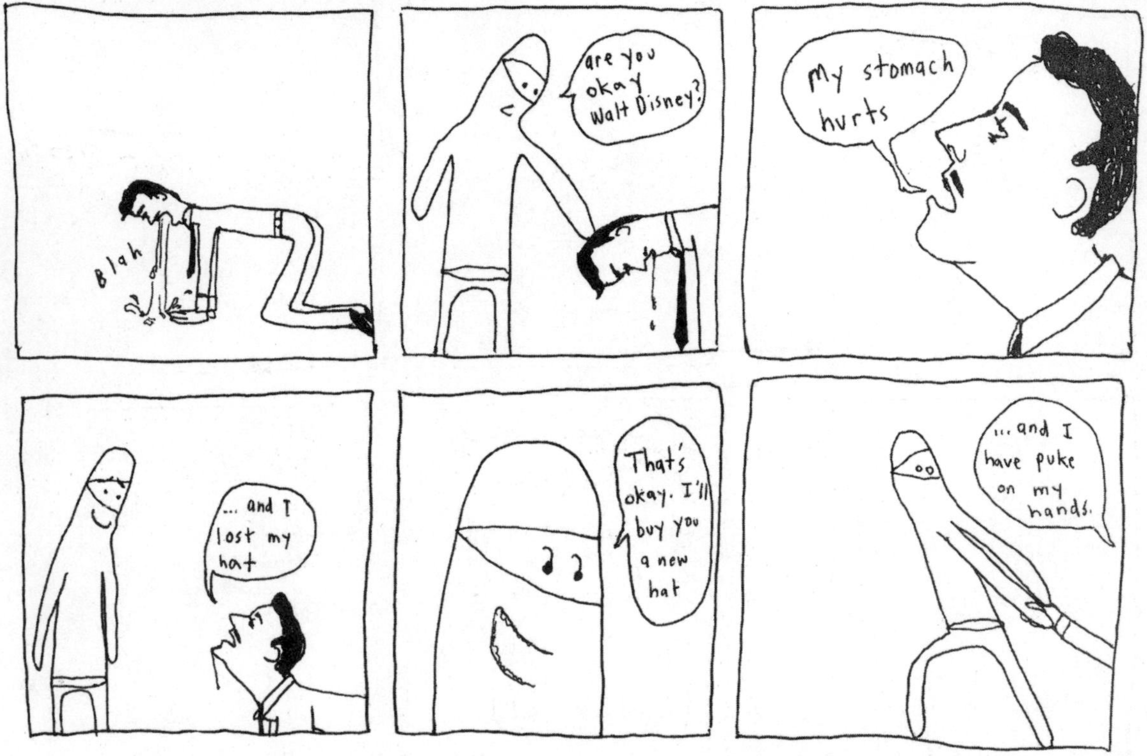
Blah
are you okay Walt Disney?
My stomach hurts
... and I lost my hat
That's okay. I'll buy you a new hat
... and I have puke on my hands.

White Ninja Holds his breath

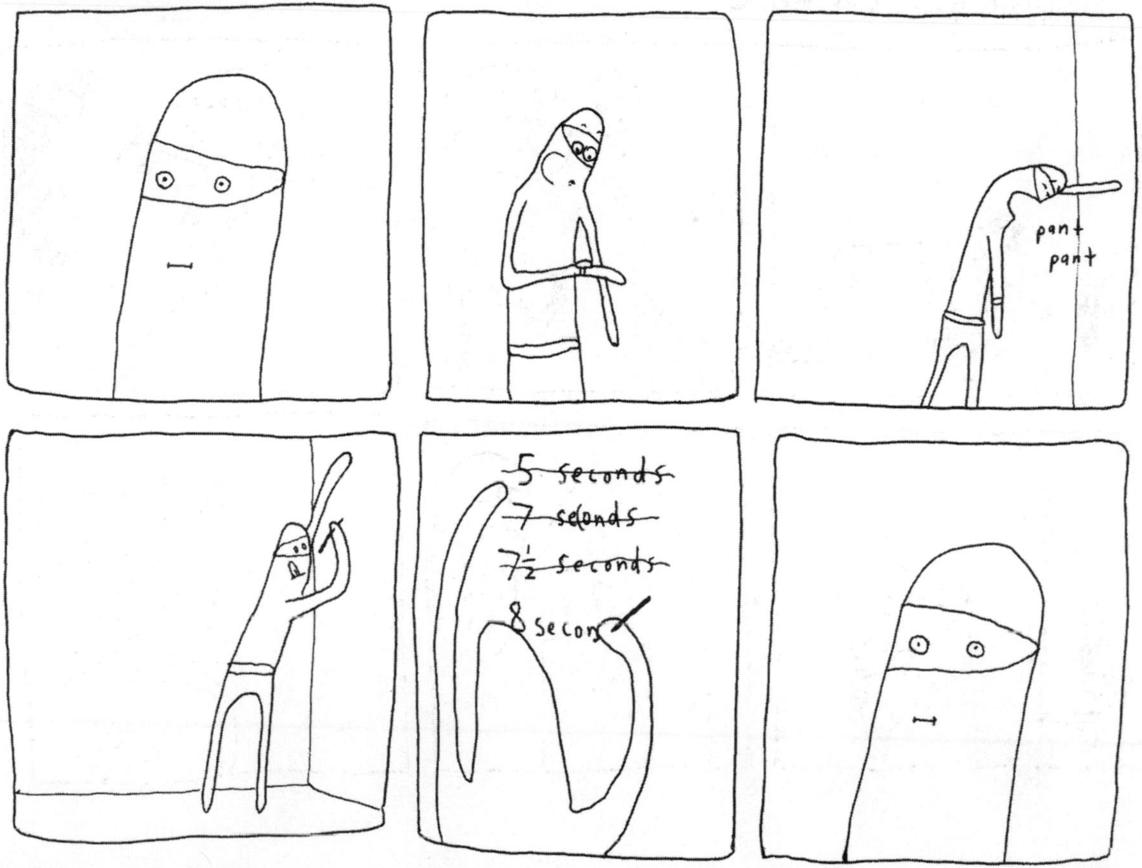
pant
pant
~~5 seconds~~
~~7 seconds~~
~~7½ seconds~~
8 secon

White Ninja's cool idea

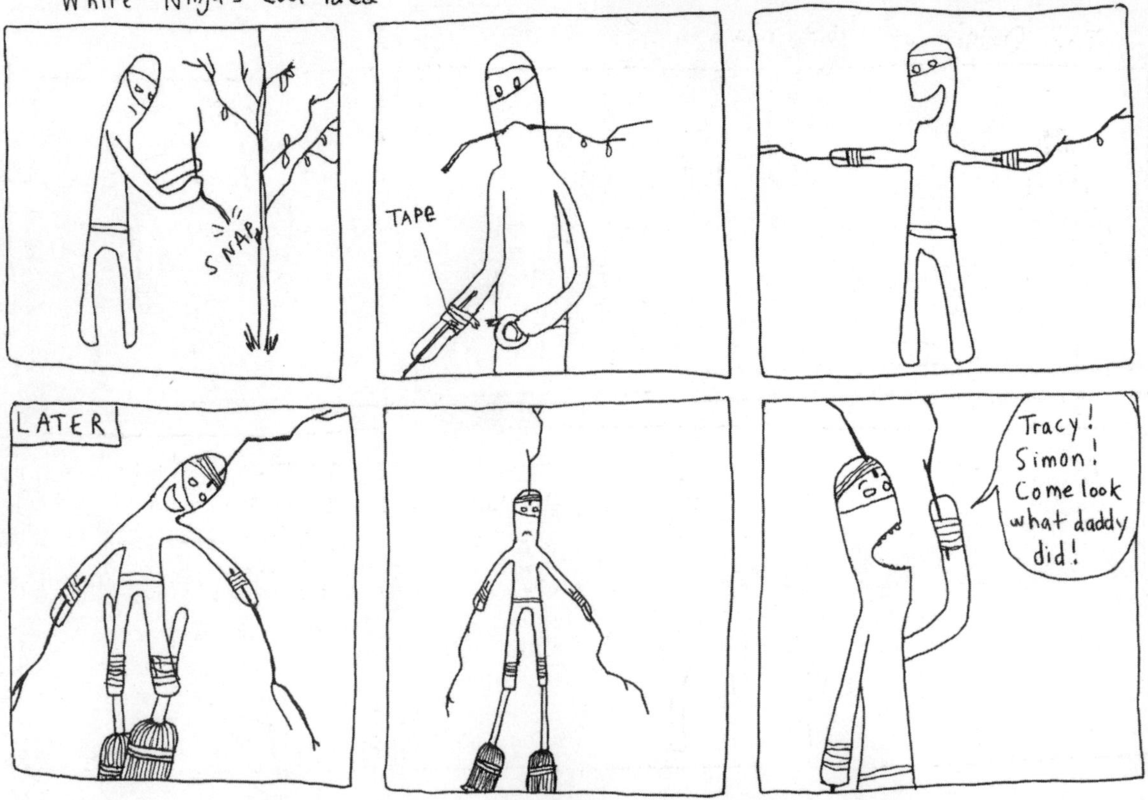
SNAP
TAPE
LATER
Tracy! Simon! Come look what daddy did!

The Origin of White Ninja

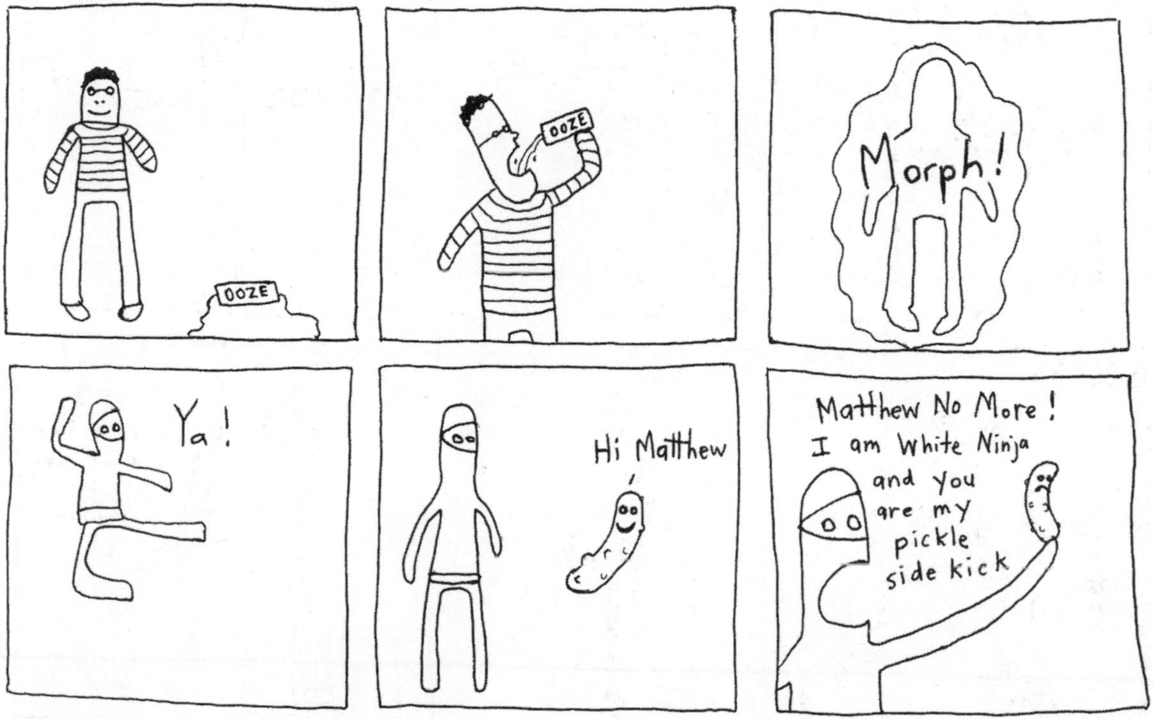

White Ninja Christmas

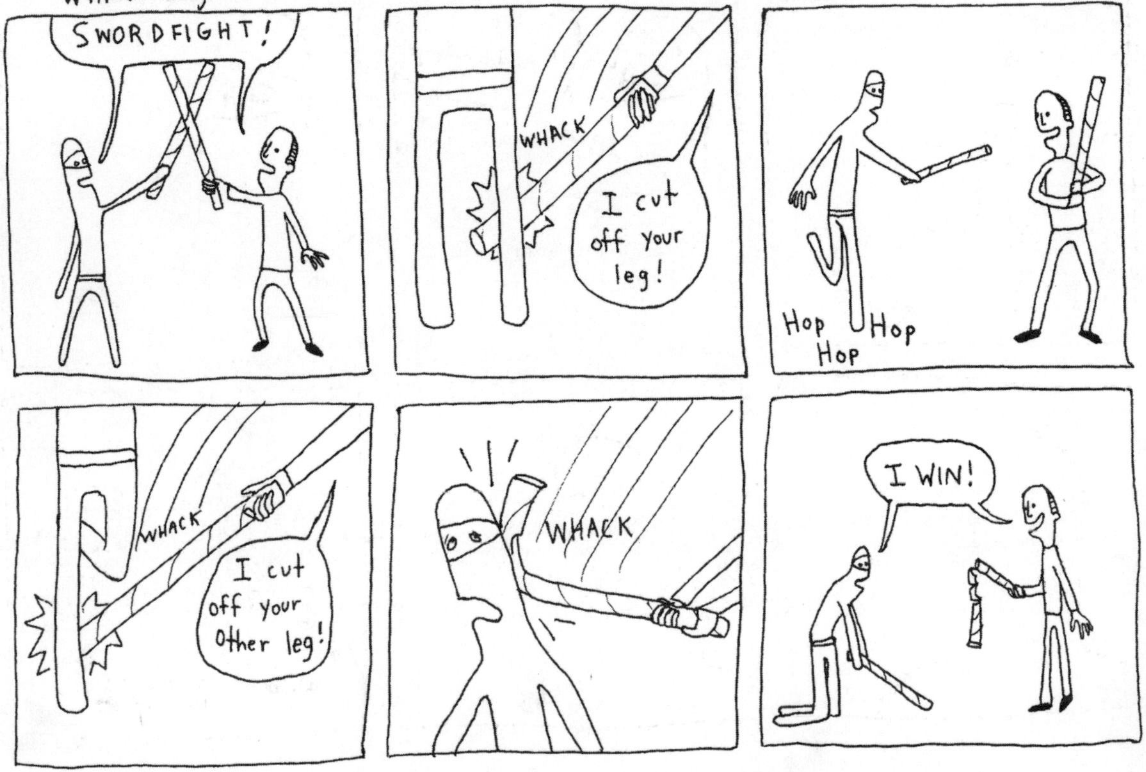
SWORDFIGHT!
WHACK
I cut off your leg!
Hop Hop Hop
WHACK
I cut off your other leg!
WHACK
I WIN!

White Ninja's Shoulder Angel

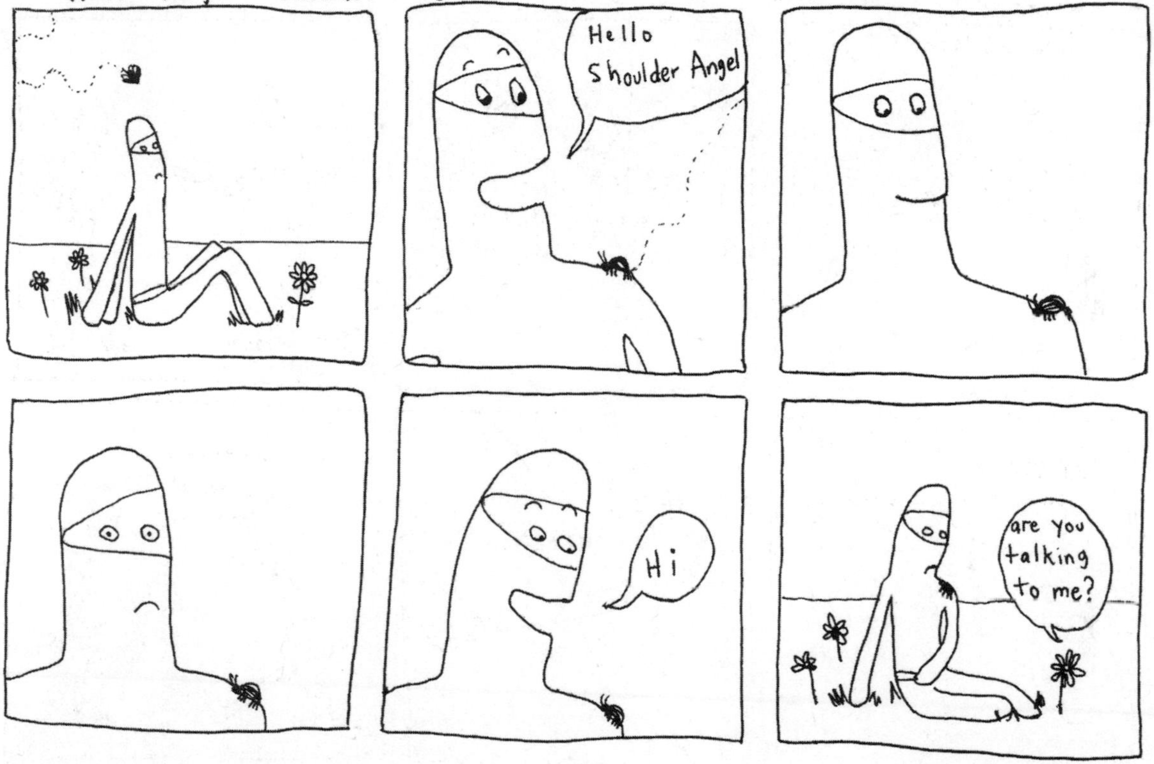
Hello Shoulder Angel
Hi
are you talking to me?

White Ninja loves baby turtles

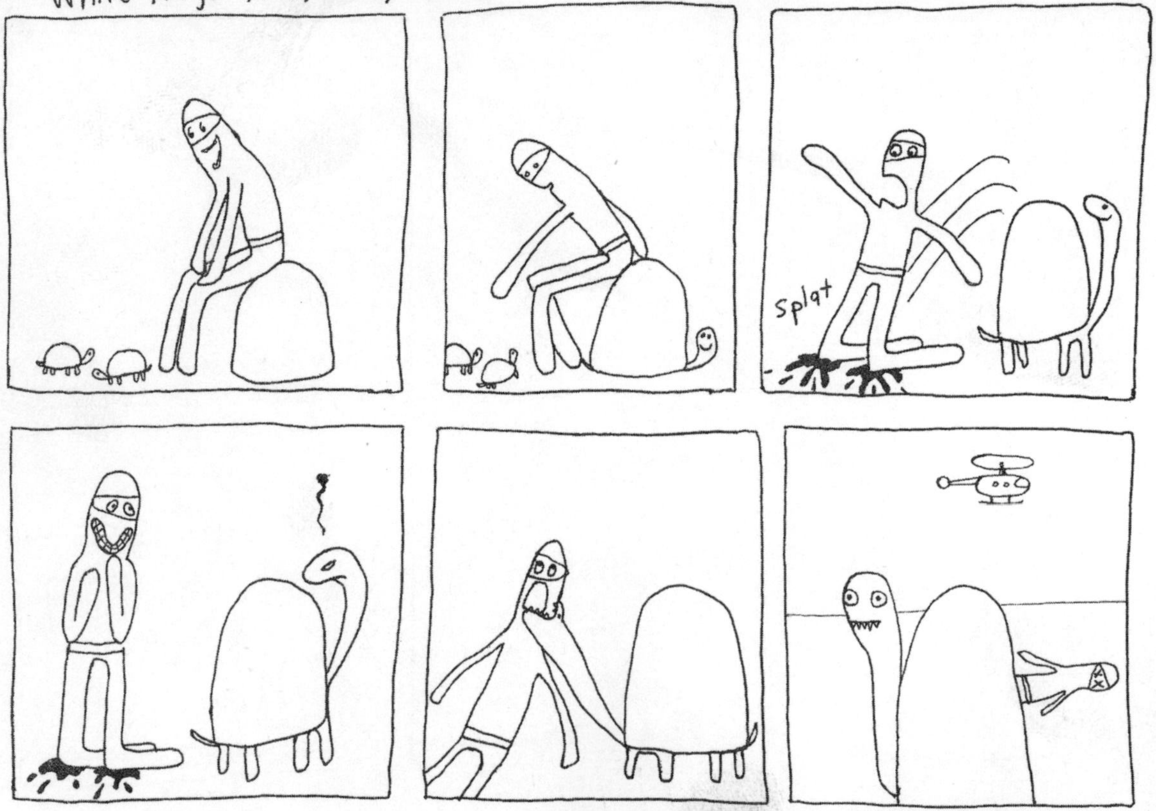
Splat

White Ninja sleeps

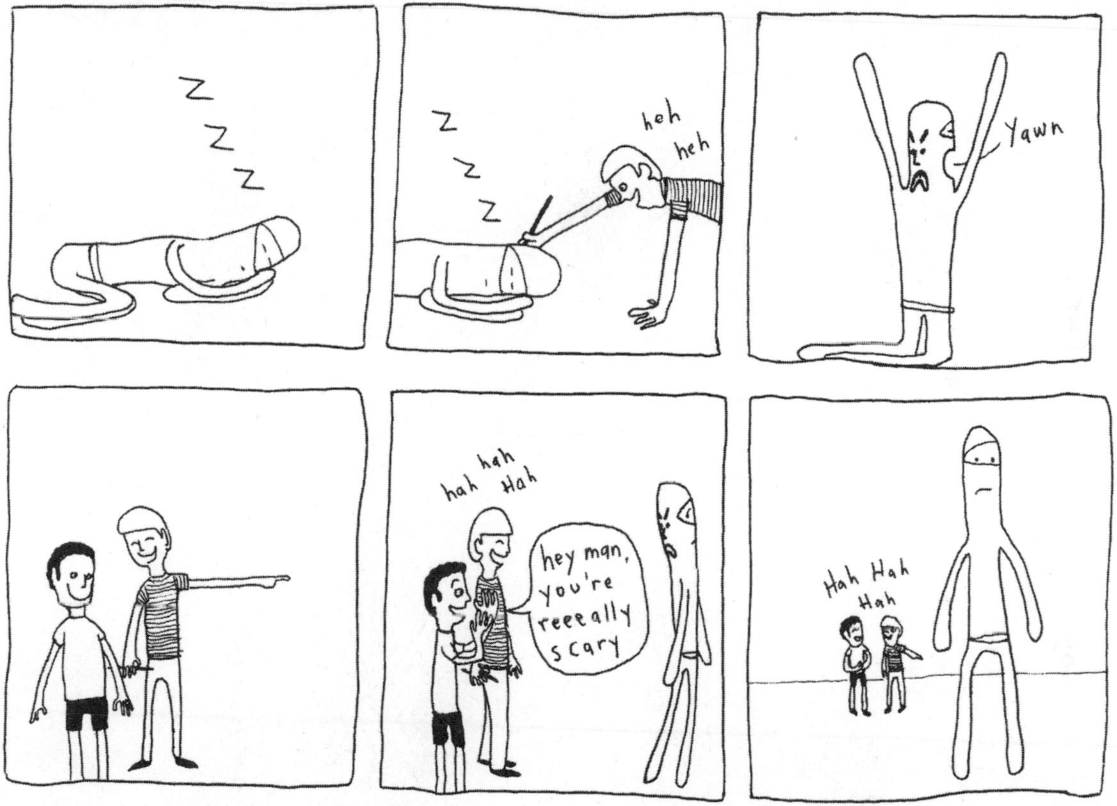
Z Z Z
Z Z Z
heh heh
Yawn
hah hah Hah
hey man, you're reeeally scary
Hah Hah Hah

White Ninja loses his Boomerang

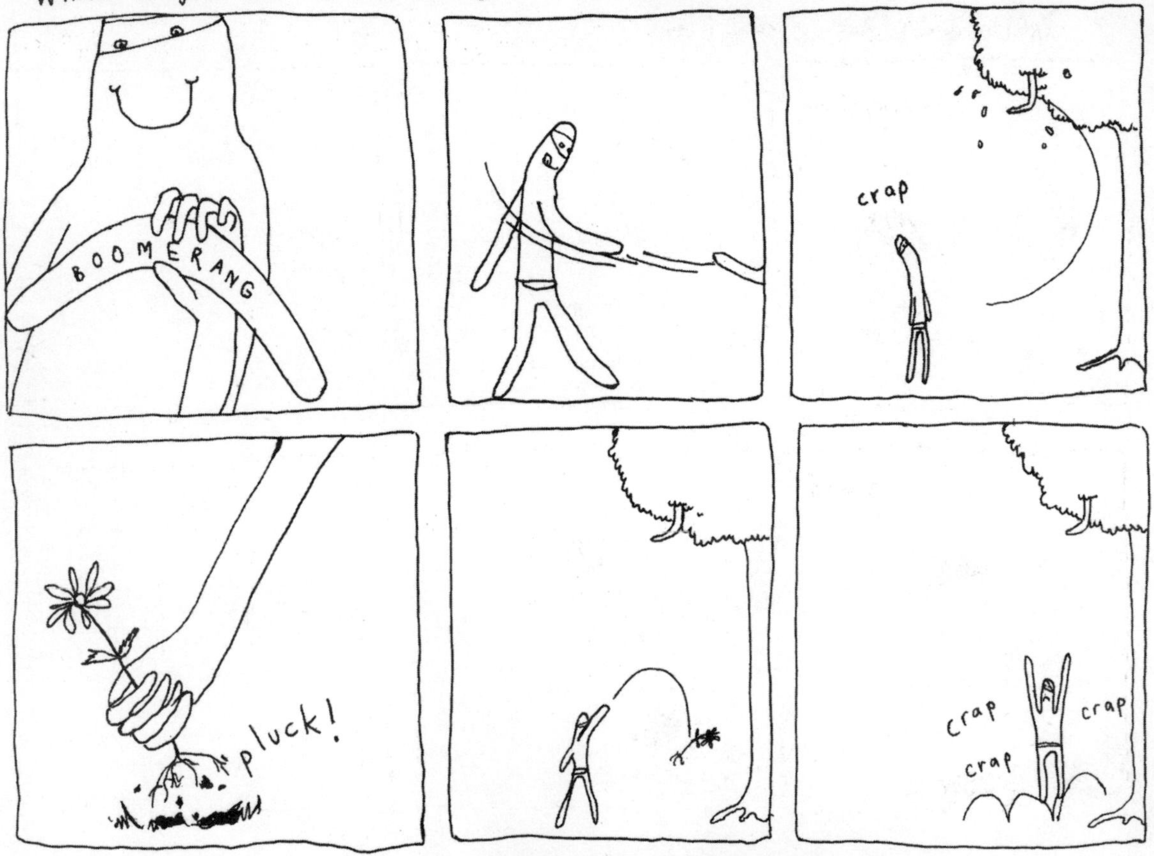
BOOMERANG
crap
pluck!
crap
crap
crap

White Ninja does a good deed

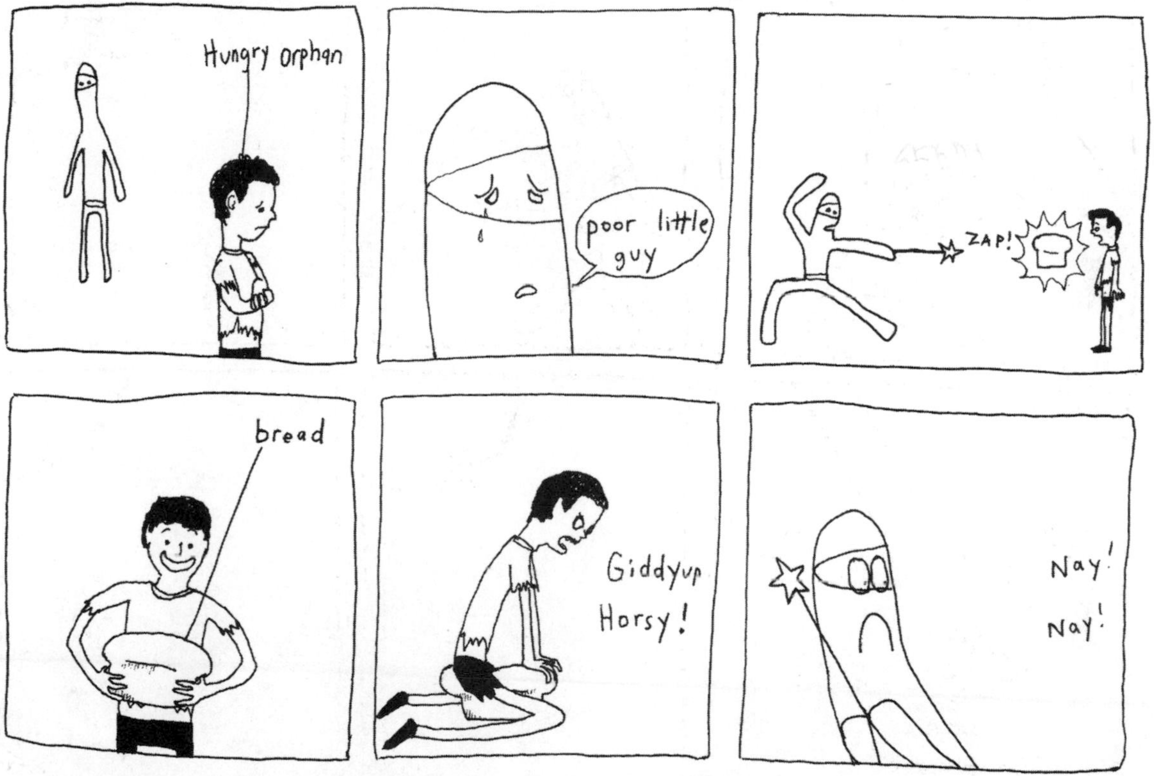
Hungry orphan
poor little guy
ZAP!
bread
Giddyup Horsy!
Nay! Nay!

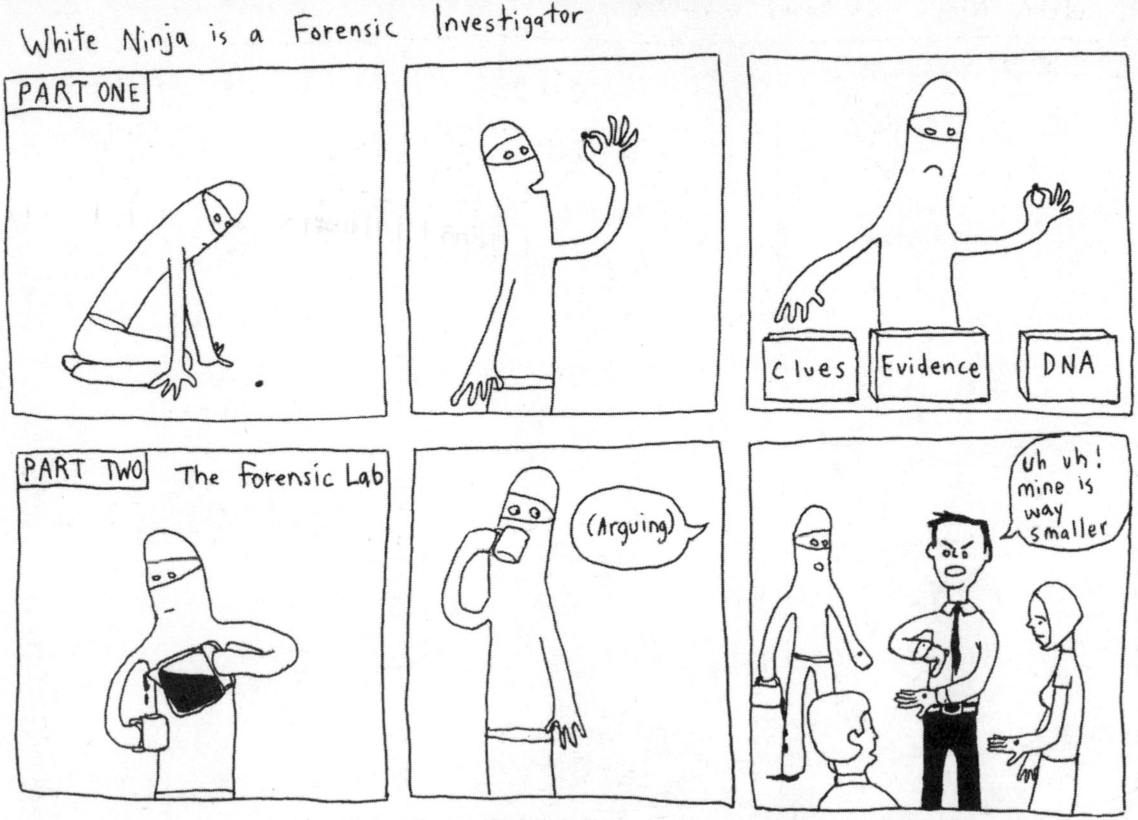
White Ninja is a Forensic Investigator
PART ONE
Clues
Evidence
DNA
PART TWO
The Forensic Lab
(Arguing)
uh uh! mine is way smaller

White Ninja is a funny babysitter

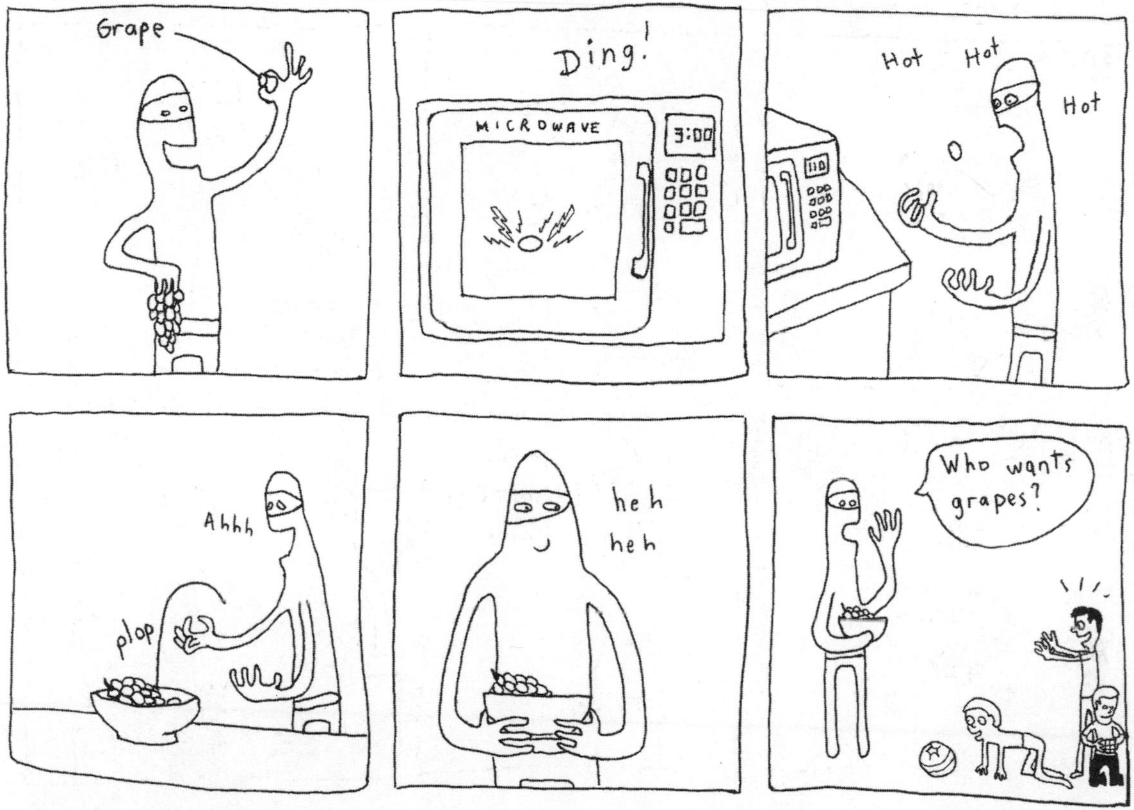
Grape
Ding!
MICROWAVE
3:00
Hot Hot
Hot
Ahhh
plop
heh
heh
Who wants grapes?

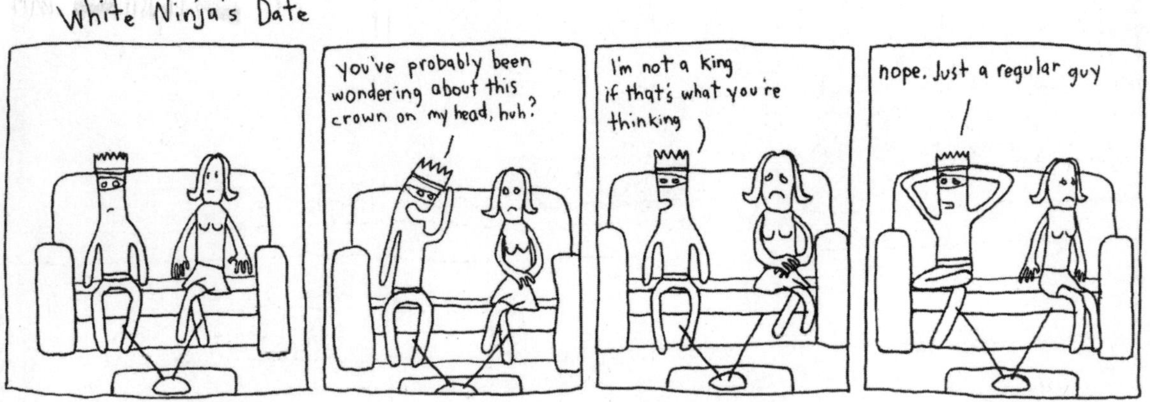
White Ninja's Date
you've probably been wondering about this crown on my head, huh?
I'm not a king if that's what you're thinking
nope. Just a regular guy

White Ninja in: Pineapple Farm

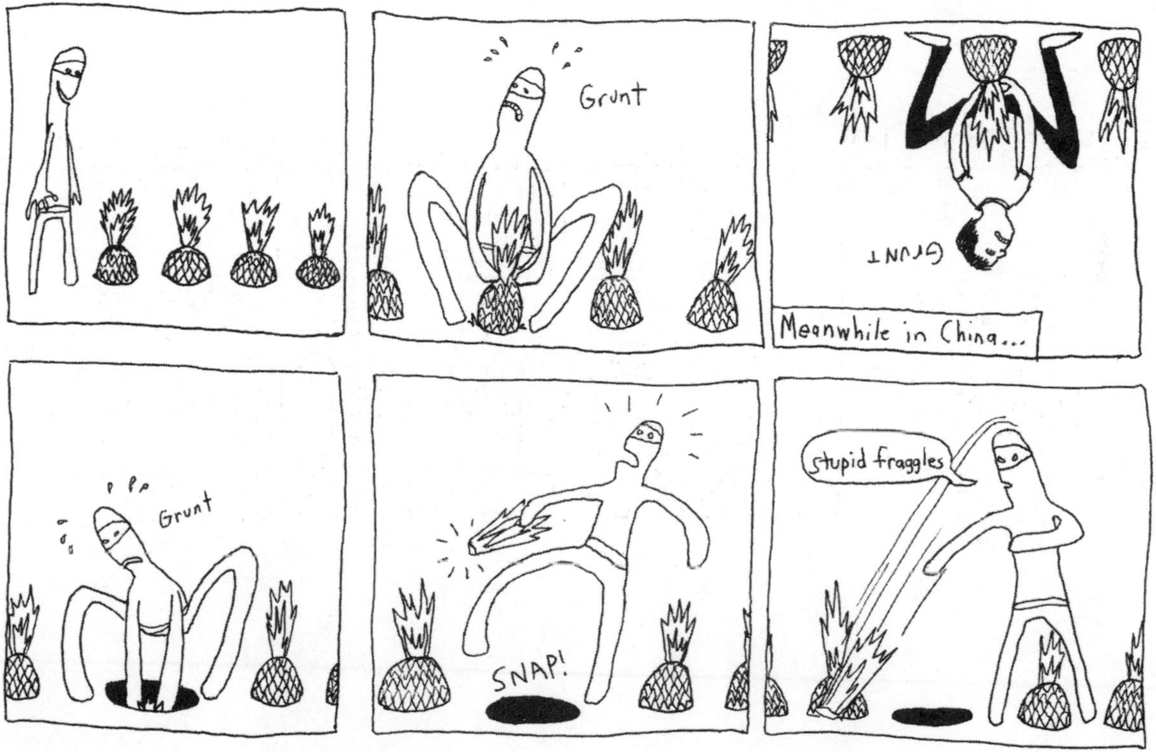
Grunt
Grunt
Meanwhile in China...
Grunt
SNAP!
stupid fraggles

White Ninja is at a funeral

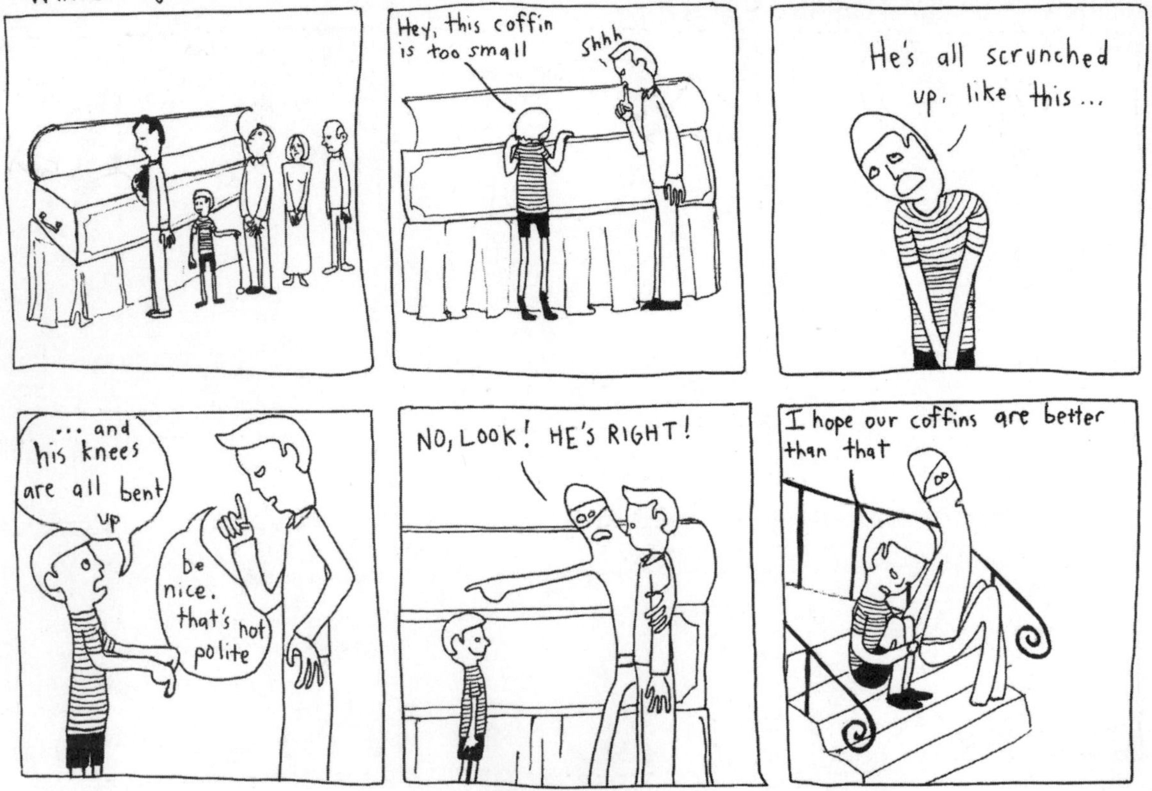

Hey, this coffin is too small
Shhh
He's all scrunched up, like this...
... and his knees are all bent up
be nice. that's not polite
NO, LOOK! HE'S RIGHT!
I hope our coffins are better than that

White Ninja and Angel of Death

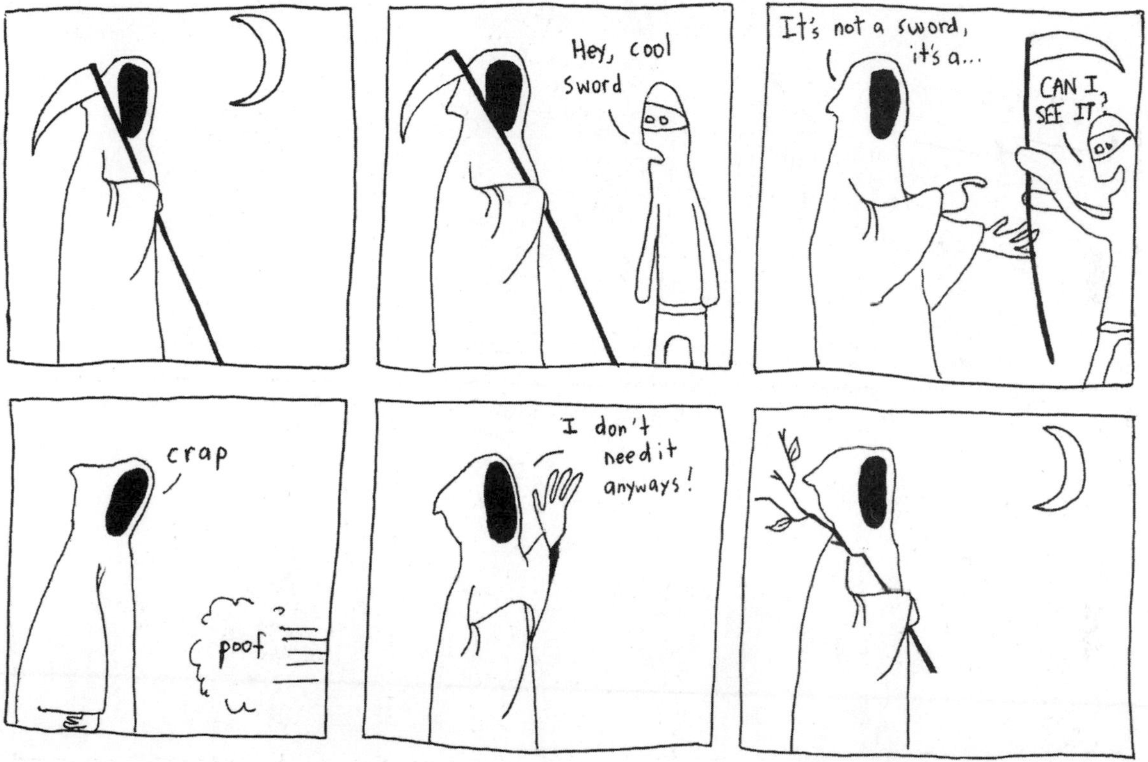
Hey, cool sword
It's not a sword, it's a...
CAN I, SEE IT?
crap
poof
I don't need it anyways!

White Ninja has a hairy face

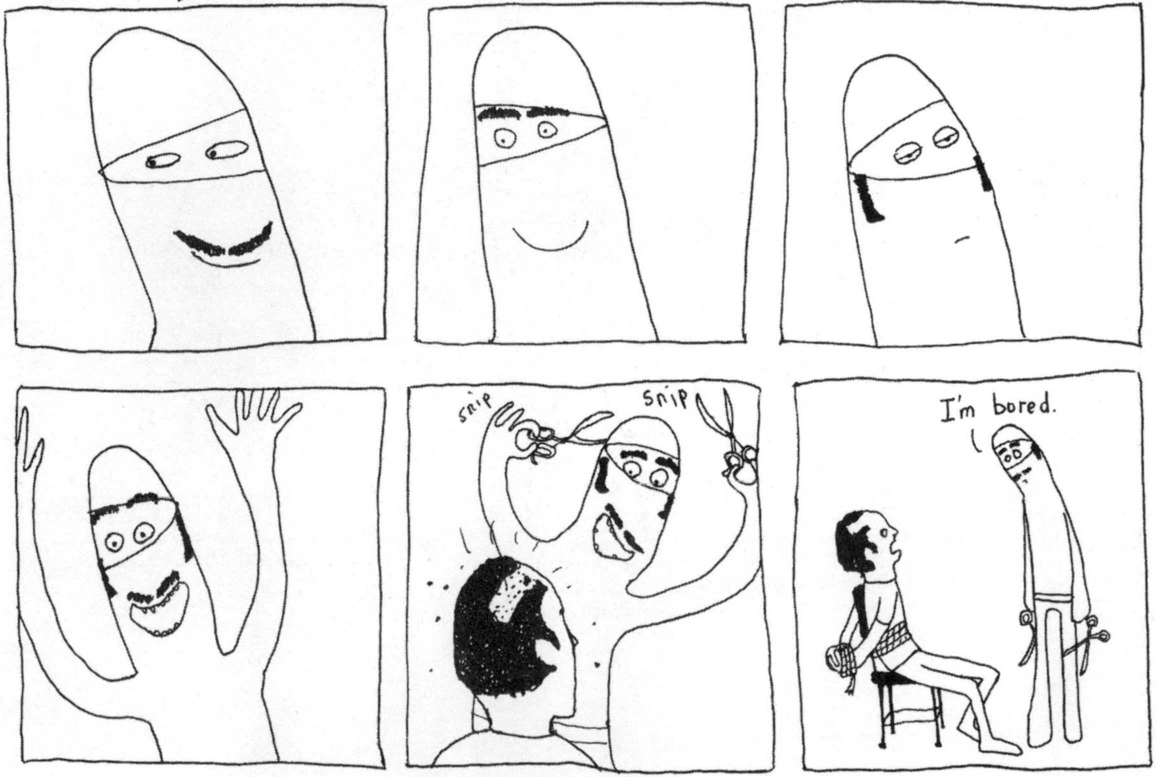
snip
snip
I'm bored.

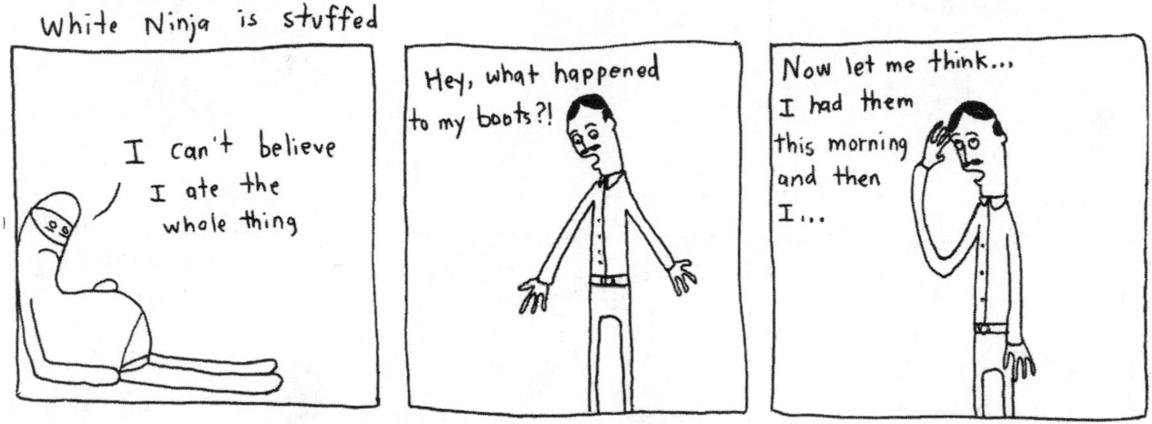
White Ninja is stuffed
I can't believe I ate the whole thing
Hey, what happened to my boots?!
Now let me think... I had them this morning and then I...

White Ninja and the Duck

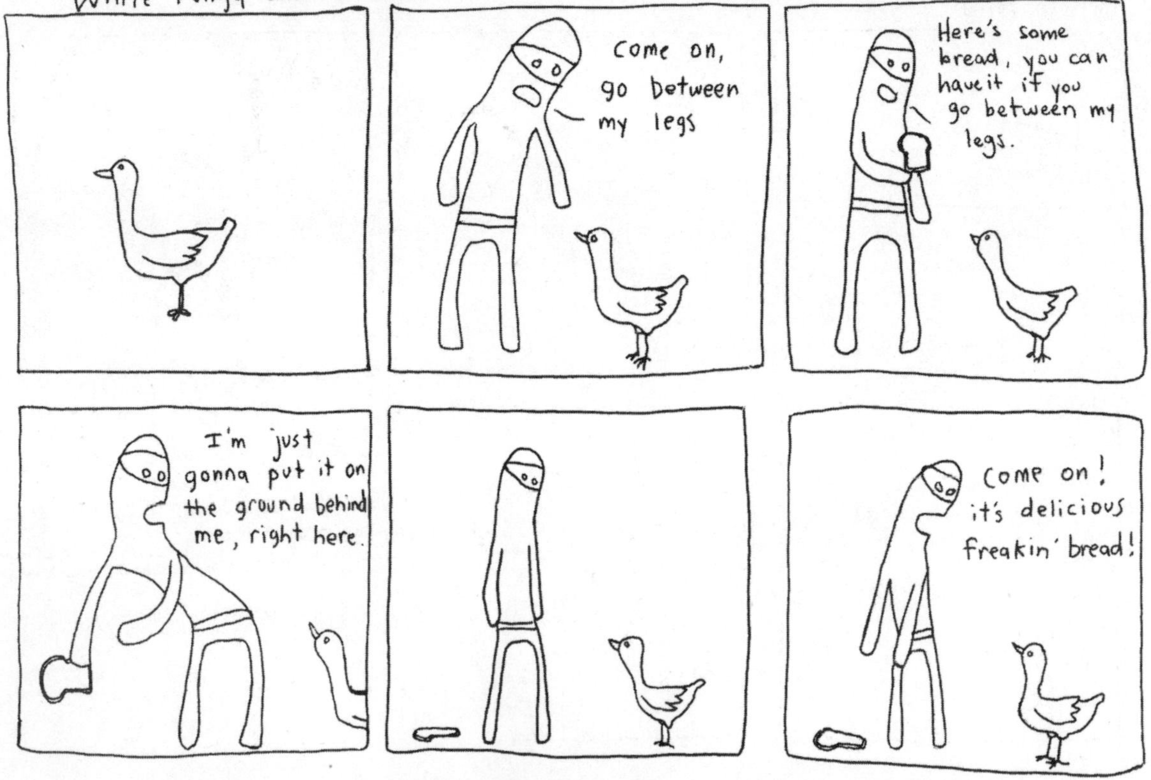

come on, go between my legs
Here's some bread, you can have it if you go between my legs.
I'm just gonna put it on the ground behind me, right here.
come on! it's delicious freakin' bread!

White Ninja in: Wet Willy

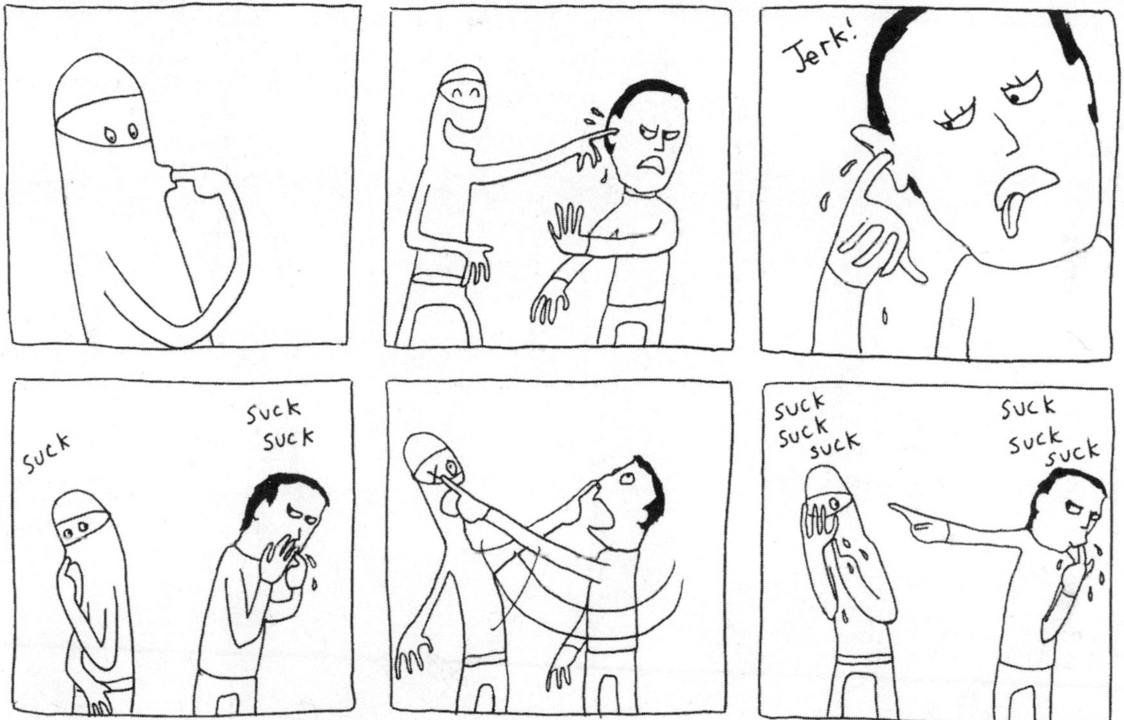
Jerk!
suck
Suck
Suck
Suck
Suck
suck
Suck
Suck
Suck

White Ninja enjoys a cookie

Wow, that looks like a good cookie!
Would you like a bite?
No, that's okay. I'll just watch

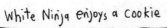

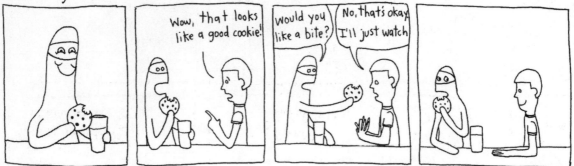

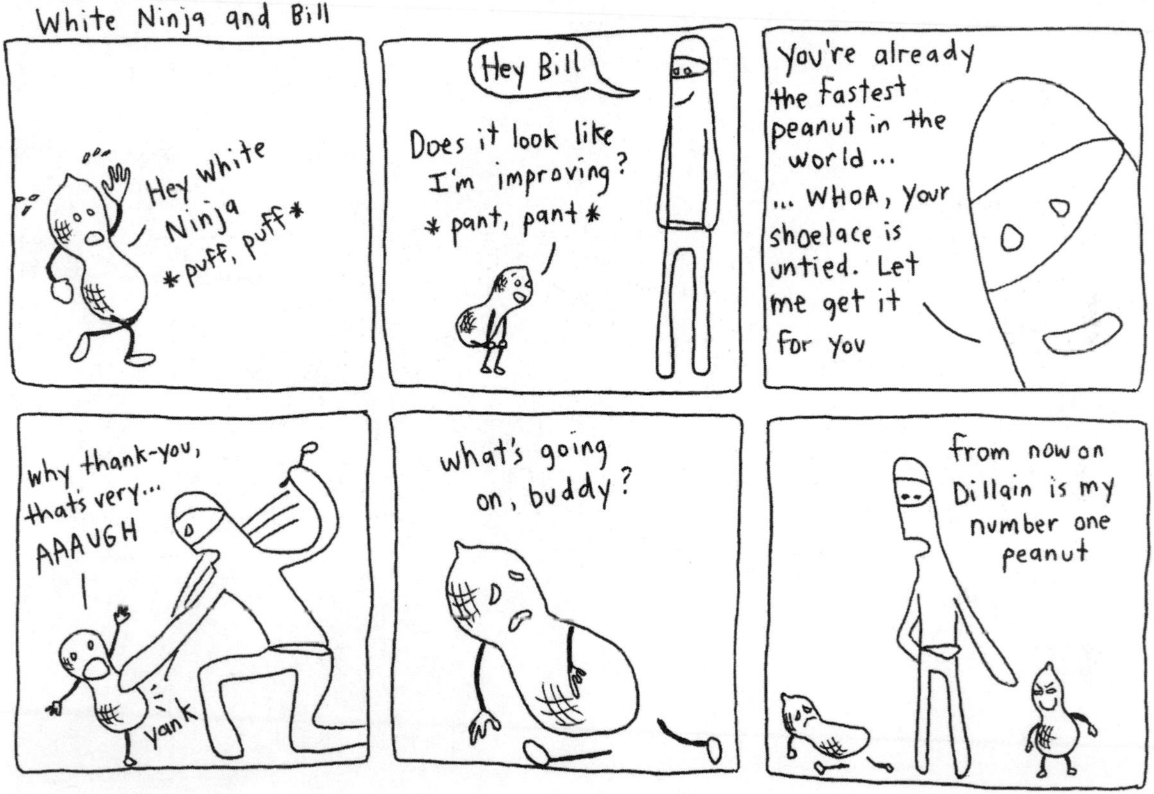
White Ninja and Bill
Hey White Ninja *puff, puff*
Hey Bill
Does it look like I'm improving? *pant, pant*
You're already the fastest peanut in the world ...
... WHOA, your shoelace is untied. Let me get it for you
why thank-you, that's very... AAAUGH
yank
what's going on, buddy?
from now on Dillain is my number one peanut

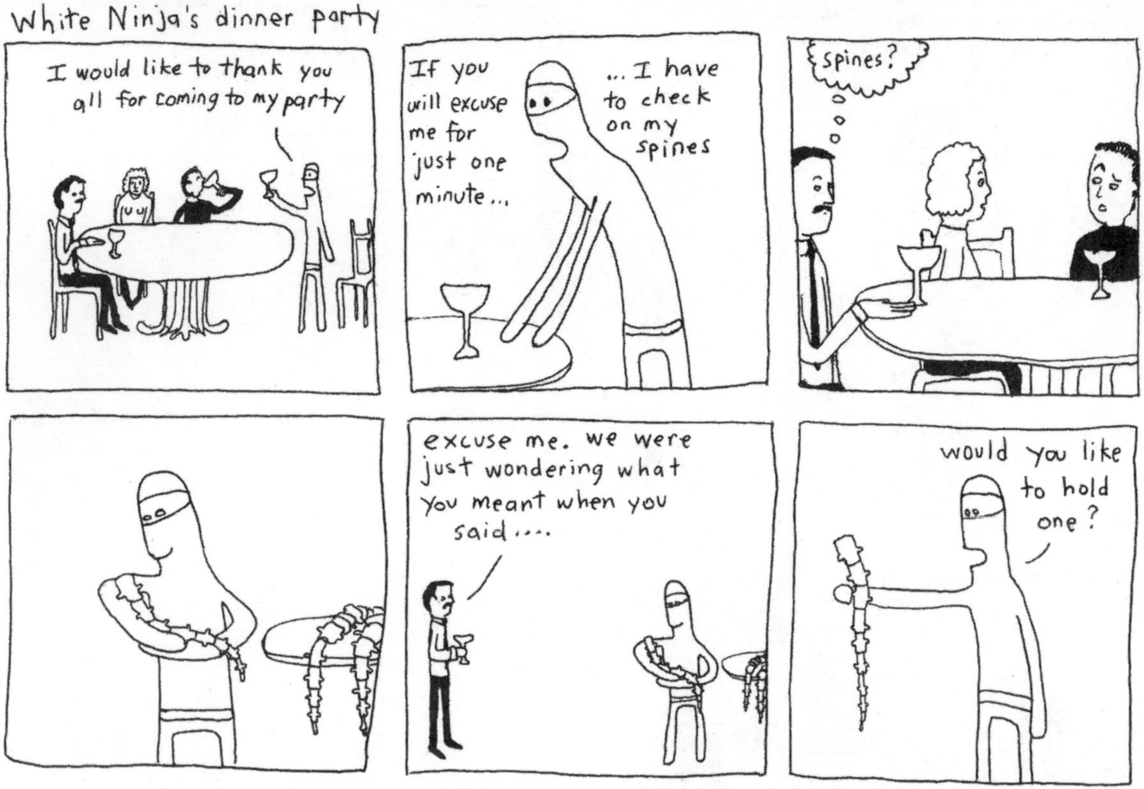
White Ninja's dinner party
I would like to thank you all for coming to my party
If you will excuse me for just one minute...
... I have to check on my spines
spines?
excuse me. we were just wondering what you meant when you said....
would you like to hold one?

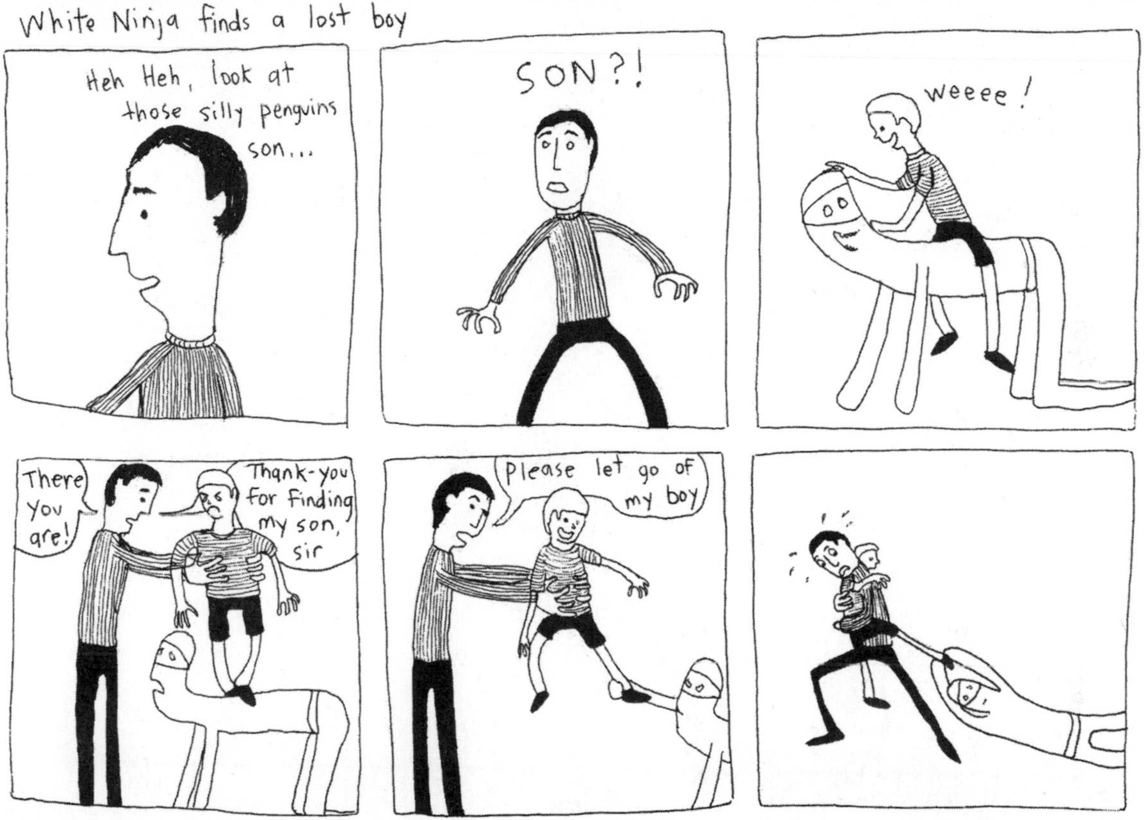
White Ninja finds a lost boy
Heh Heh, look at those silly penguins son...
SON?!
weeee!
There you are!
Thank-you for finding my son, sir
Please let go of my boy

White Ninja Goes to the Doctor

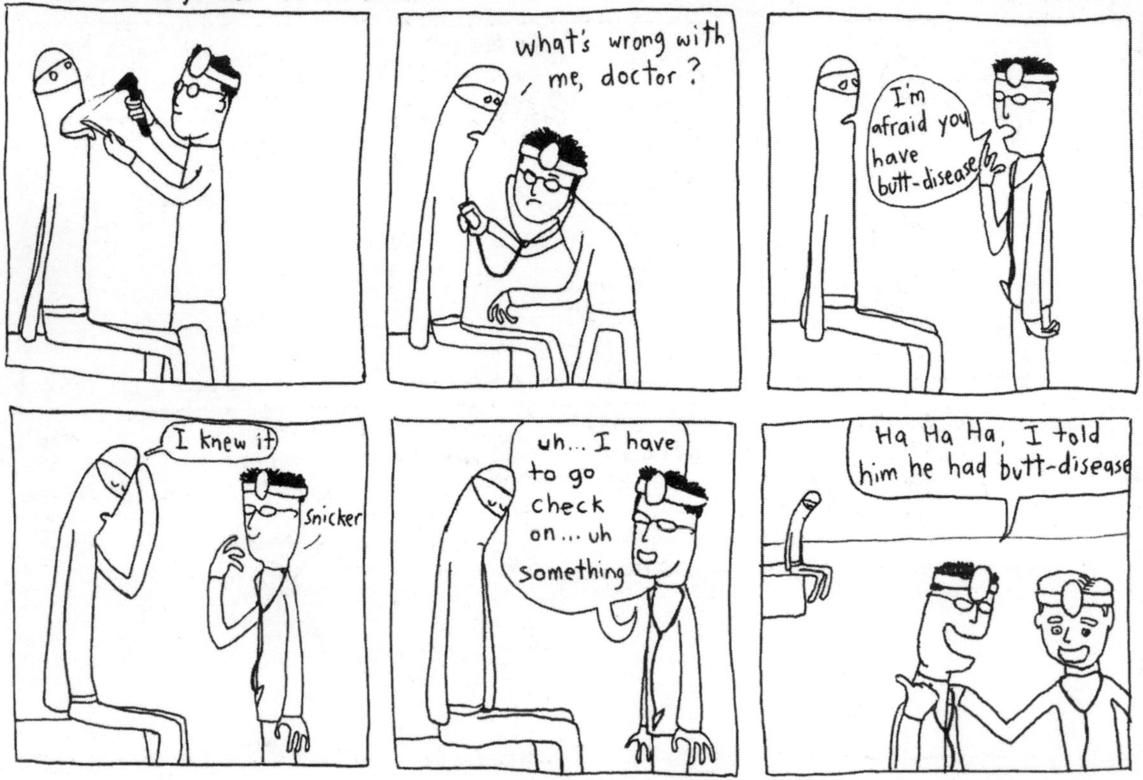

what's wrong with me, doctor?
I'm afraid you have butt-disease
I knew it
snicker
uh... I have to go check on... uh something
Ha Ha Ha, I told him he had butt-disease

White Ninja and the Magic Lamp

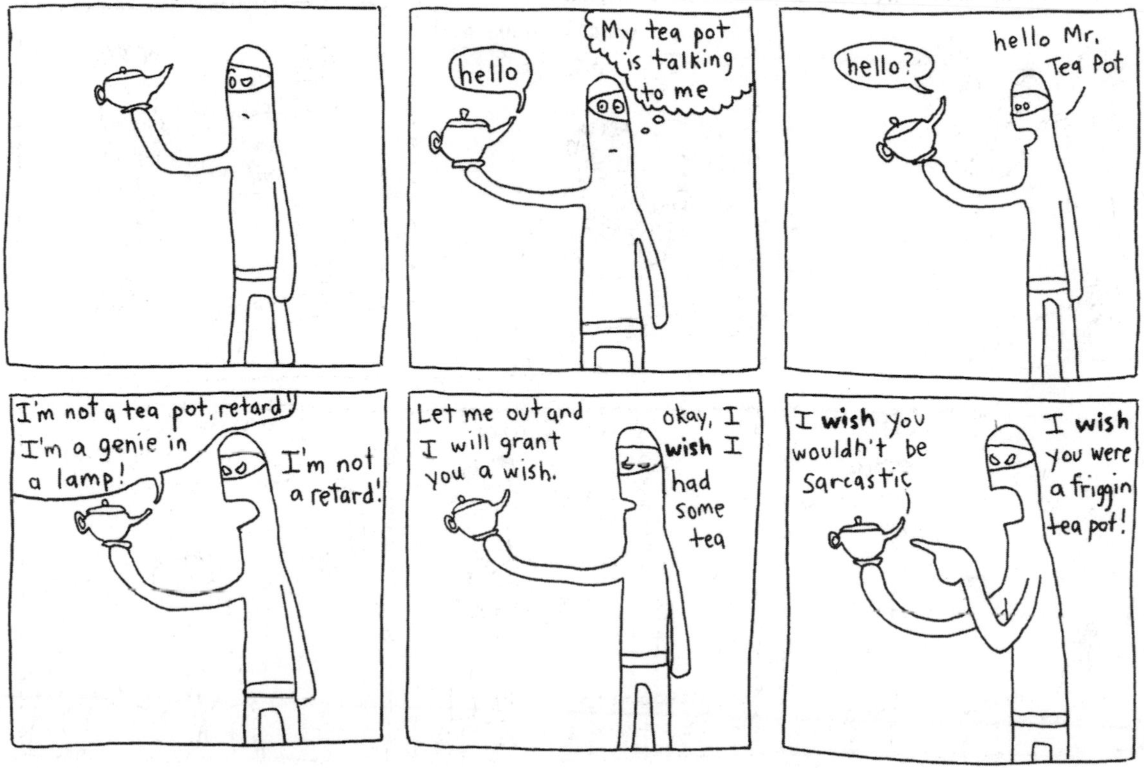

hello
My tea pot is talking to me
hello?
hello Mr. Tea Pot
I'm not a tea pot, retard! I'm a genie in a lamp!
I'm not a retard!
Let me out and I will grant you a wish.
okay, I **wish** I had some tea
I **wish** you wouldn't be sarcastic
I **wish** you were a friggin tea pot!

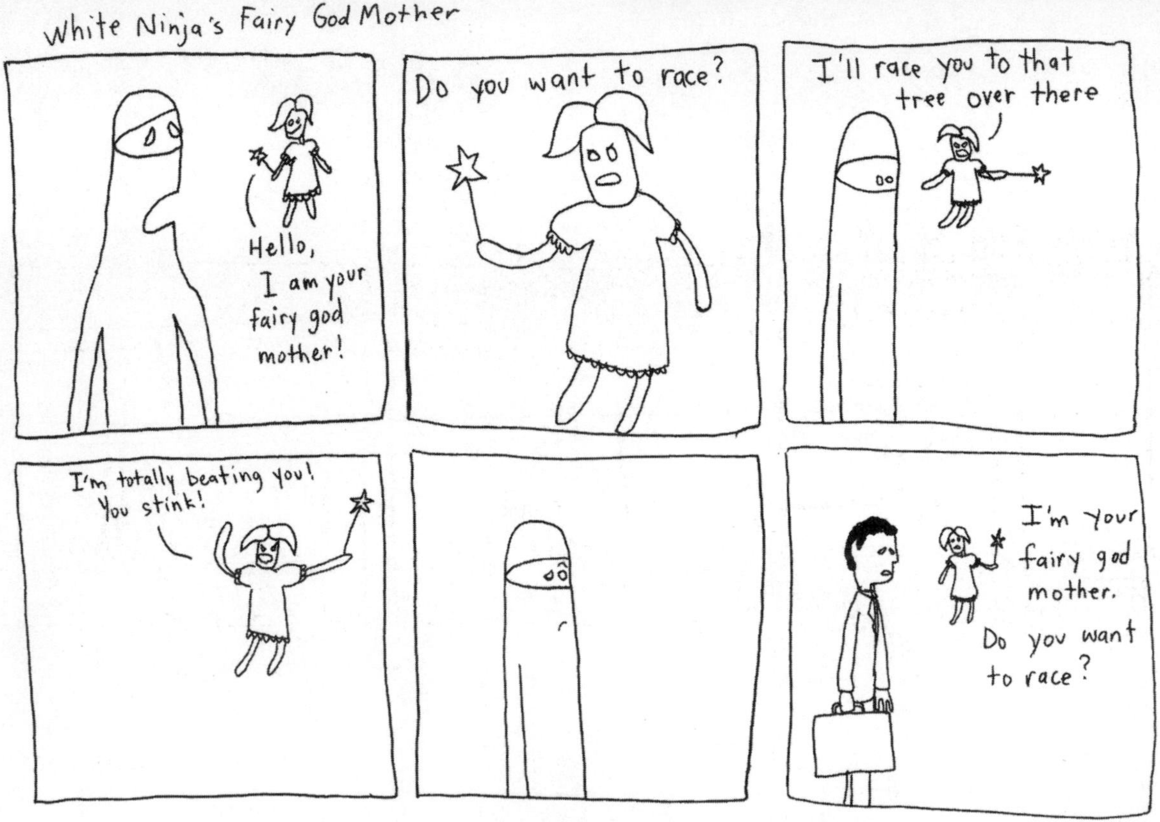
White Ninja's Fairy God Mother
Hello, I am your fairy god mother!
Do you want to race?
I'll race you to that tree over there
I'm totally beating you! You stink!
I'm your fairy god mother.
Do you want to race?

White Ninja gets drive-thru

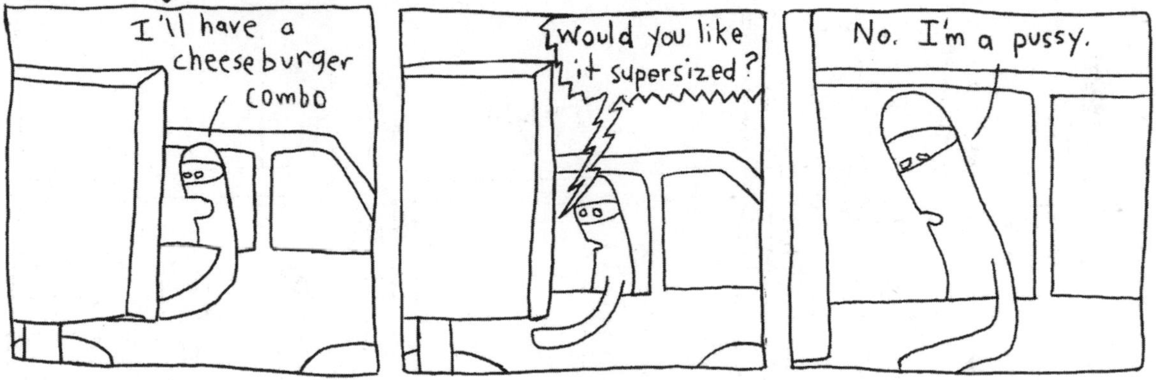

I'll have a cheeseburger combo
Would you like it supersized?
No. I'm a pussy.

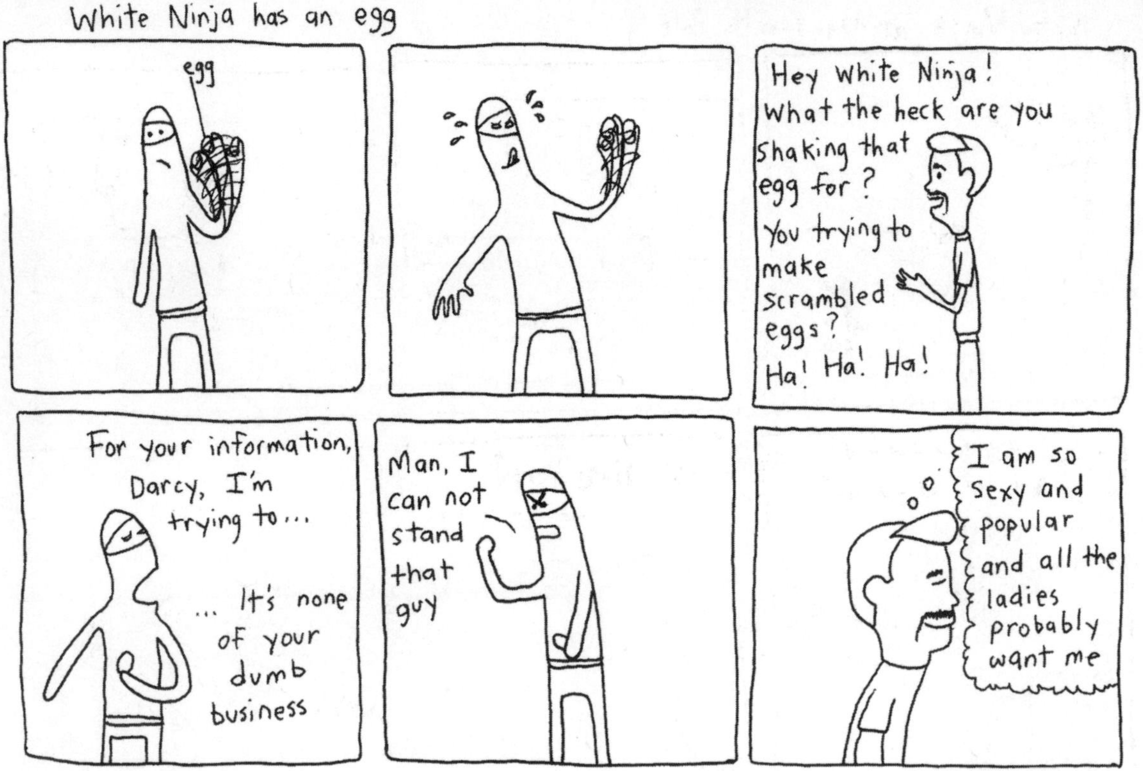
White Ninja has an egg
egg
Hey White Ninja! What the heck are you shaking that egg for? You trying to make scrambled eggs? Ha! Ha! Ha!
For your information, Darcy, I'm trying to...
... It's none of your dumb business
Man, I can not stand that guy
I am so sexy and popular and all the ladies probably want me

White Ninja at the North Pole

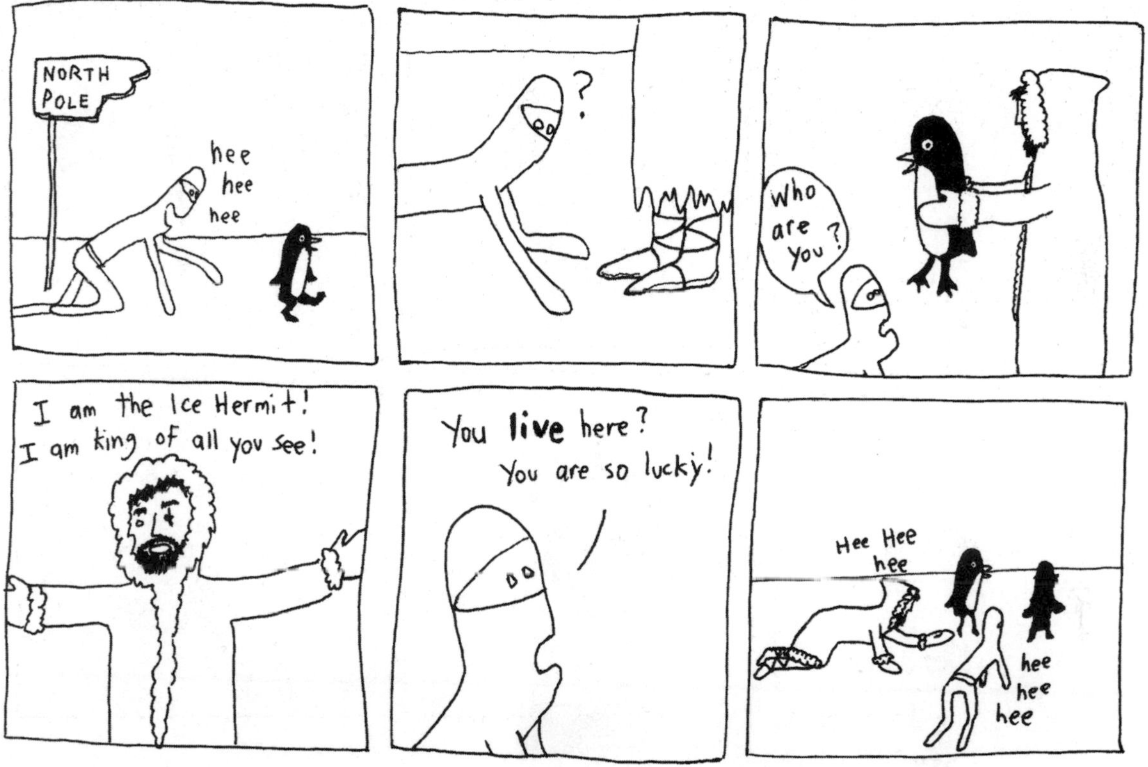
NORTH POLE
hee hee hee
?
Who are you?
I am the Ice Hermit! I am king of all you see!
You **live** here?
You are so lucky!
Hee Hee hee
hee hee hee

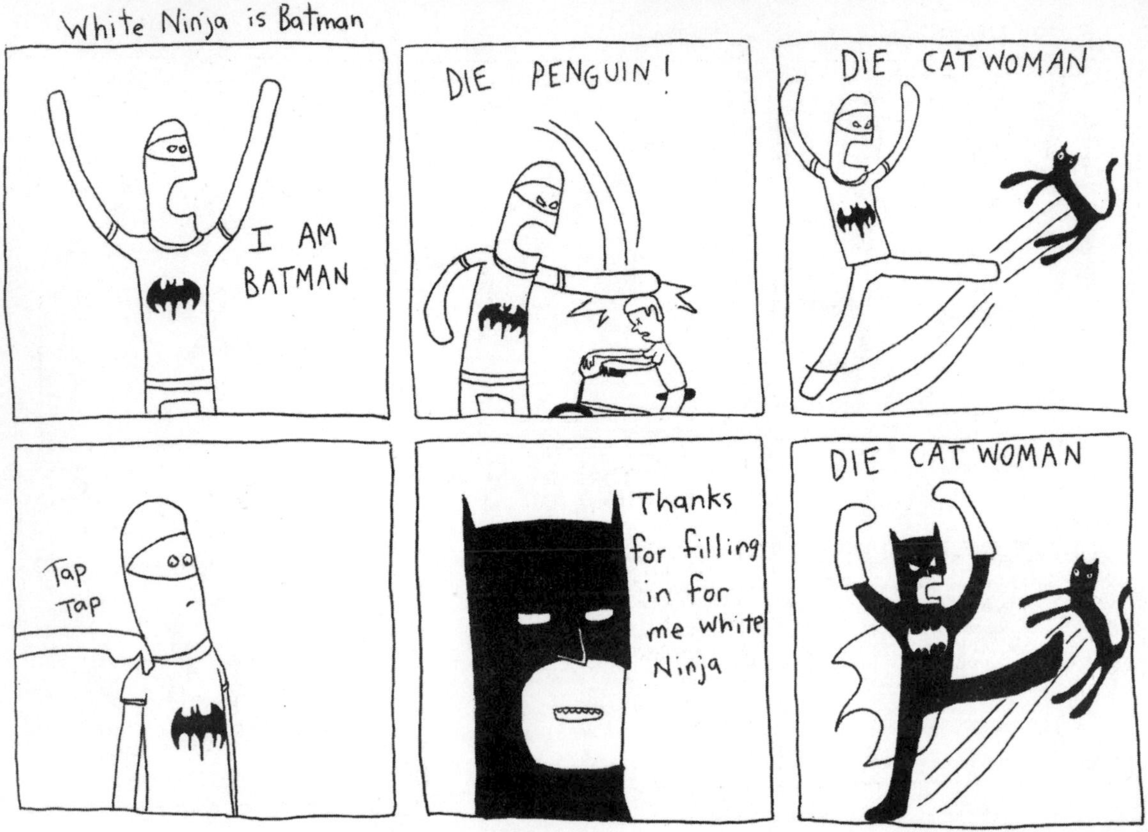
White Ninja is Batman
I AM BATMAN
DIE PENGUIN!
DIE CATWOMAN
Tap Tap
Thanks for filling in for me white Ninja
DIE CATWOMAN

White Ninja draws horses better

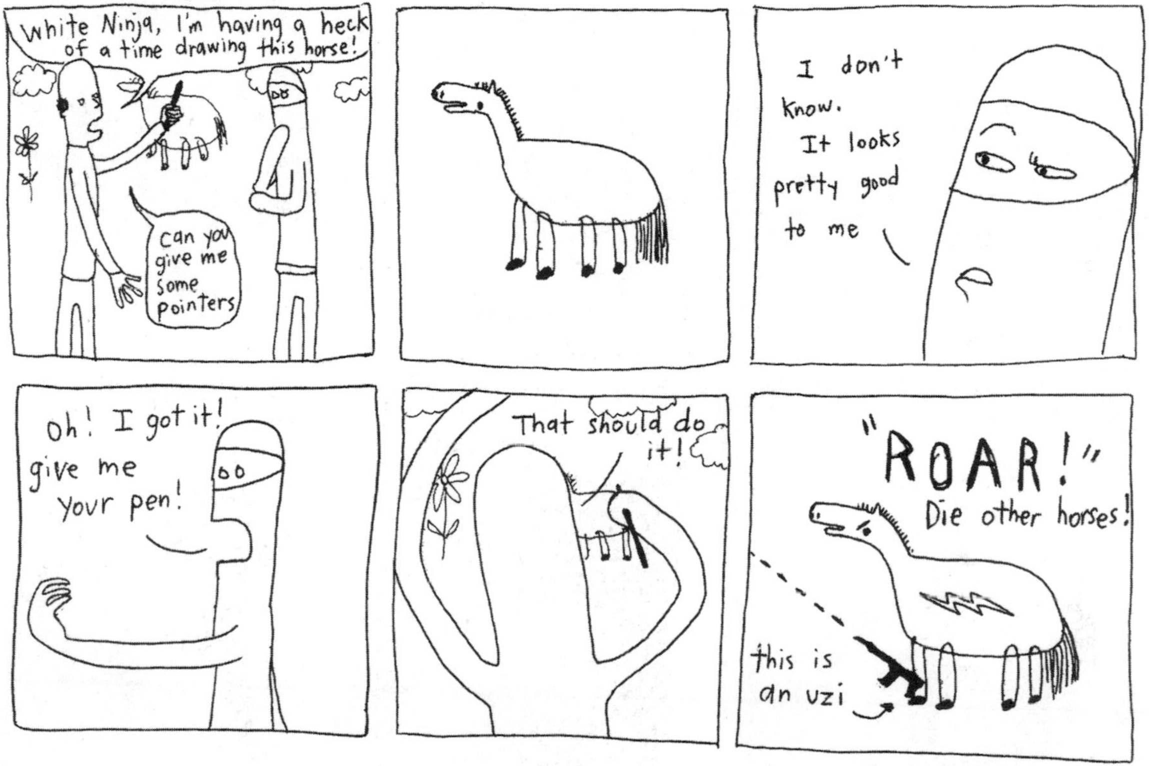
White Ninja, I'm having a heck of a time drawing this horse!
Can you give me some pointers
I don't know. It looks pretty good to me
Oh! I got it! give me your pen!
That should do it!
"ROAR!"
Die other horses!
this is an uzi

White Ninja takes care of Lyle

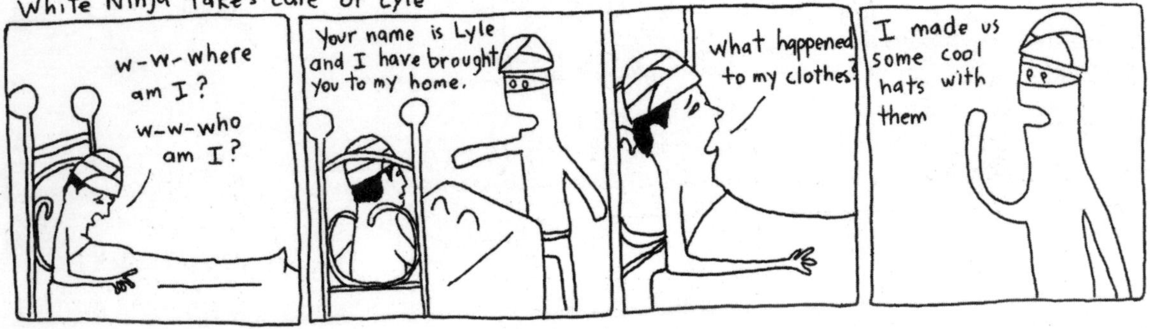
w-w-where am I?
w-w-who am I?
Your name is Lyle and I have brought you to my home.
what happened to my clothes?
I made us some cool hats with them

White Ninja and the gross little boy

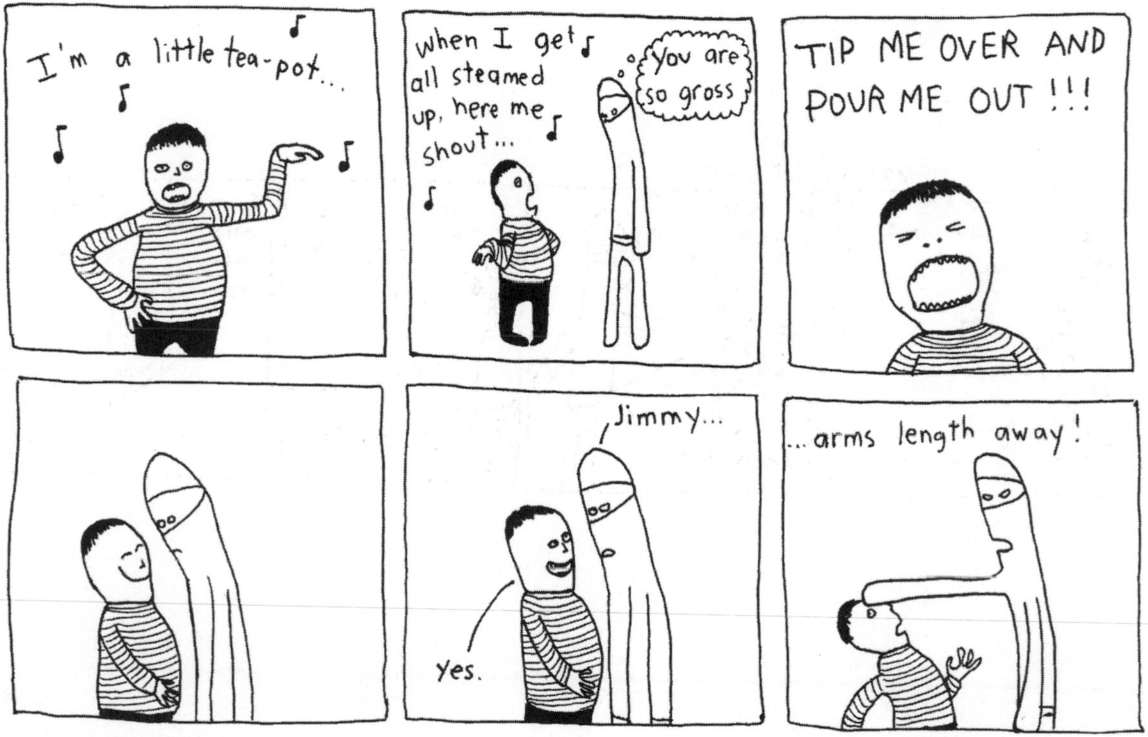
I'm a little tea-pot...
when I get all steamed up, here me shout...
you are so gross
TIP ME OVER AND POUR ME OUT !!!
Jimmy...
yes.
...arms length away!

White Ninja walks a cat

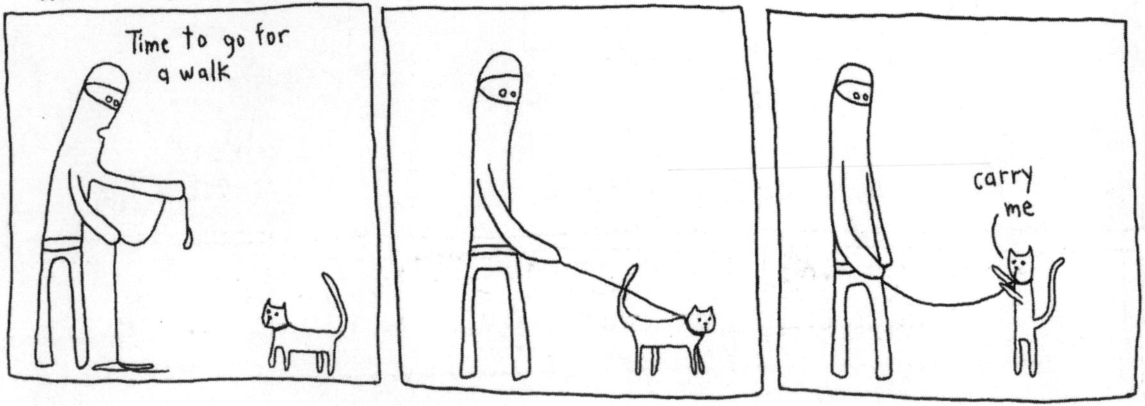
Time to go for a walk
carry me

White Ninja's Brew

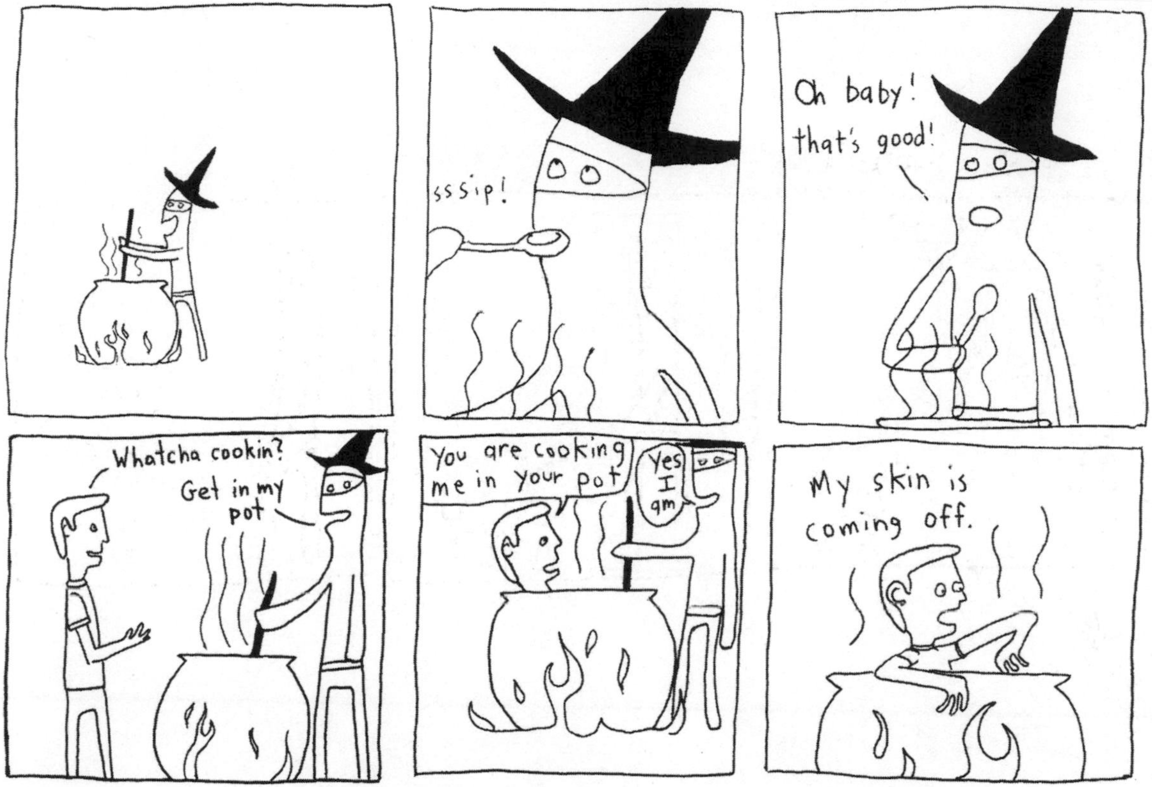

sssip!
Oh baby! that's good!
Whatcha cookin?
Get in my pot
You are cooking me in your pot
Yes I am
My skin is coming off.

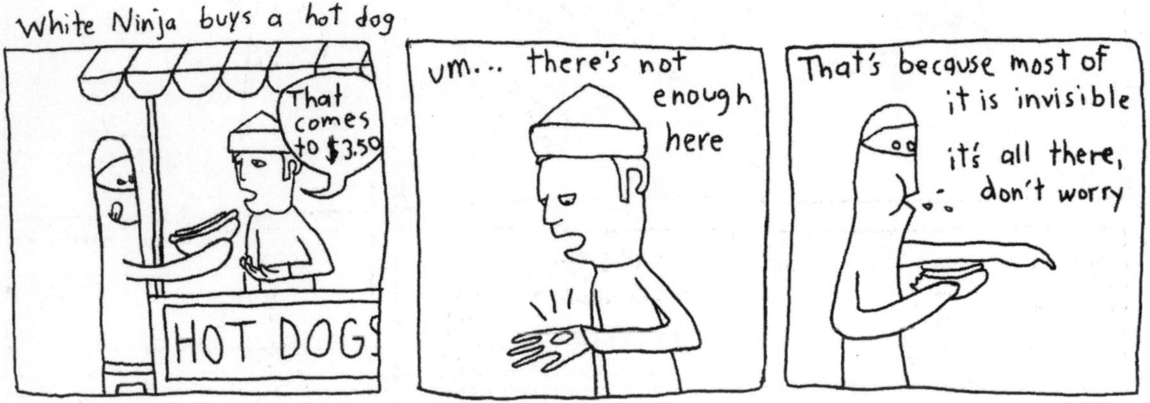
White Ninja buys a hot dog
That comes to $3.50
HOT DOGS
um... there's not enough here
That's because most of it is invisible
it's all there, don't worry

White Ninja in: Predicament

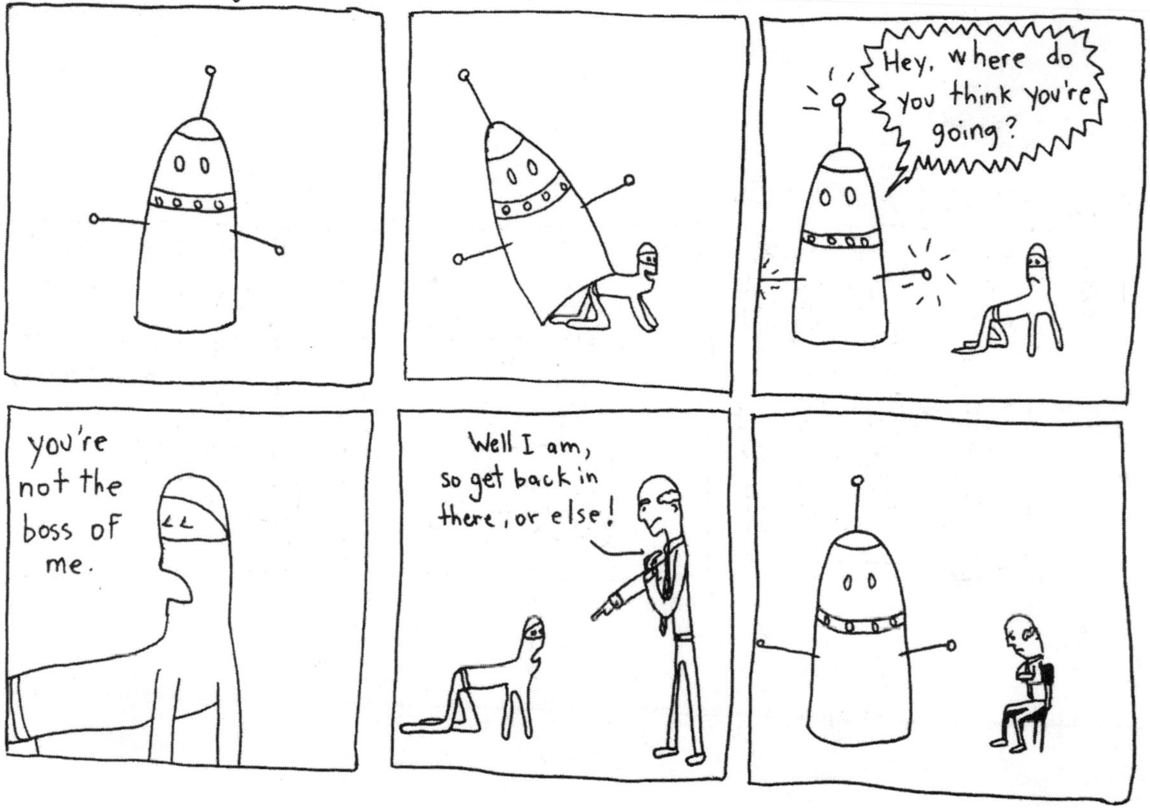

Hey, where do you think you're going?
you're not the boss of me.
Well I am, so get back in there, or else!

White Ninja enjoys a record

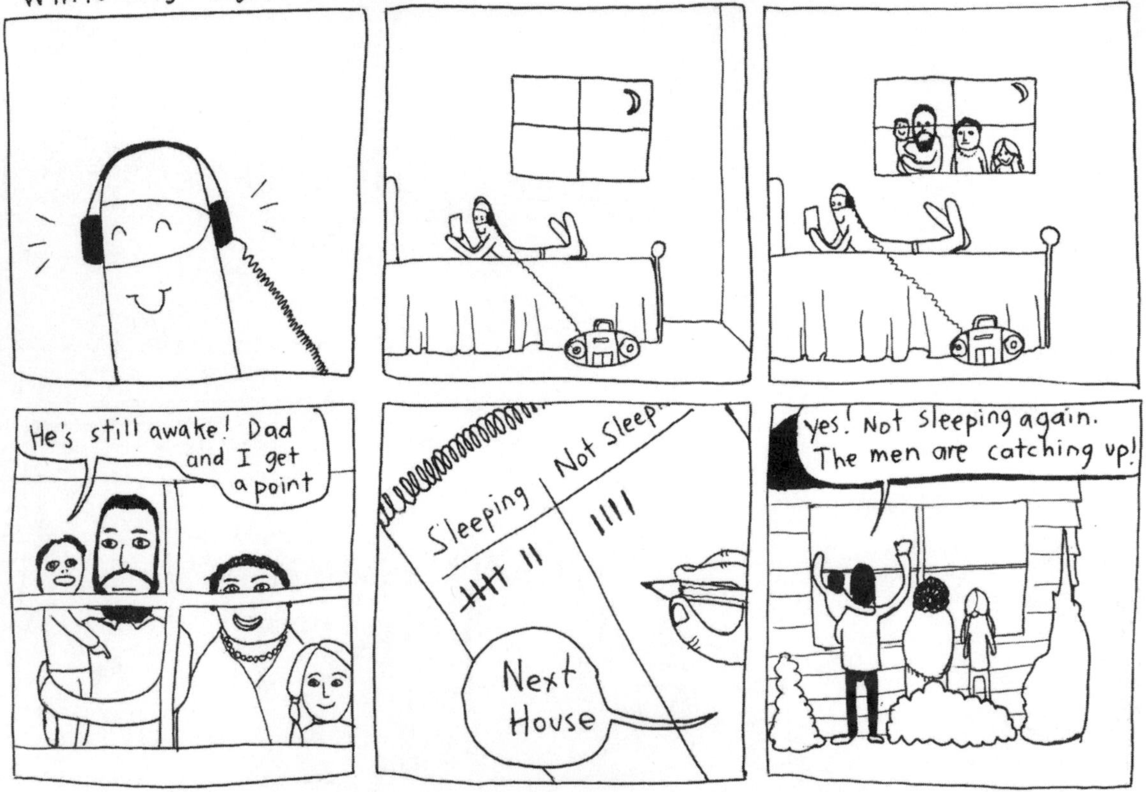
He's still awake! Dad and I get a point
Sleeping
Not Sleep
Next House
yes! Not sleeping again. The men are catching up!

White Ninja is the man

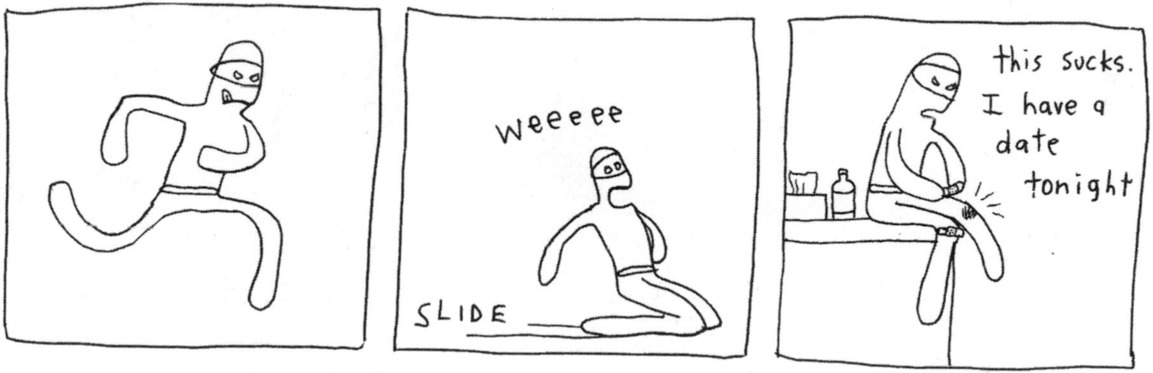
weeeee
SLIDE
this sucks. I have a date tonight

White Ninja's Skunk costume

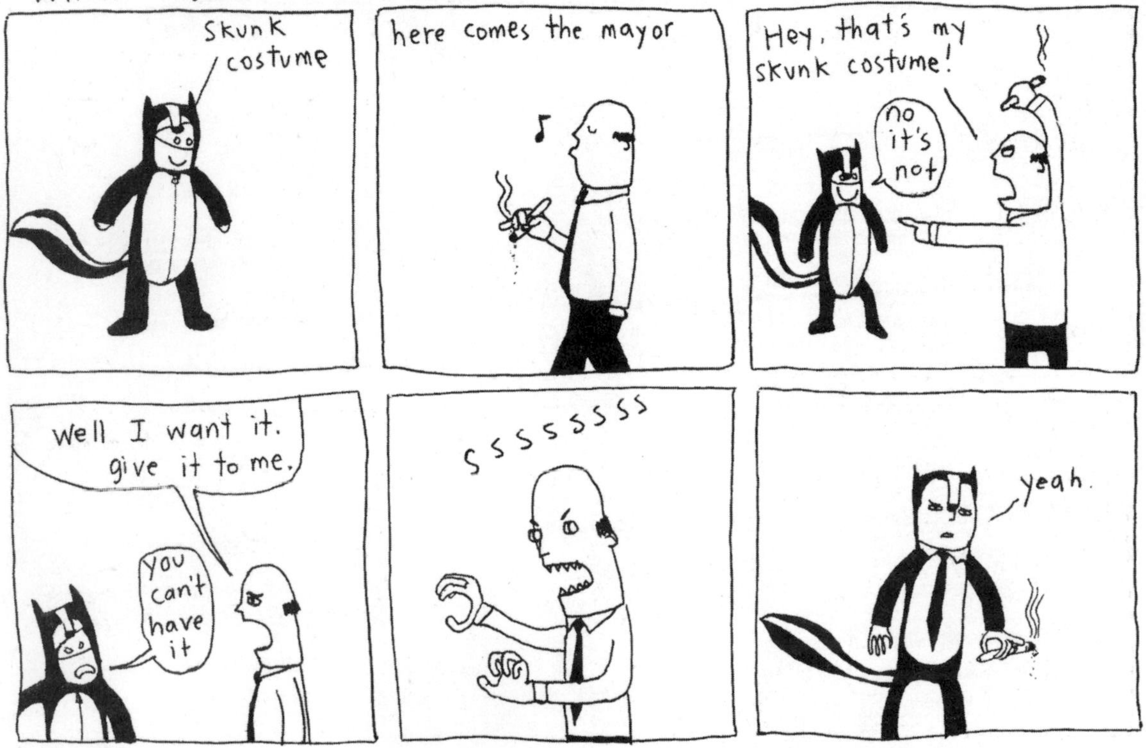
Skunk costume
here comes the mayor
Hey, that's my skunk costume!
no it's not
well I want it. give it to me.
you can't have it
sssssssss
yeah.

White Ninja meets the Tin Man

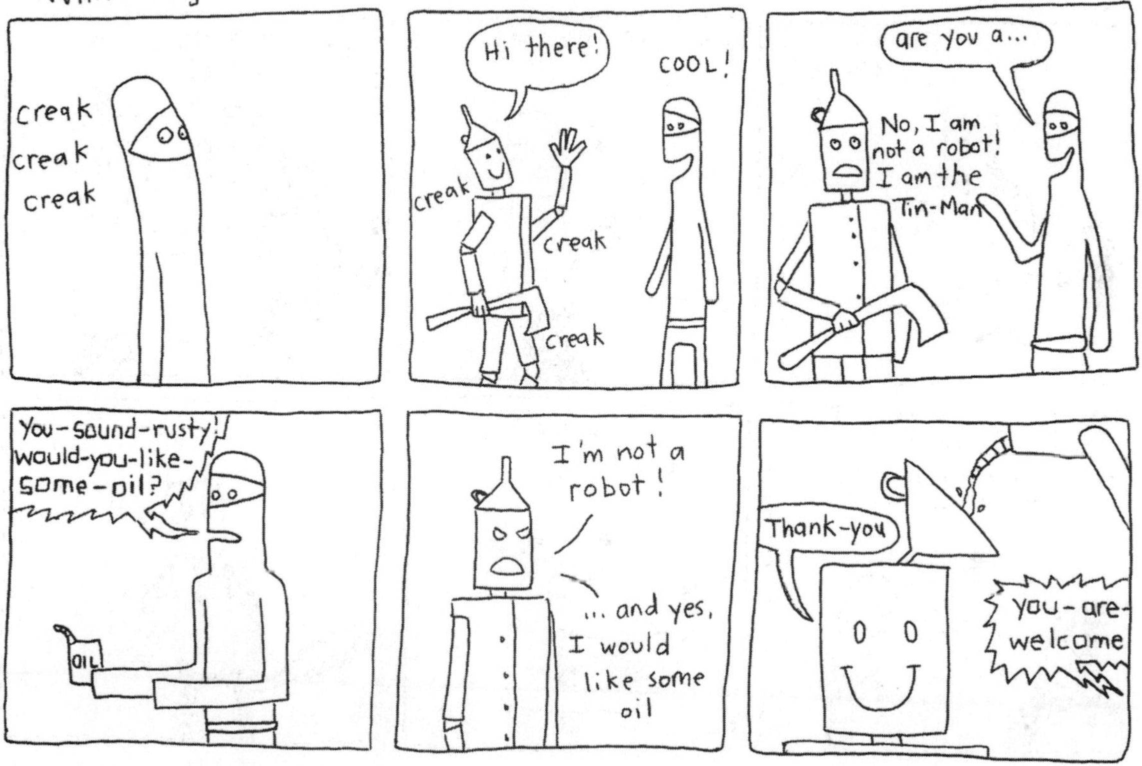
creak
creak
creak
Hi there!
COOL!
creak
creak
creak
are you a...
No, I am not a robot! I am the Tin-Man
You-sound-rusty! would-you-like-some-oil?
OIL
I'm not a robot!
... and yes, I would like some oil
Thank-you
you-are-welcome

White Ninja is parched

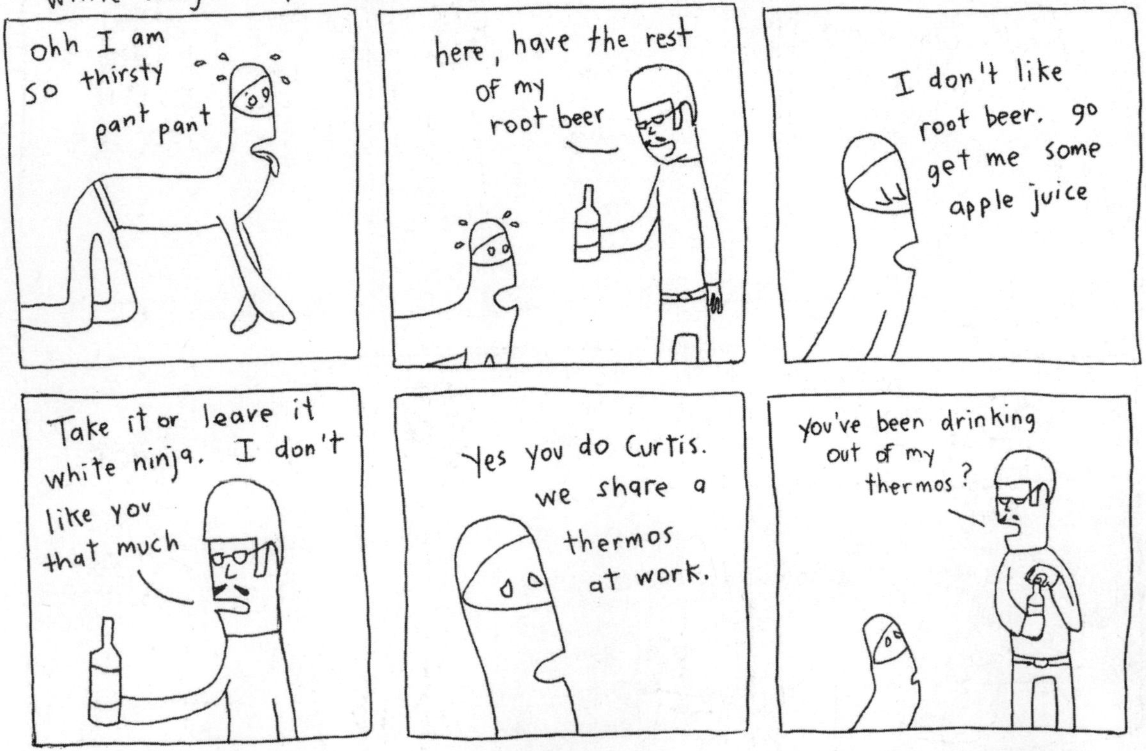
ohh I am so thirsty
pant pant
here, have the rest of my root beer
I don't like root beer. go get me some apple juice
Take it or leave it white ninja. I don't like you that much
Yes you do Curtis. we share a thermos at work.
you've been drinking out of my thermos?

White Ninja has a scar.

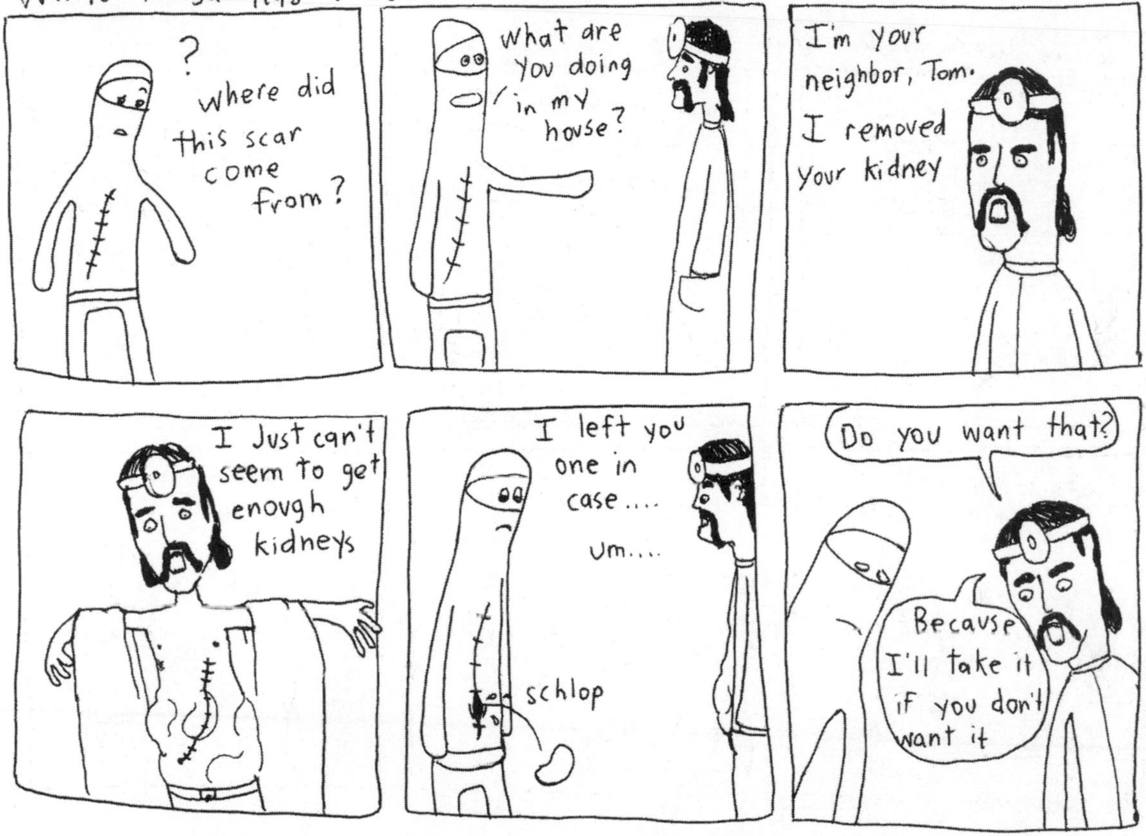
?
where did this scar come from?
what are you doing in my house?
I'm your neighbor, Tom.
I removed your kidney
I Just can't seem to get enough kidneys
I left you one in case....
um....
schlop
Do you want that?
Because I'll take it if you don't want it

White Ninja helps a blind man

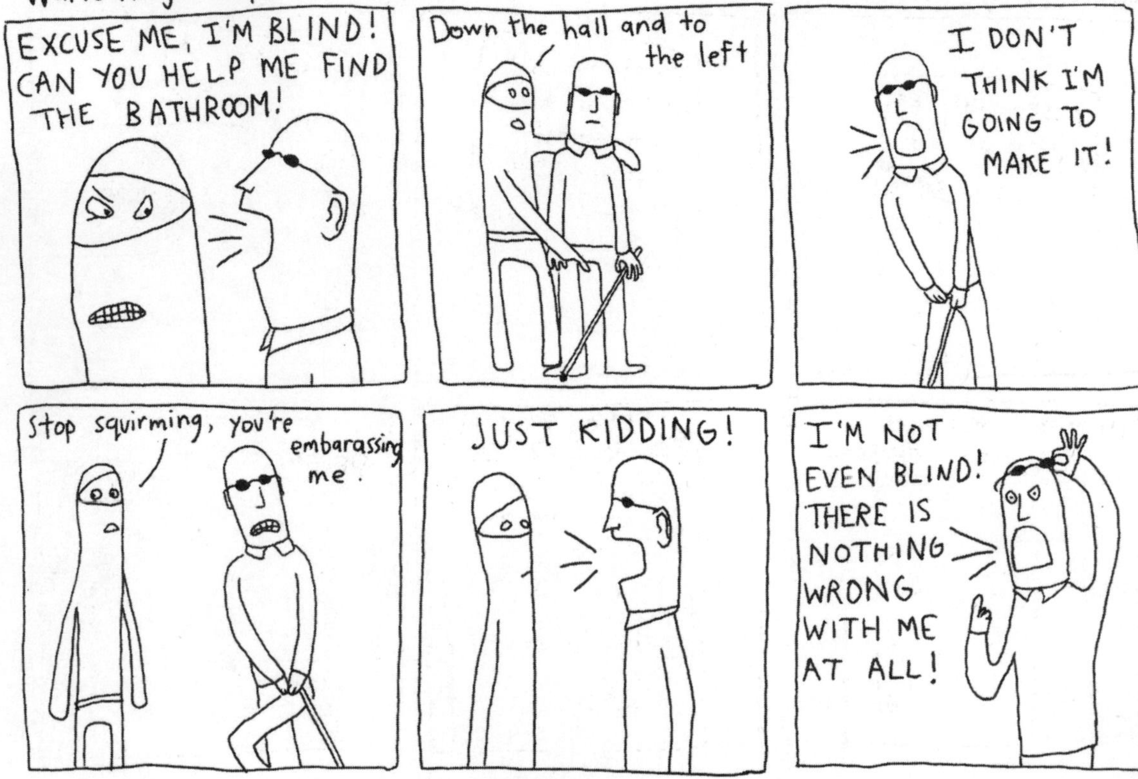
EXCUSE ME, I'M BLIND! CAN YOU HELP ME FIND THE BATHROOM!
Down the hall and to the left
I DON'T THINK I'M GOING TO MAKE IT!
Stop squirming, you're embarassing me.
JUST KIDDING!
I'M NOT EVEN BLIND! THERE IS NOTHING WRONG WITH ME AT ALL!

White Ninja writes a poem

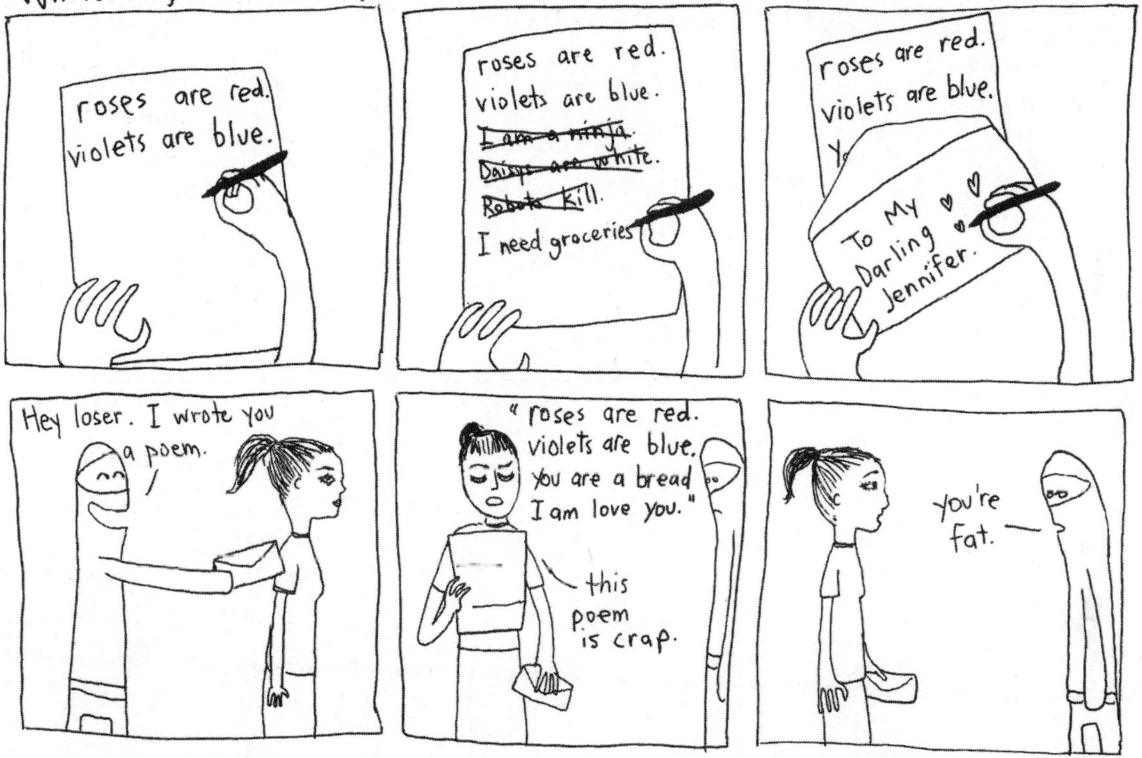

roses are red.
violets are blue.
roses are red.
violets are blue.
~~I am a ninja.~~
~~Daisys are white.~~
~~Robots kill.~~
I need groceries
roses are red.
violets are blue.
To My Darling Jennifer.
Hey loser. I wrote you a poem.
"roses are red. violets are blue. you are a bread I am love you."
this poem is crap.
you're fat.

White Ninja is in Jail

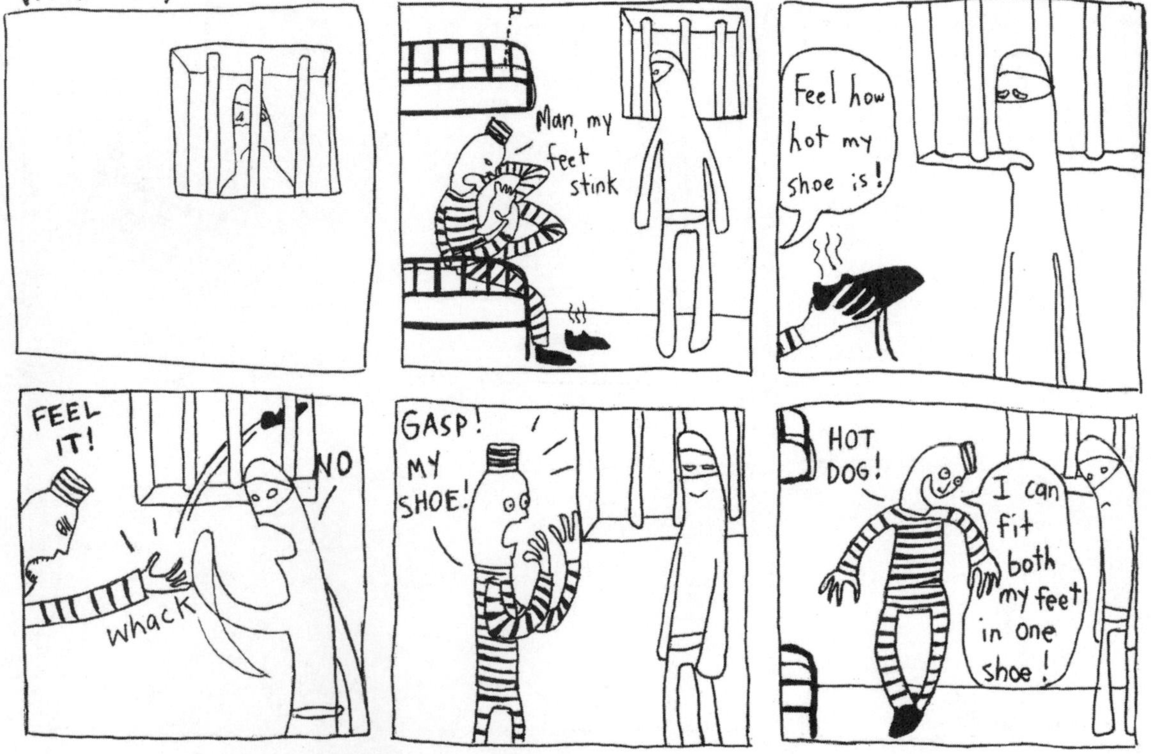
Man, my feet stink
Feel how hot my shoe is!
FEEL IT!
NO
whack
GASP! MY SHOE!
HOT DOG!
I can fit both my feet in one shoe!

White Ninja and the mummy

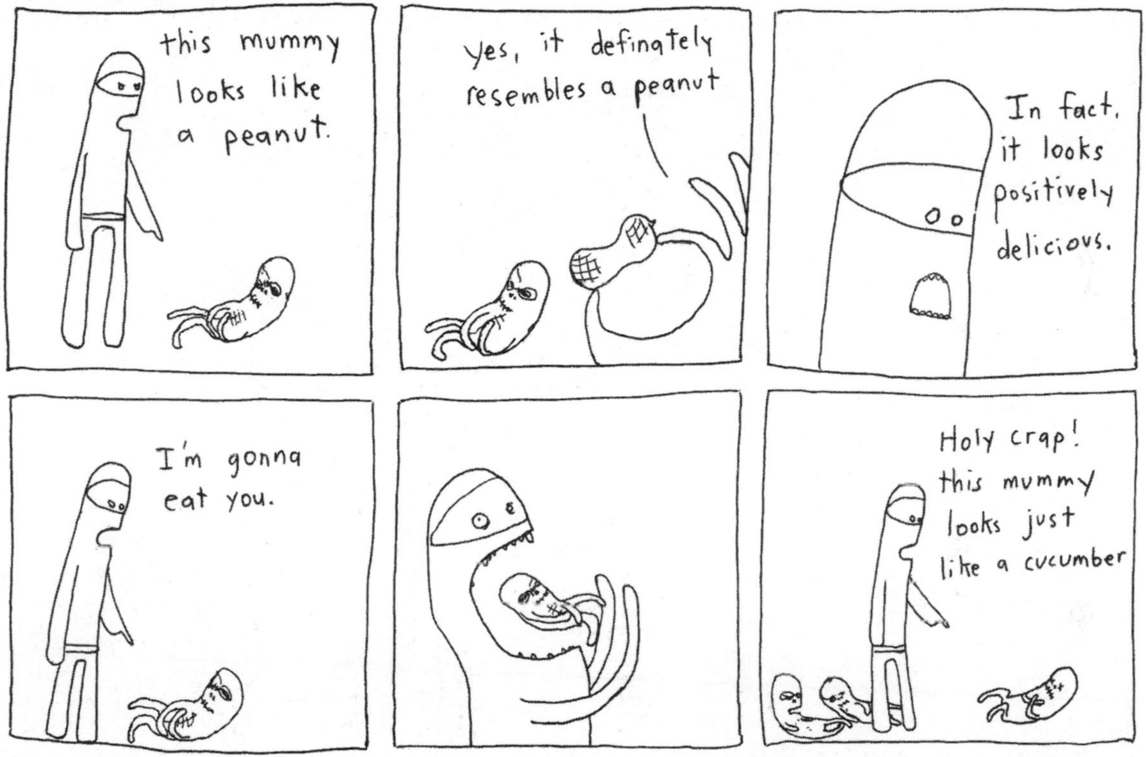
this mummy looks like a peanut.
yes, it definately resembles a peanut
In fact, it looks positively delicious.
I'm gonna eat you.
Holy crap! this mummy looks just like a cucumber

White Ninja sets a trap

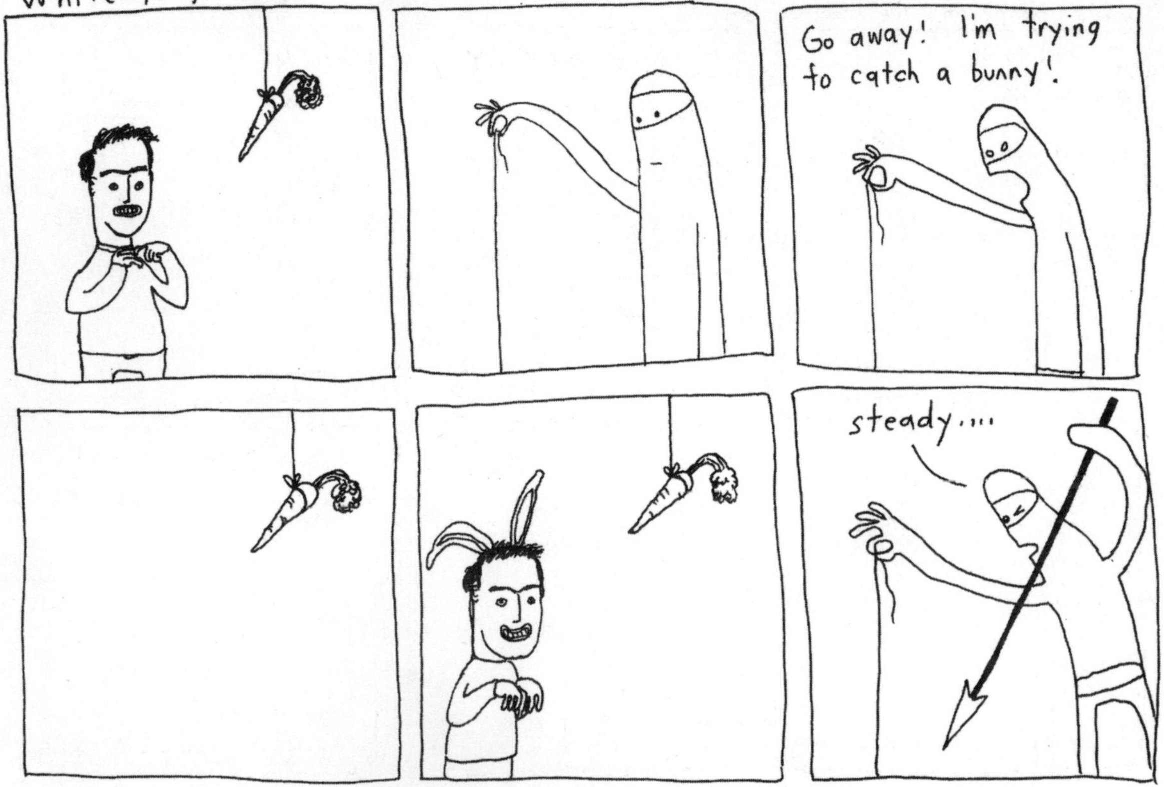
Go away! I'm trying to catch a bunny!
steady....

White Ninja and the floating boy

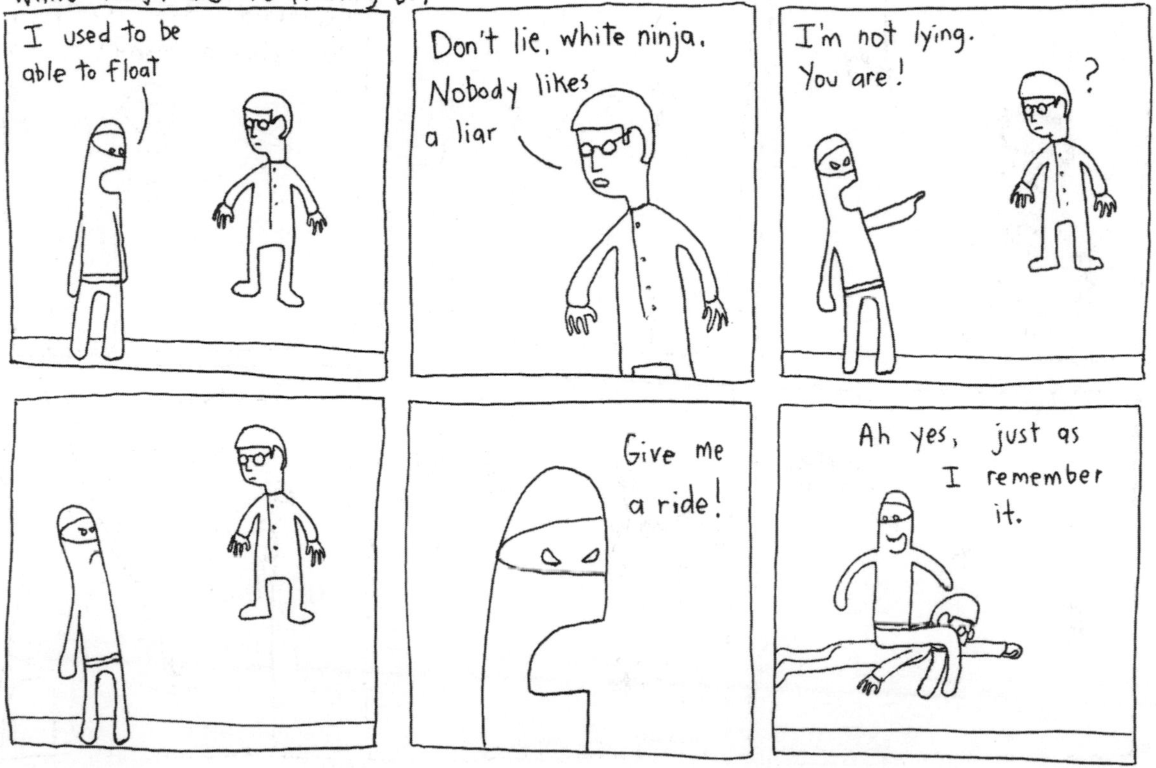
I used to be able to float
Don't lie, white ninja. Nobody likes a liar
I'm not lying. You are!
?
Give me a ride!
Ah yes, just as I remember it.

White Ninja has warts

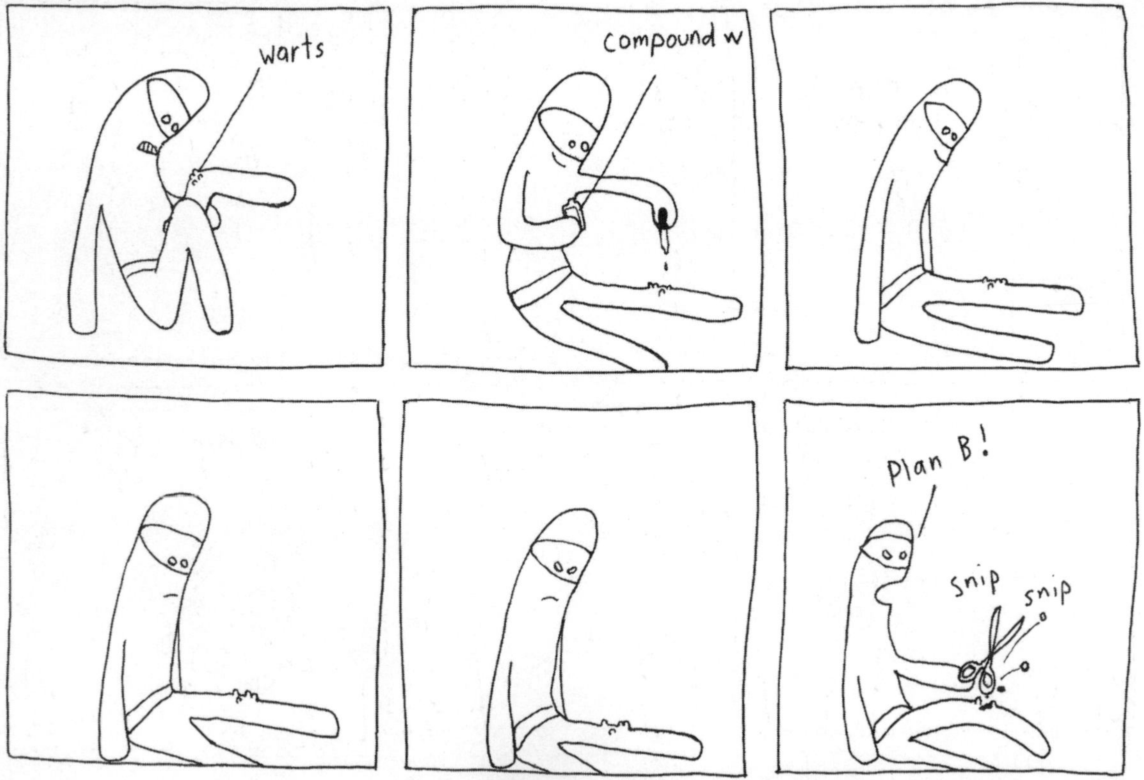
warts
compound w
Plan B!
snip
snip

White Ninja and the wizard

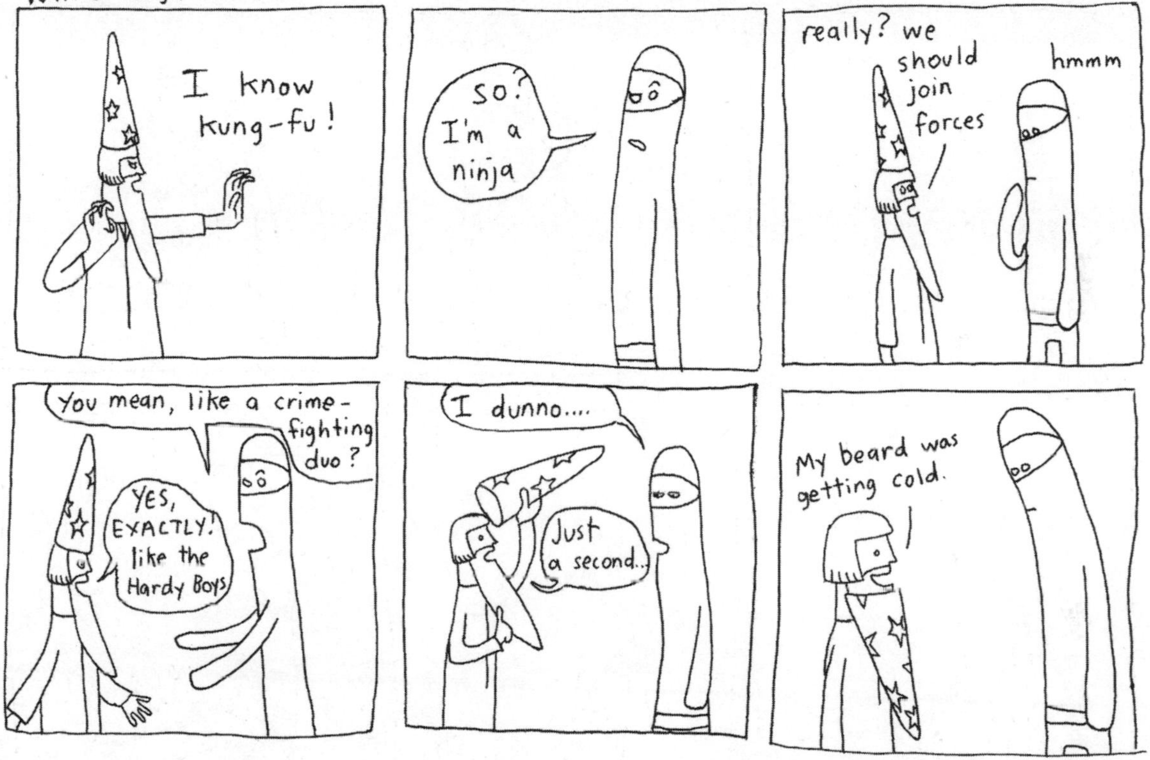

White Ninja gets robbed

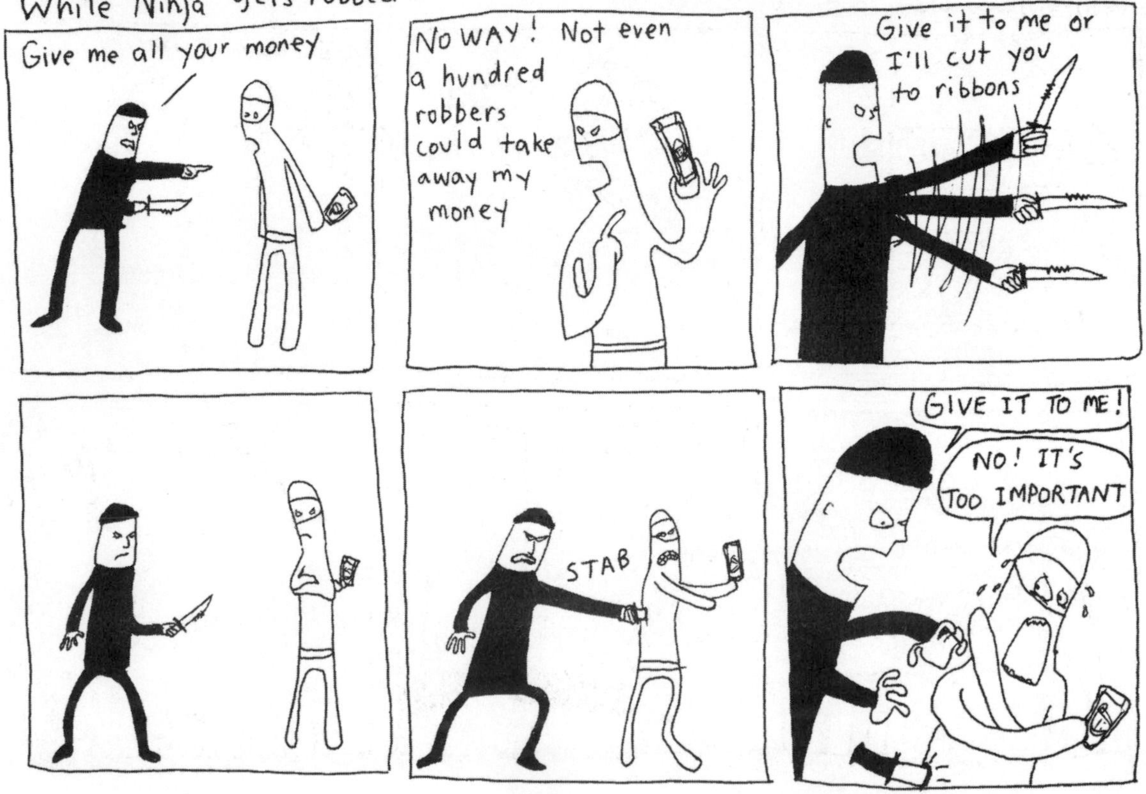
Give me all your money
NO WAY! Not even a hundred robbers could take away my money
Give it to me or I'll cut you to ribbons
STAB
GIVE IT TO ME!
NO! IT'S TOO IMPORTANT

White Ninja plays a trick.

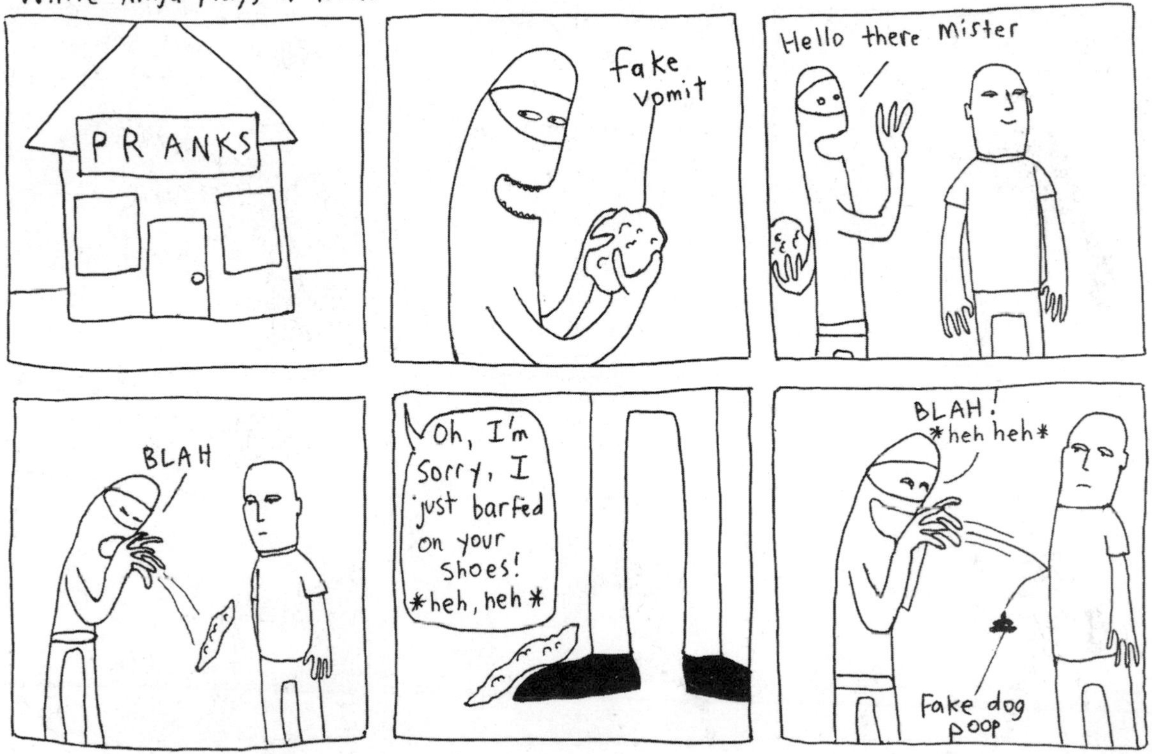
PRANKS
fake vomit
Hello there Mister
BLAH
Oh, I'm sorry, I just barfed on your shoes! *heh, heh*
BLAH! *heh heh*
Fake dog poop

white Ninja and the mystery beast

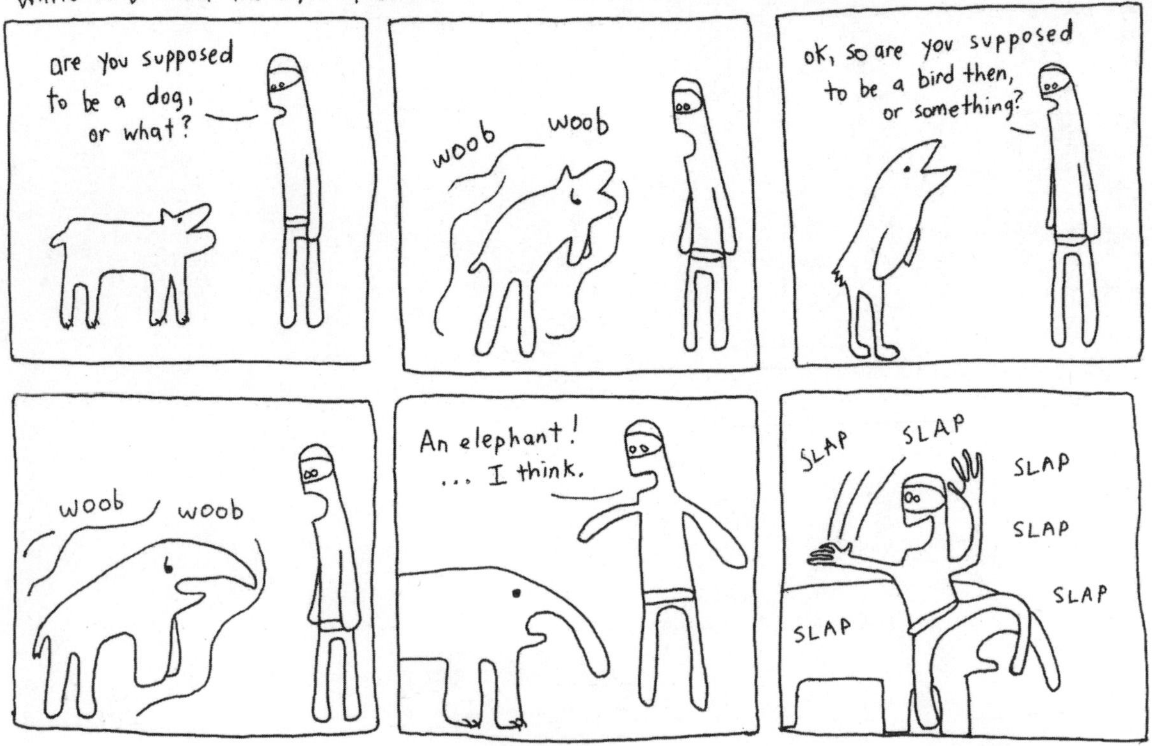
are you supposed to be a dog, or what?
woob woob
ok, so are you supposed to be a bird then, or something?
woob woob
An elephant! ... I think.
SLAP SLAP SLAP SLAP SLAP SLAP

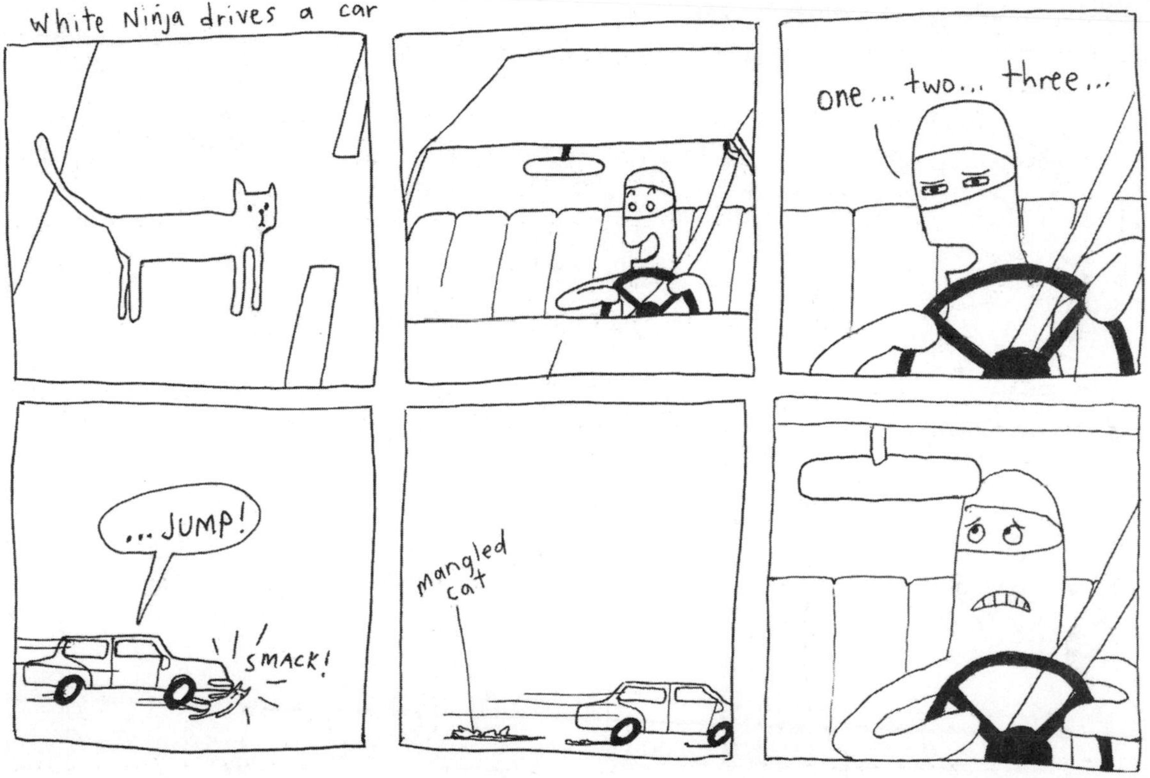
white Ninja drives a car
one... two... three...
...JUMP!
SMACK!
mangled cat

white Ninja gets punched in the Face

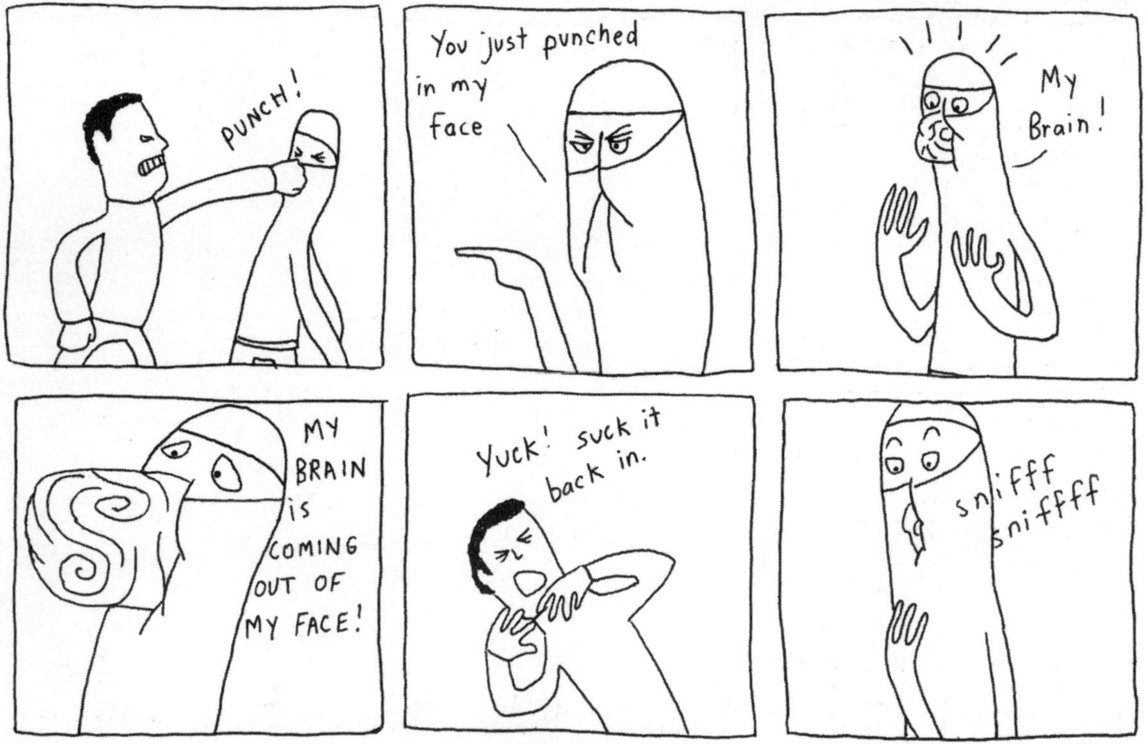
PUNCH!
You just punched in my face
My Brain!
MY BRAIN is COMING OUT OF MY FACE!
Yuck! suck it back in.
snifff snifffff

White Ninja and the mask

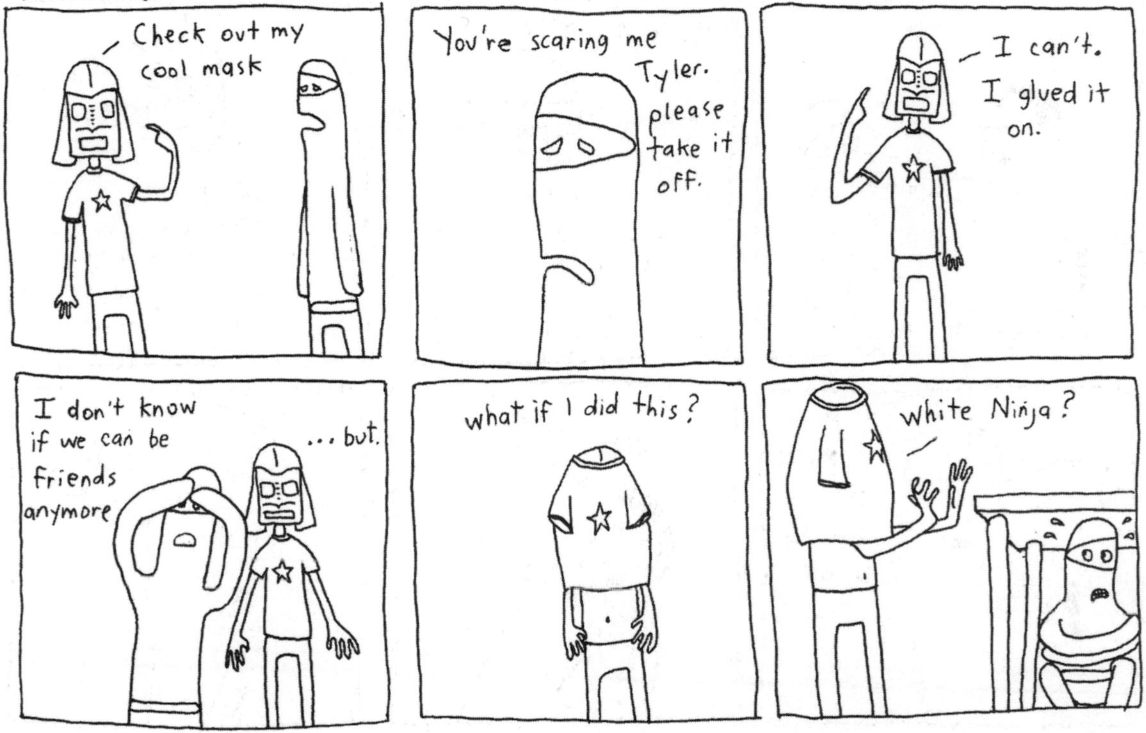
Check out my cool mask
You're scaring me Tyler. please take it off.
I can't. I glued it on.
I don't know if we can be friends anymore
... but.
what if I did this?
White Ninja?

White Ninja and the rainy day

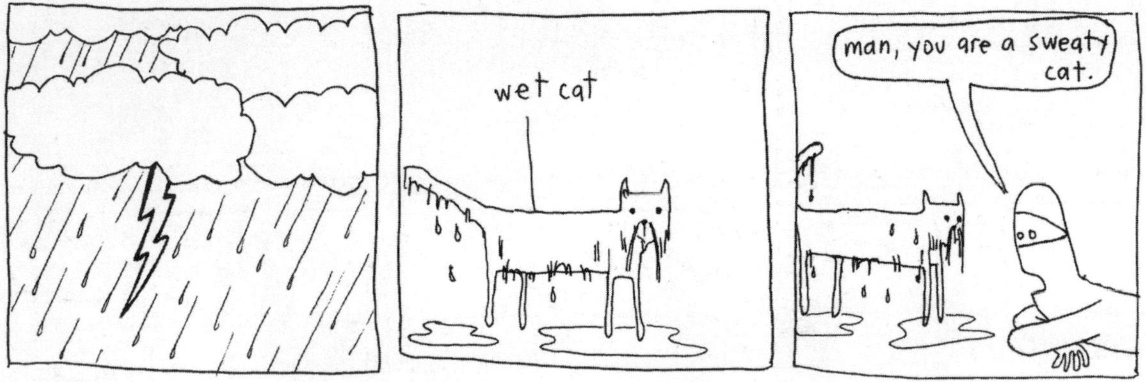
wet cat
man, you are a sweaty cat.

White Ninja's new belt

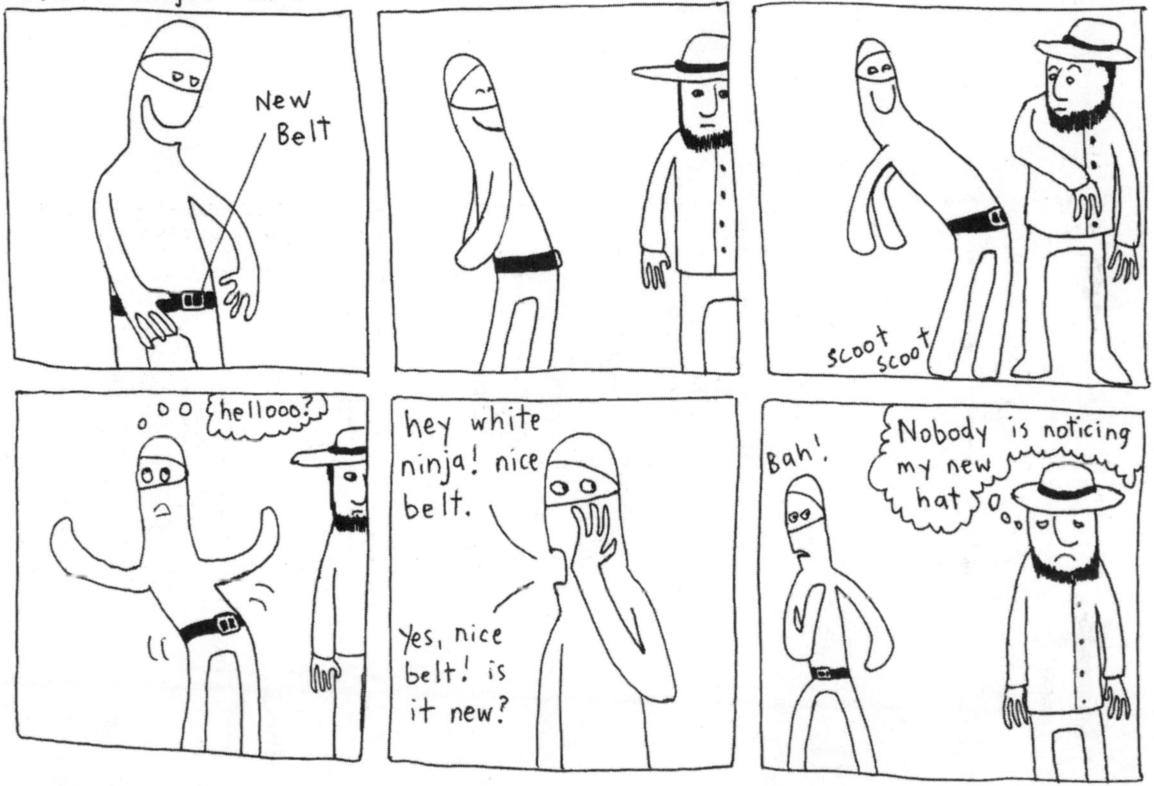

New Belt
scoot scoot
hellooo?
hey white ninja! nice belt.
Yes, nice belt! is it new?
Bah!
Nobody is noticing my new hat

White Ninja smells something gross

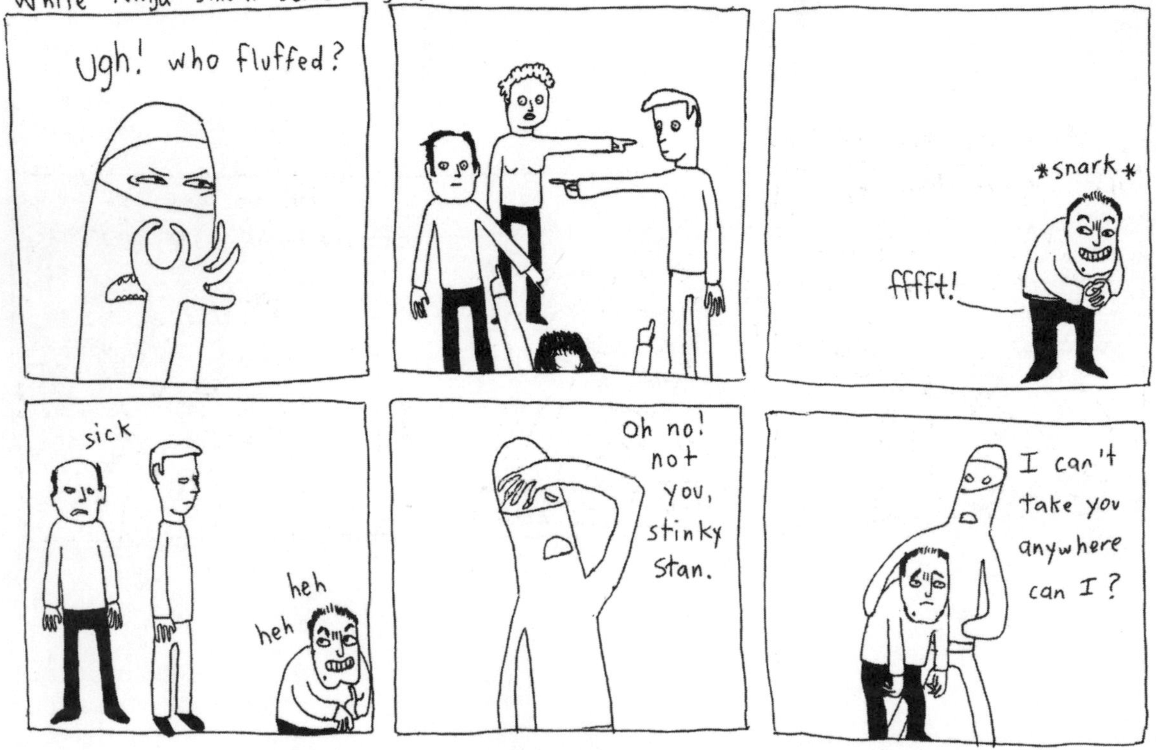
ugh! who fluffed?
snark
fffft!
sick
heh heh
Oh no! not you, stinky Stan.
I can't take you anywhere can I?

White Ninja stands too close

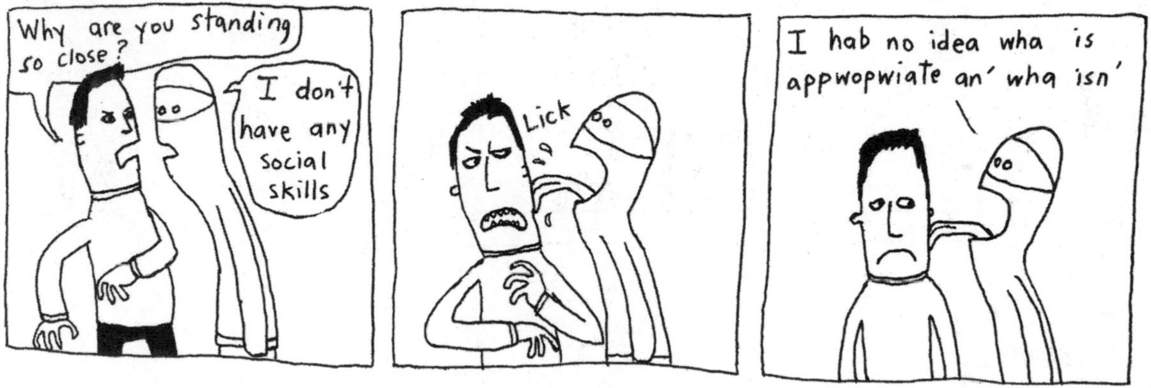
Why are you standing so close?
I don't have any social skills
Lick
I hab no idea wha is appwopwiate an' wha isn'

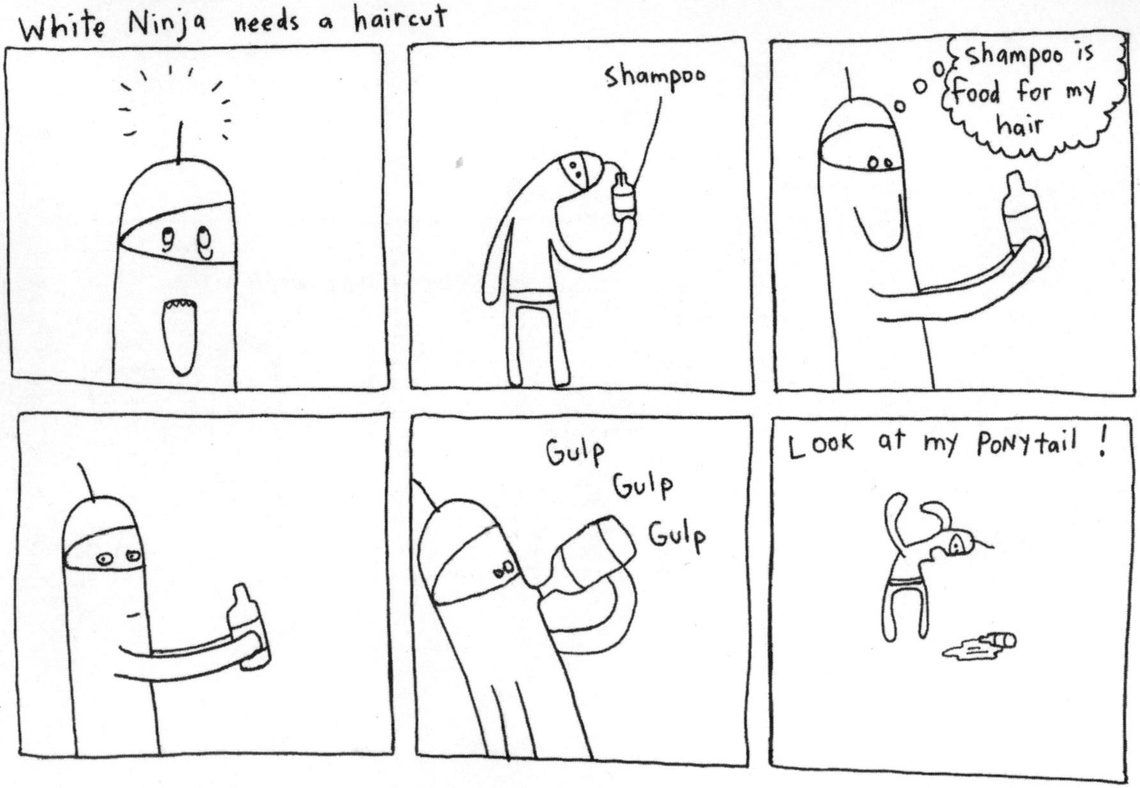
White Ninja needs a haircut
Shampoo
Shampoo is food for my hair
Gulp
Gulp
Gulp
Look at my PONYtail !

White Ninja builds a dam

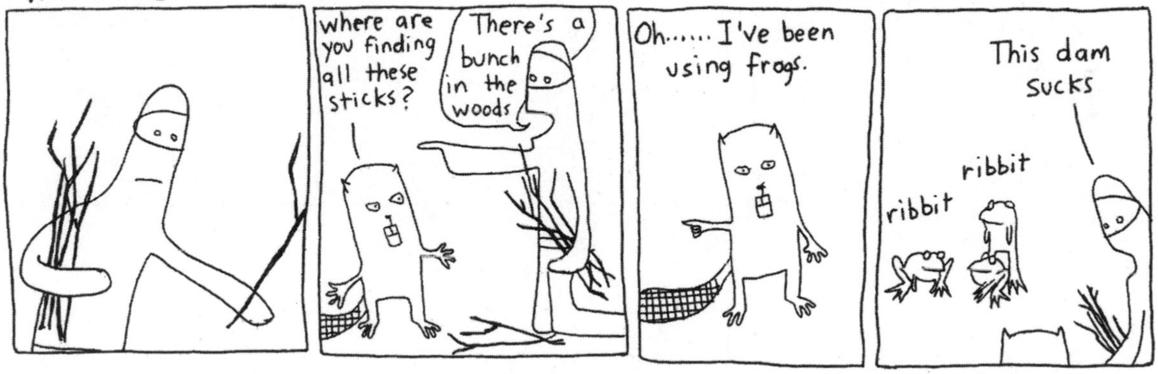
where are you finding all these sticks?
There's a bunch in the woods
Oh...... I've been using frogs.
This dam sucks
ribbit
ribbit

White Ninja is tired at Dinner

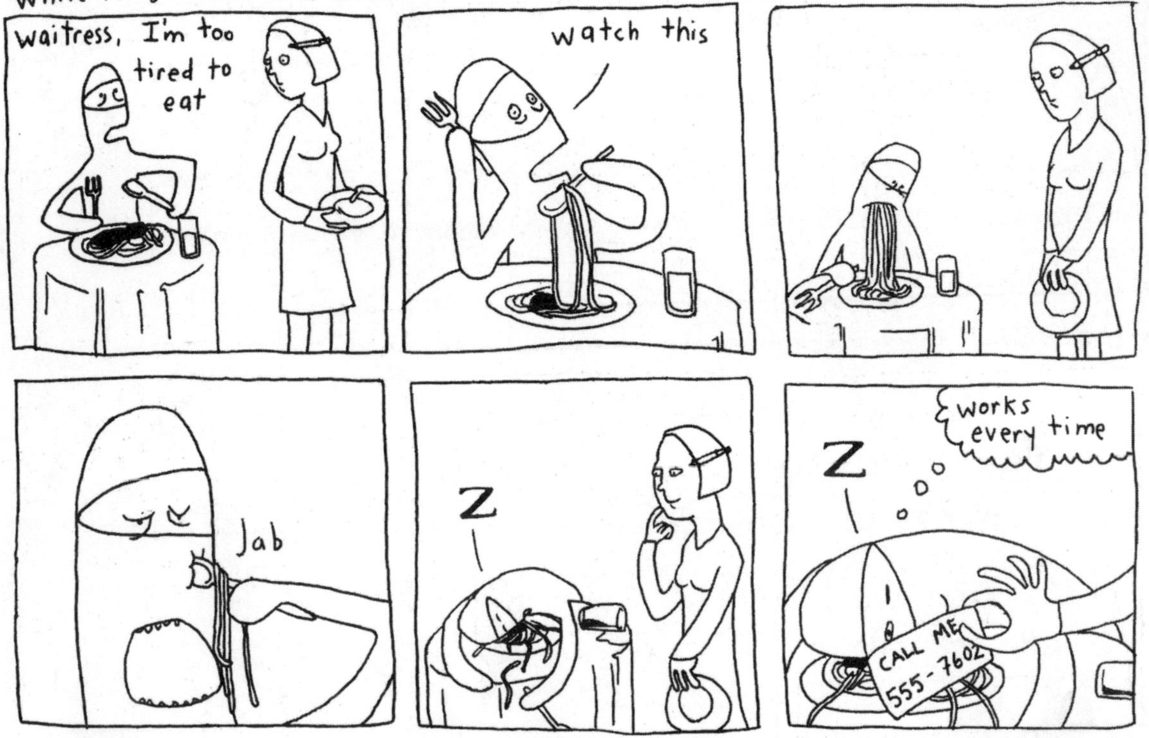
waitress, I'm too tired to eat
watch this
Jab
Z
Z
works every time
CALL ME 555-7602

White Ninja gets a Kiwi

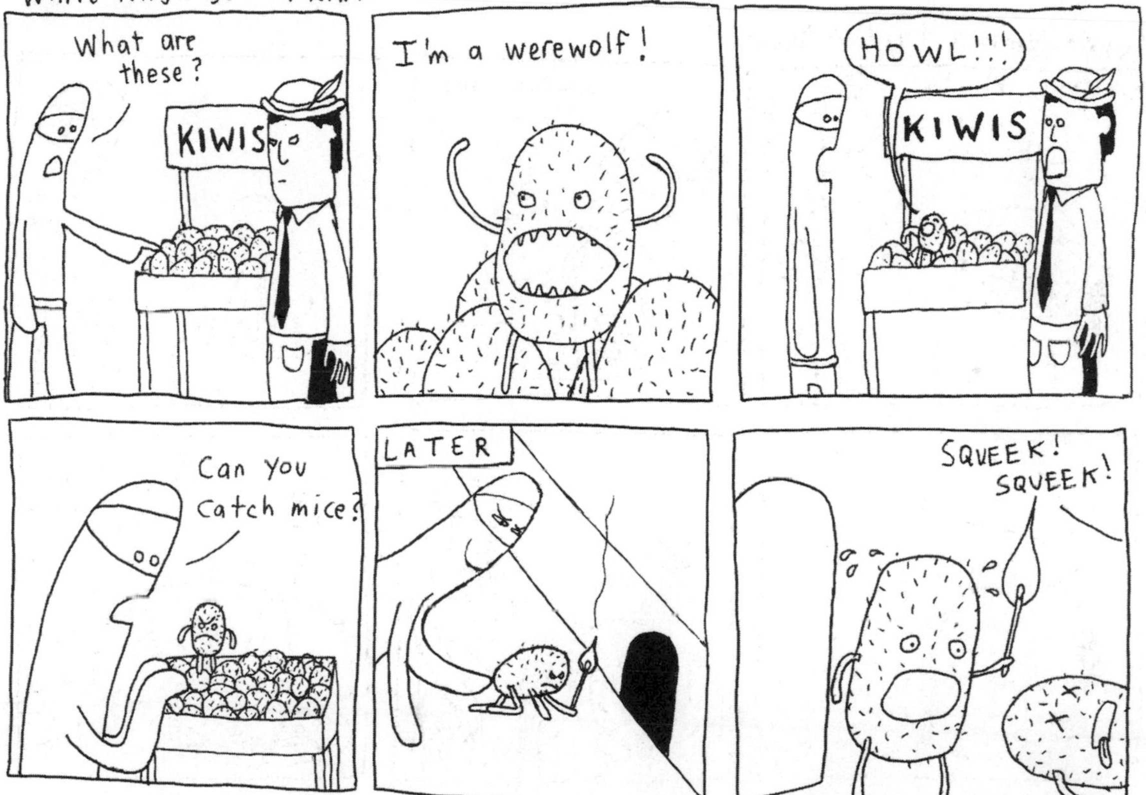
What are these?
KIWIS
I'm a werewolf!
HOWL!!!
KIWIS
Can you catch mice?
LATER
SQUEEK!
SQUEEK!

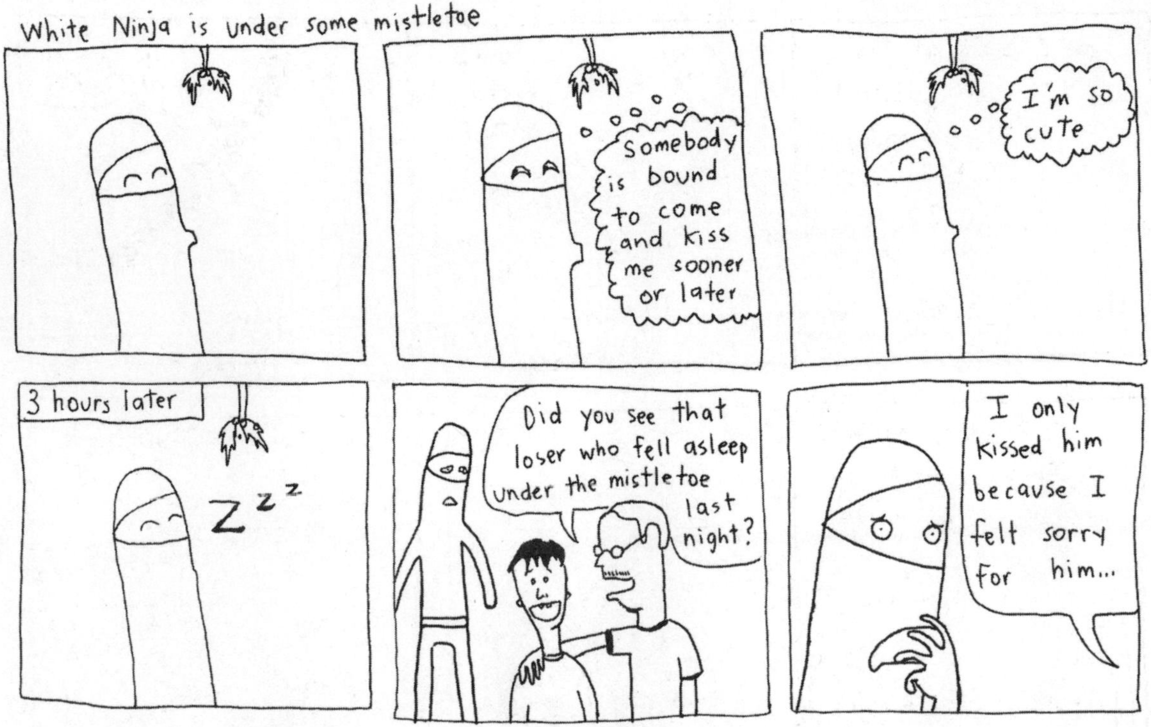
White Ninja is under some mistletoe
Somebody is bound to come and kiss me sooner or later
I'm so cute
3 hours later
Z z z
Did you see that loser who fell asleep under the mistletoe last night?
I only kissed him because I felt sorry for him...

White Ninja and the darling puppy

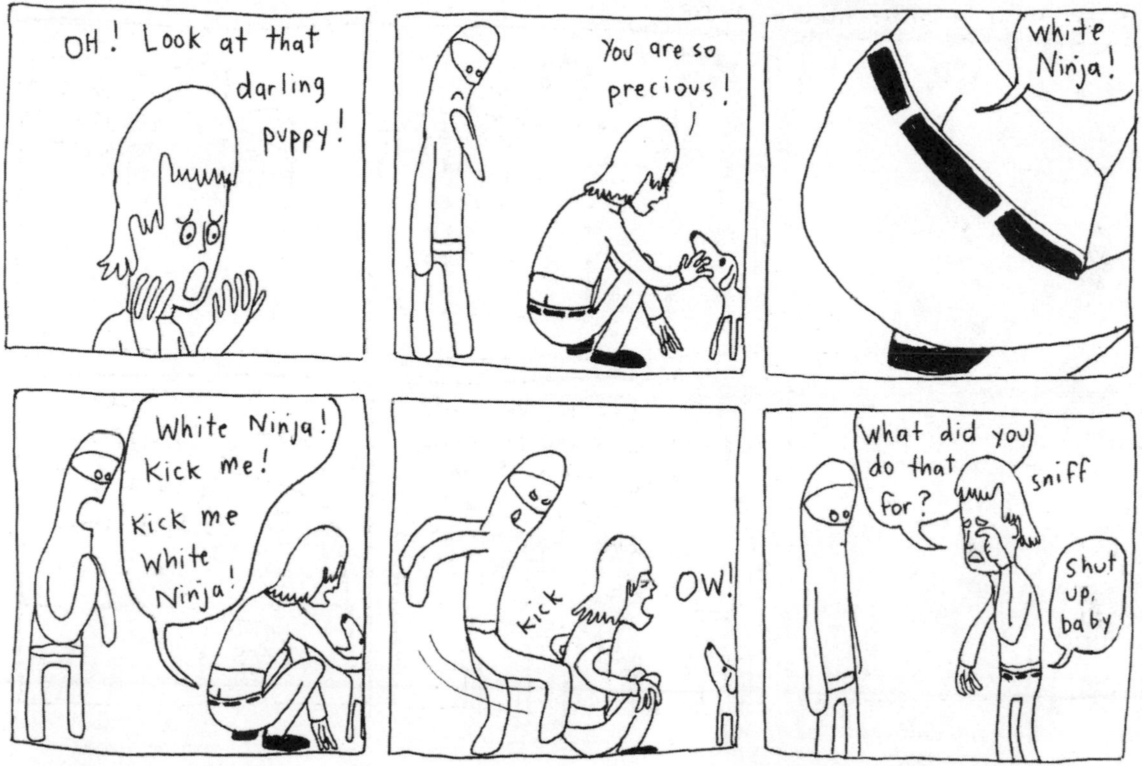
OH! Look at that darling puppy!
You are so precious!
White Ninja!
White Ninja! Kick me!
Kick me White Ninja!
kick
OW!
What did you do that for?
sniff
Shut up, baby

White Ninja shows off

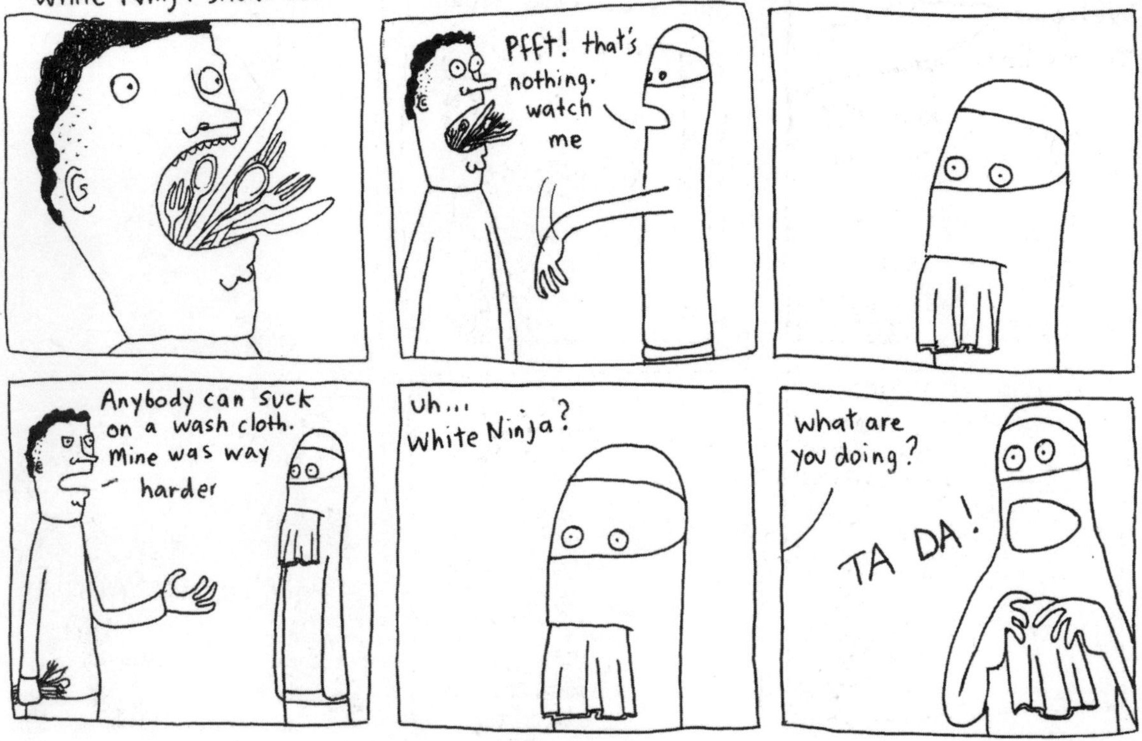

Pfft! that's nothing. watch me
Anybody can suck on a wash cloth. Mine was way harder
uh... White Ninja?
what are you doing?
TA DA!

White Ninja on the farm

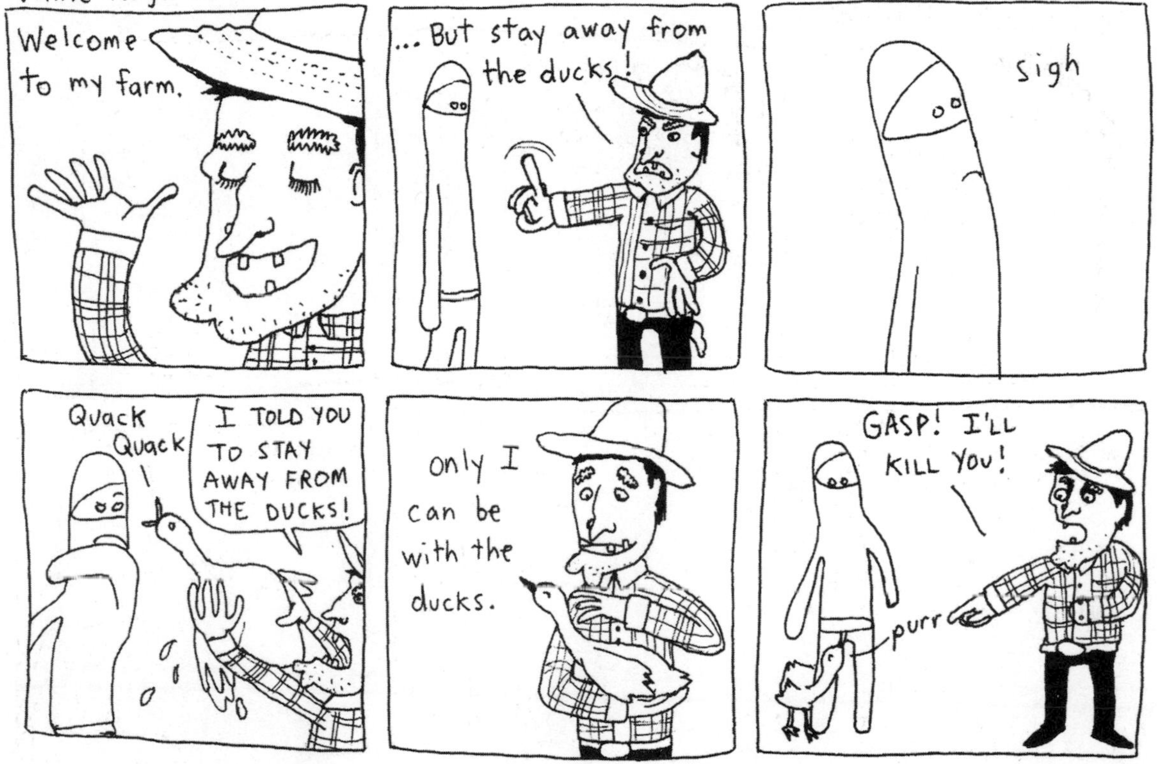
Welcome to my farm.
... But stay away from the ducks!
sigh
Quack Quack
I TOLD YOU TO STAY AWAY FROM THE DUCKS!
only I can be with the ducks.
GASP! I'LL KILL YOU!
purr

White Ninja's mouse died

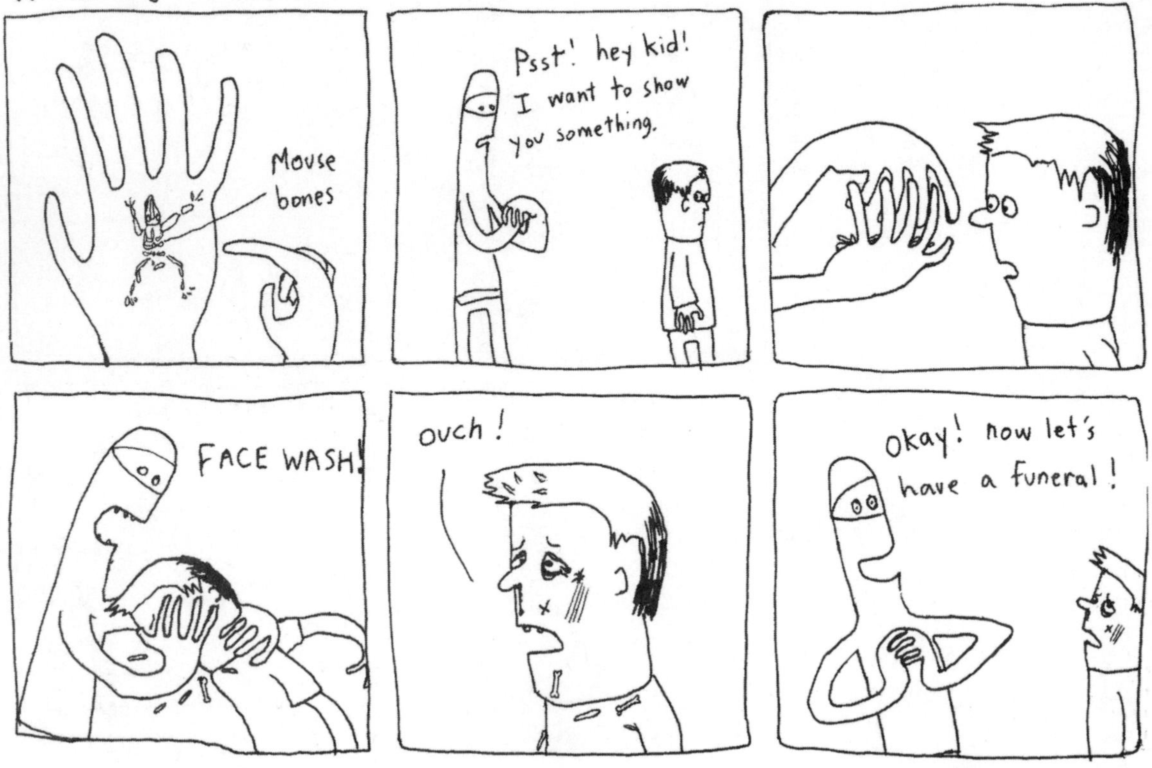
Mouse bones
Psst! hey kid! I want to show you something.
FACE WASH!
ouch!
Okay! now let's have a funeral!

White Ninja's new jacket

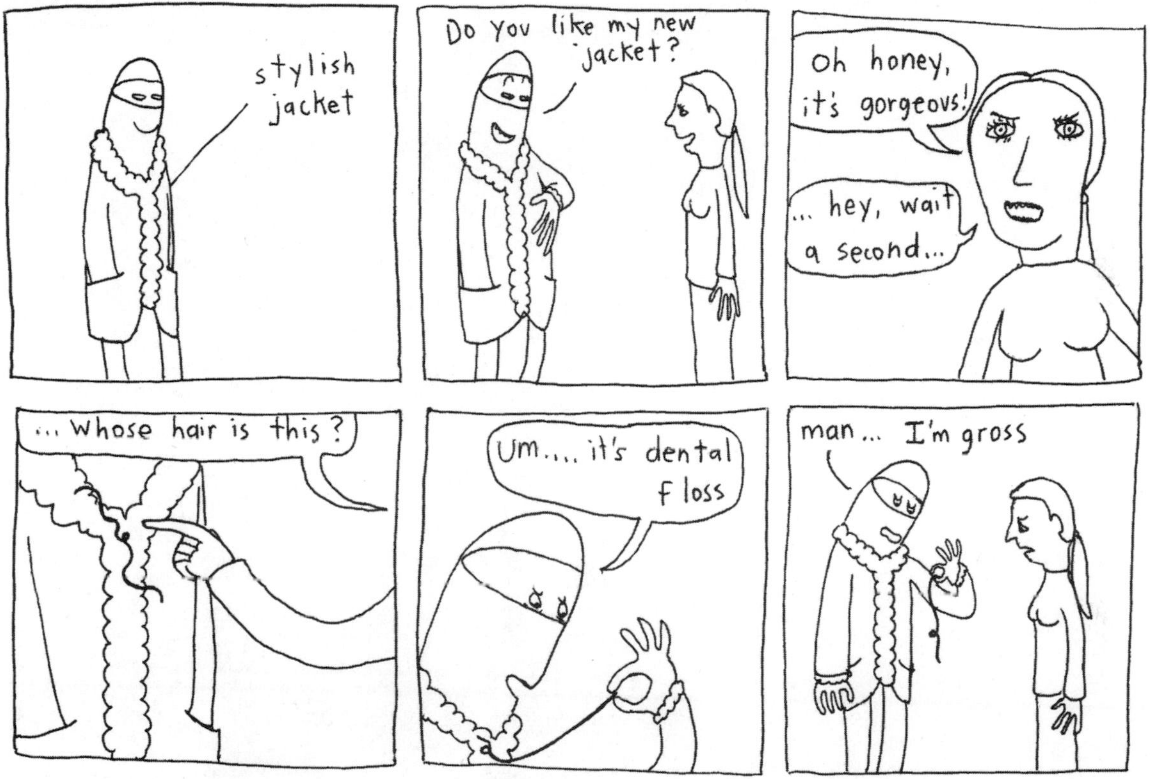
stylish jacket
Do you like my new jacket?
Oh honey, it's gorgeous!
... hey, wait a second...
... whose hair is this?
Um.... it's dental floss
man... I'm gross

White Ninja and the lion

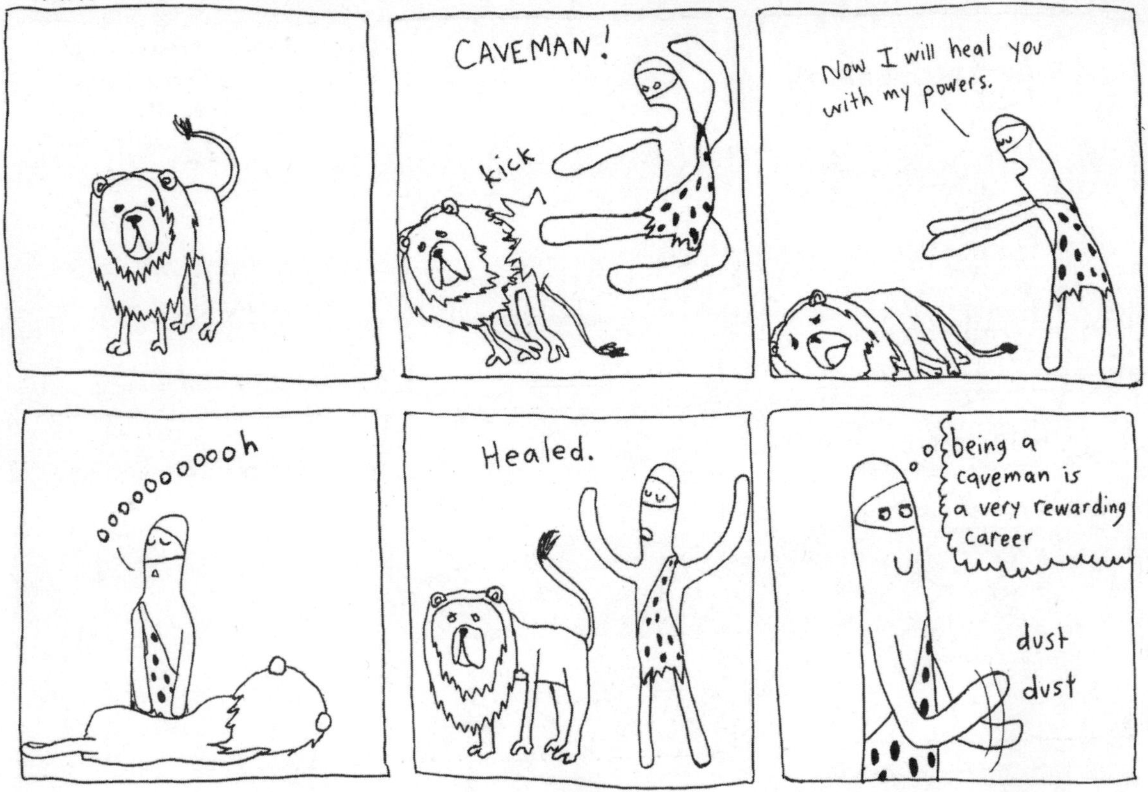
CAVEMAN!
kick
Now I will heal you with my powers.
ooooooooooooh
Healed.
being a caveman is a very rewarding career
dust
dust

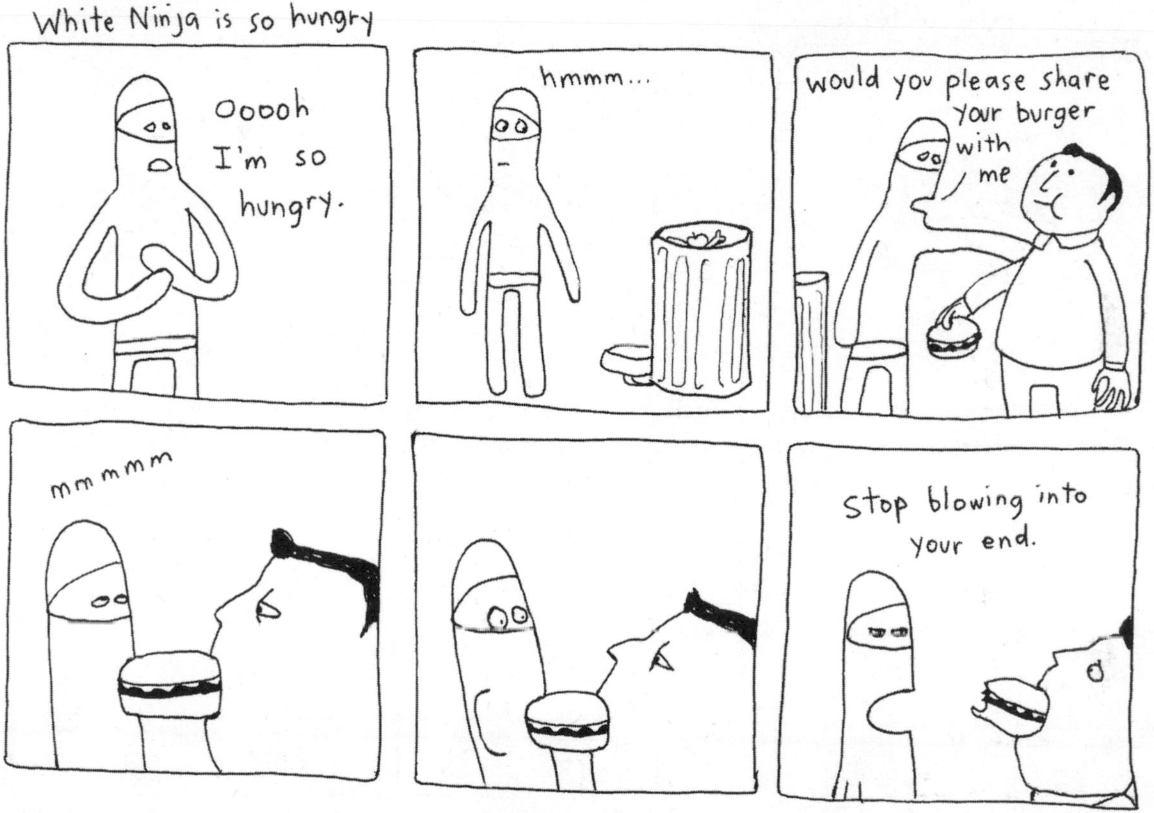
White Ninja is so hungry
Ooooh I'm so hungry.
hmmm...
would you please share your burger with me
mmmmm
Stop blowing into your end.

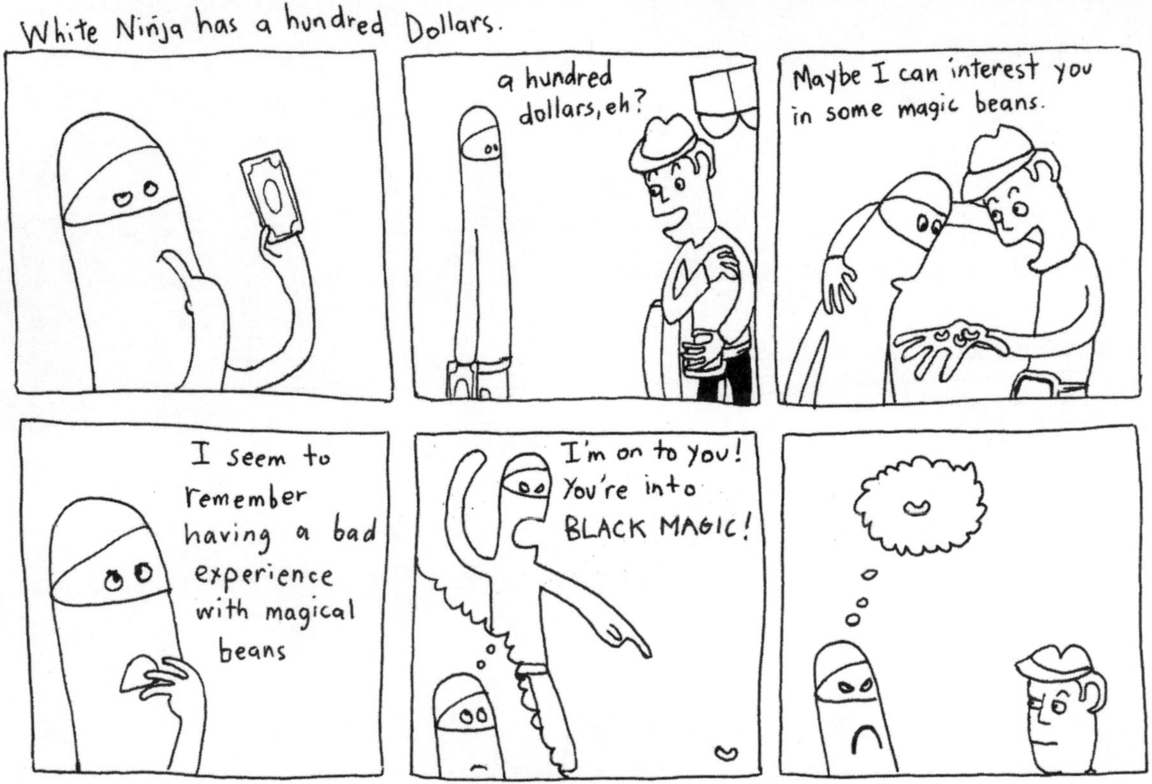
White Ninja has a hundred Dollars.
a hundred dollars, eh?
Maybe I can interest you in some magic beans.
I seem to remember having a bad experience with magical beans
I'm on to you! You're into BLACK MAGIC!

White Ninja is content.

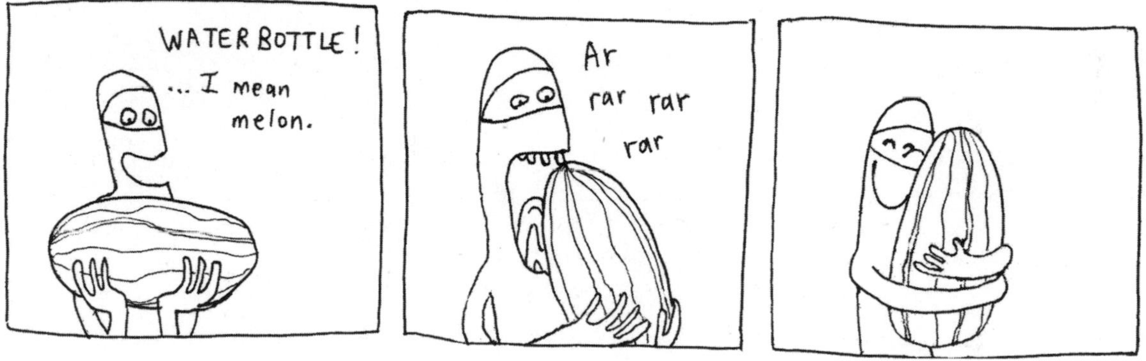
WATER BOTTLE!
... I mean melon.
Ar rar rar rar

White Ninja is home

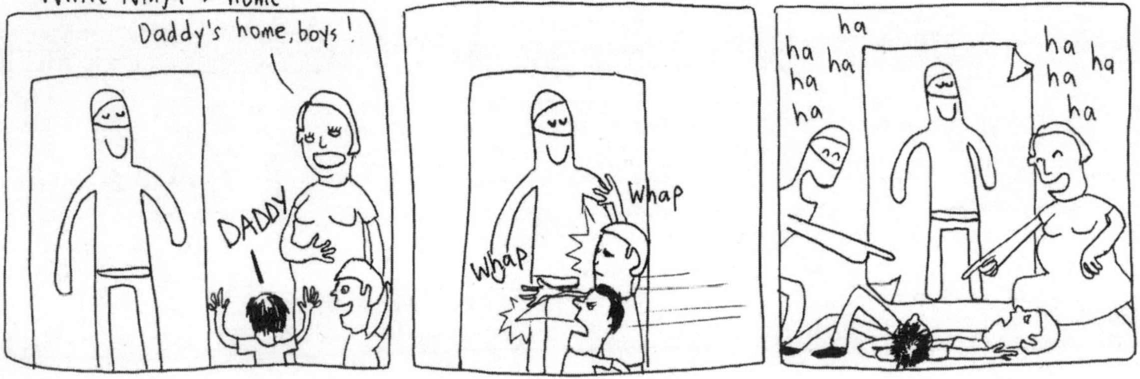
Daddy's home, boys!
DADDY
Whap
Whap
ha
ha
ha
ha
ha
ha
ha
ha
ha
ha

White Ninja gives a lecture.

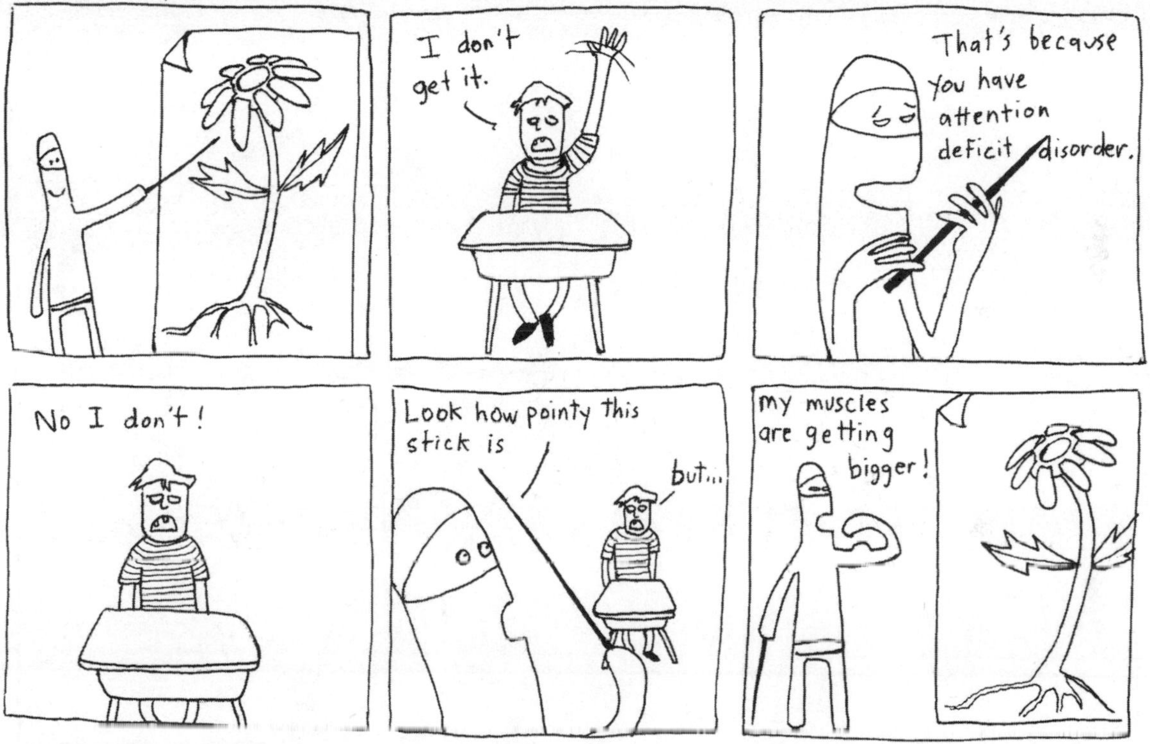

White Ninja's Mysterious third eye!

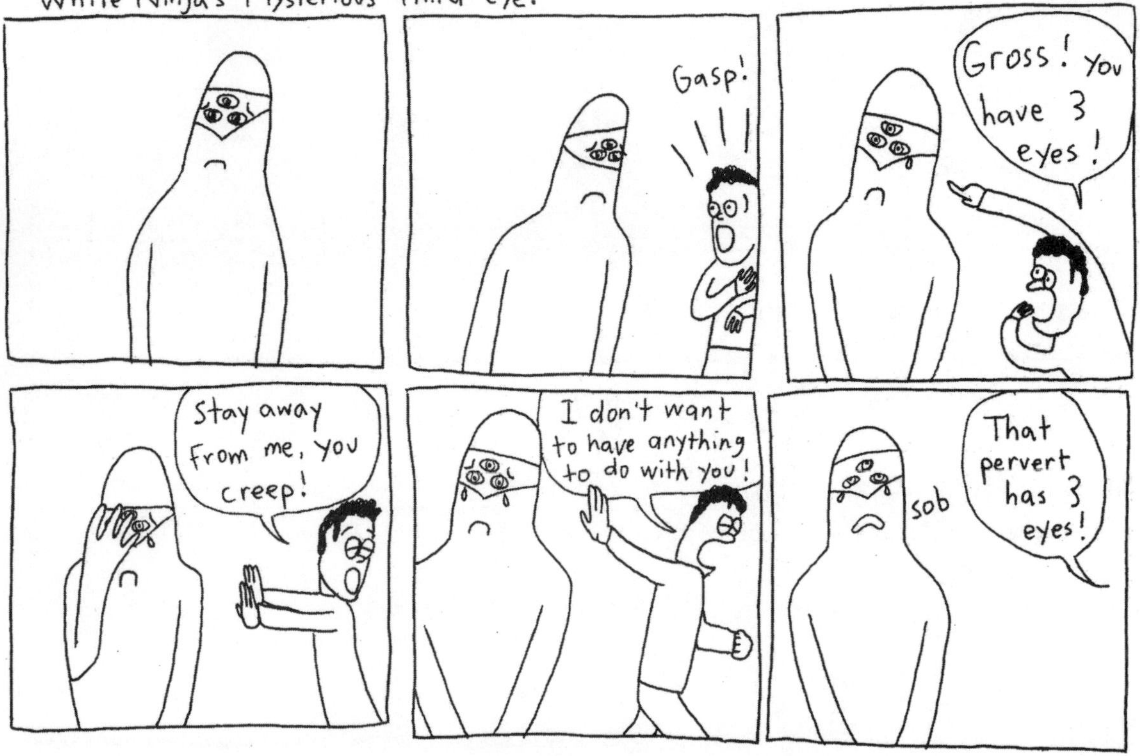
Gasp!
Gross! You have 3 eyes!
Stay away from me, you creep!
I don't want to have anything to do with you!
sob
That pervert has 3 eyes!

White Ninja and the munchkins

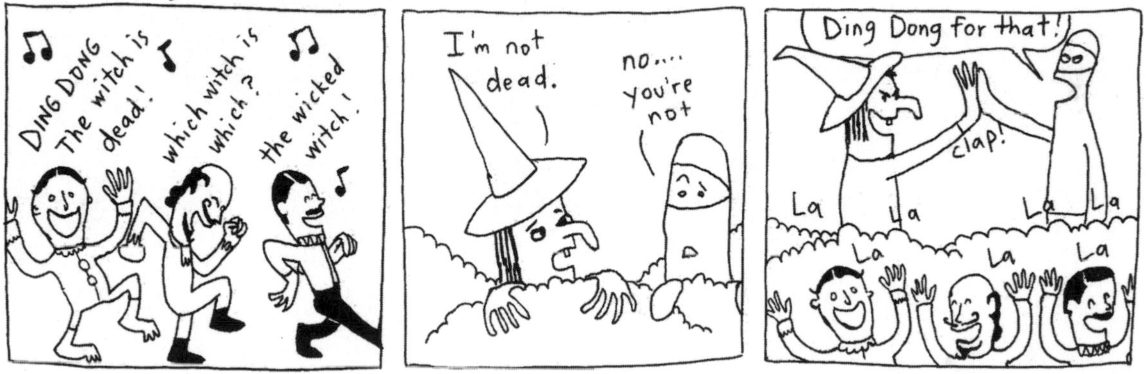

DING DONG The witch is dead!
which witch is which?
the wicked witch!
I'm not dead.
no.... you're not
Ding Dong for that!
clap!
La
La
La
La
La
La
La

White Ninja and the best stick

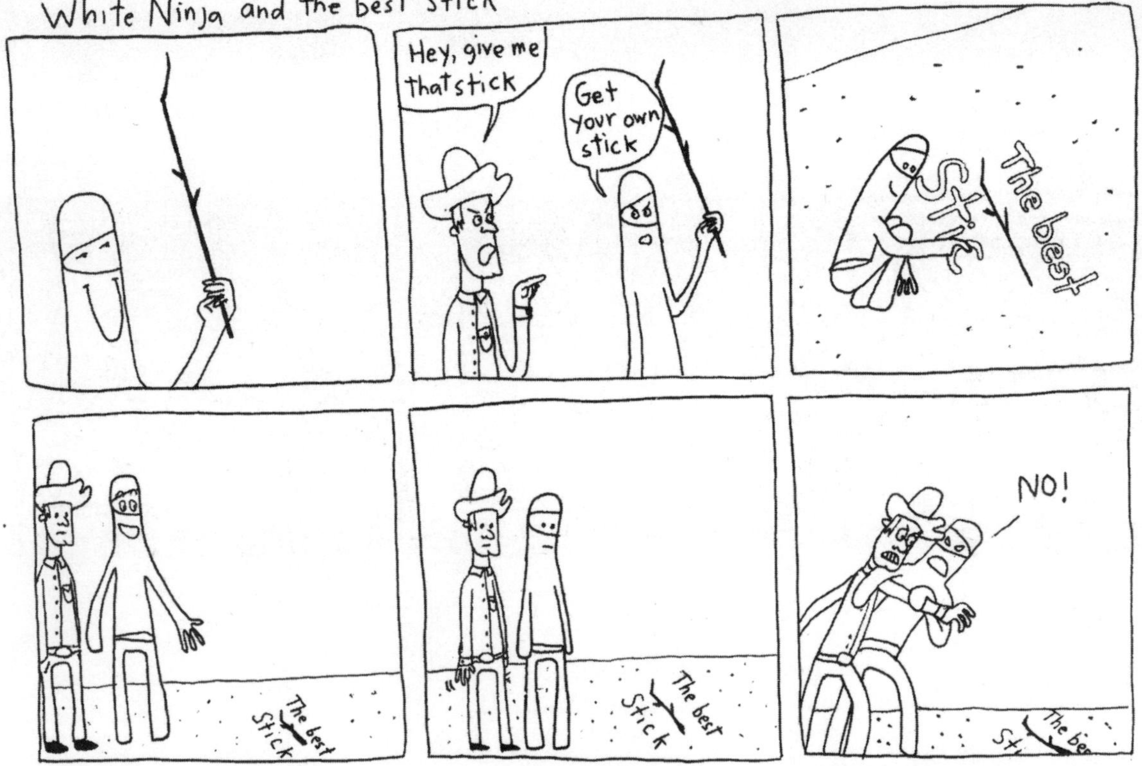
Hey, give me that stick
Get your own stick
The best Stick
The best Stick
The best Stick
NO!

White Ninja witnesses an accident

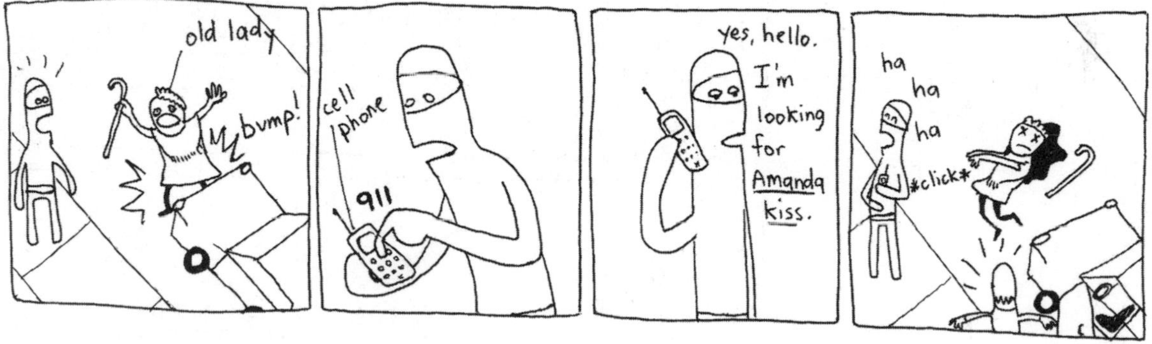
old lady
bump!
cell phone
911
yes, hello.
I'm looking for Amanda kiss.
ha
ha
ha
click

White Ninja's moustache

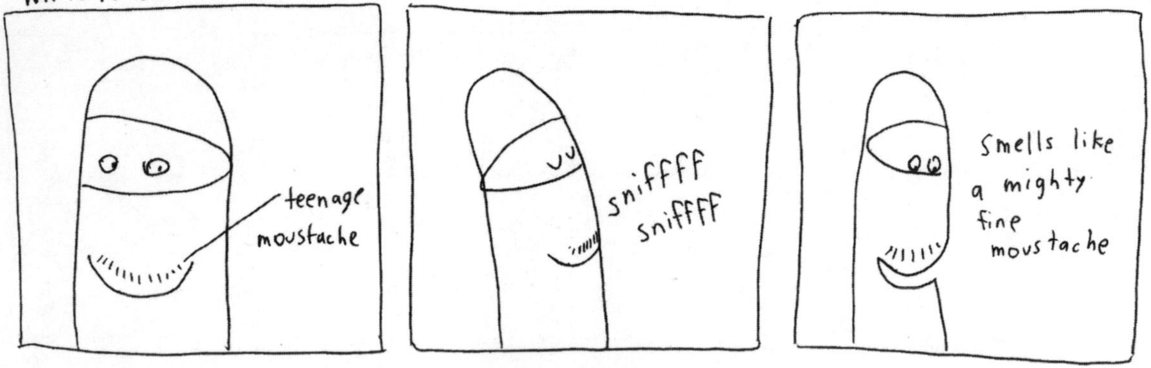
teenage moustache
sniffff
sniffff
Smells like a mighty fine moustache

White Ninja and the acrobats

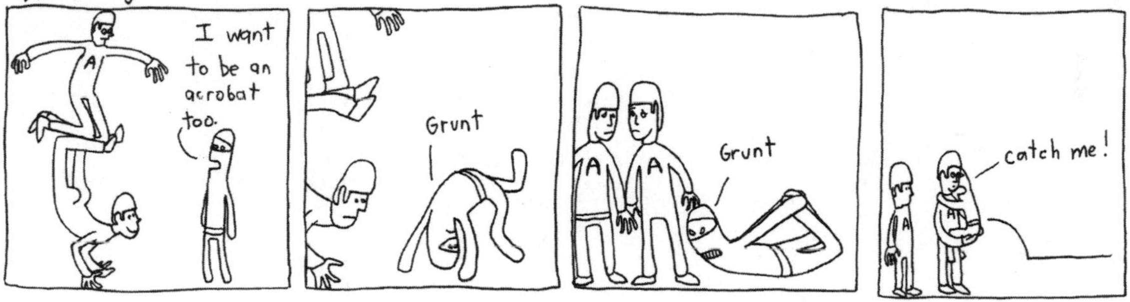
I want to be an acrobat too.
Grunt
Grunt
catch me!

White Ninja warns a cat

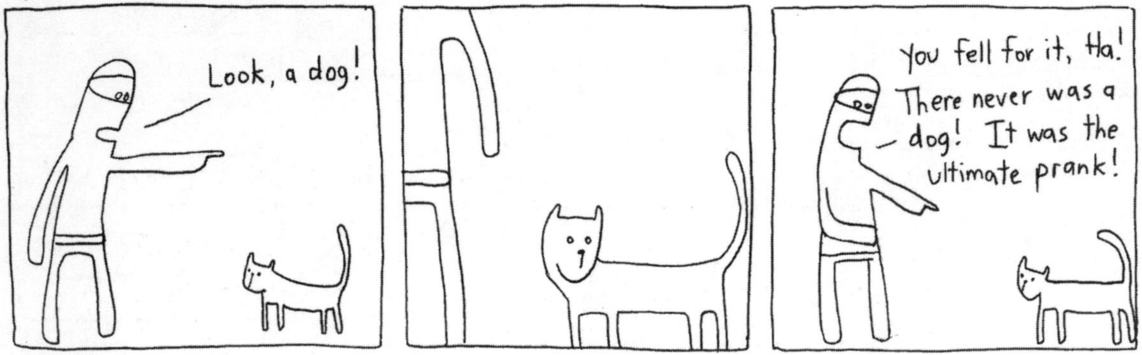
Look, a dog!
You fell for it, Ha! There never was a dog! It was the ultimate prank!

White Ninja is a Pelican

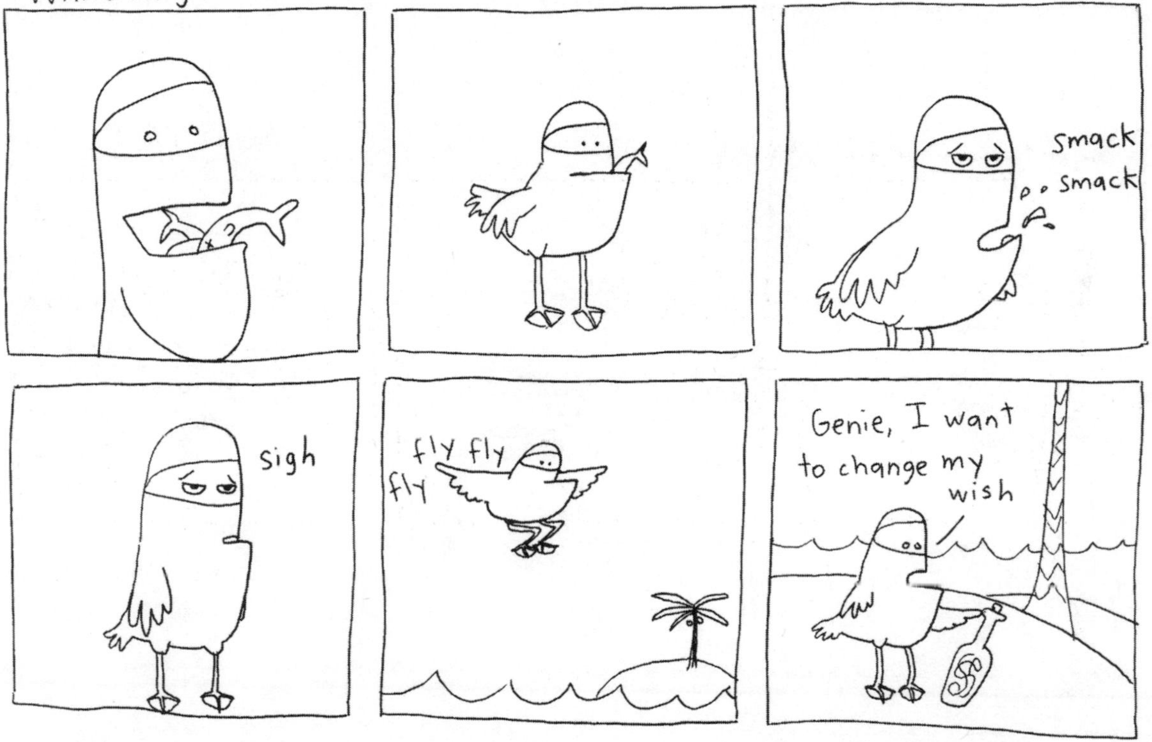
smack
smack
sigh
fly fly
fly
Genie, I want to change my wish

White Ninja learns the alphabet

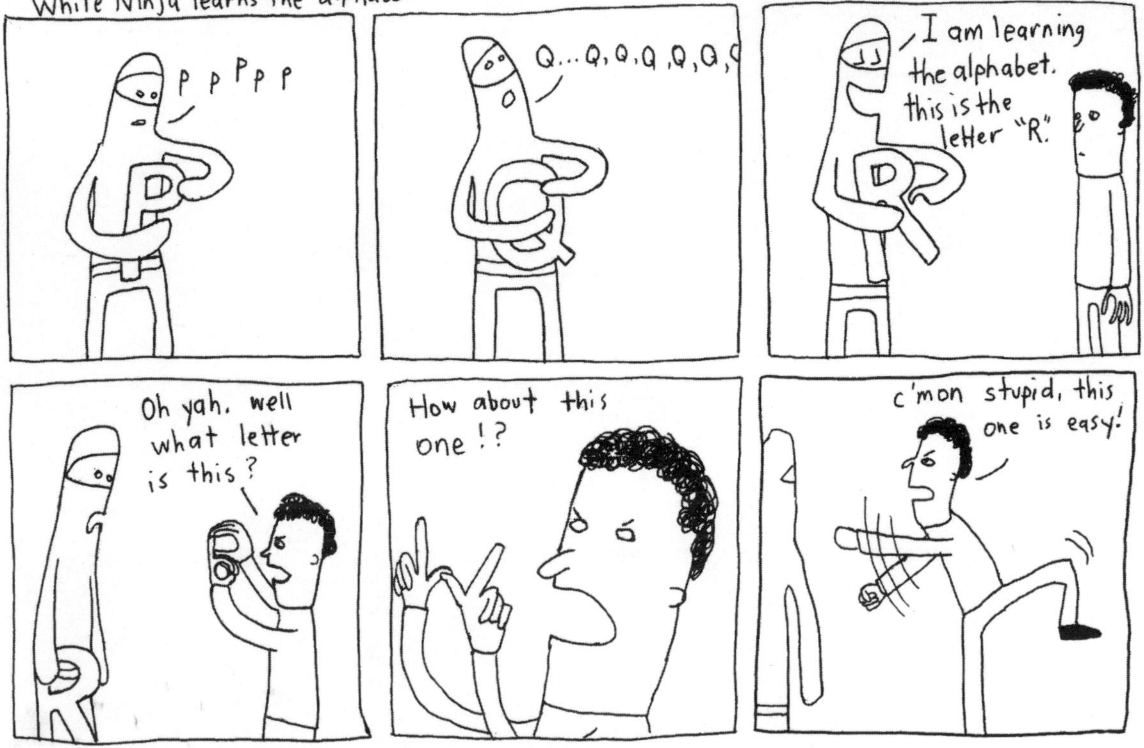
P P P P P
Q... Q, Q, Q, Q, Q,
I am learning the alphabet. this is the letter "R."
Oh yah. well what letter is this?
How about this one!?
c'mon stupid, this one is easy!

White Ninja has breakfast

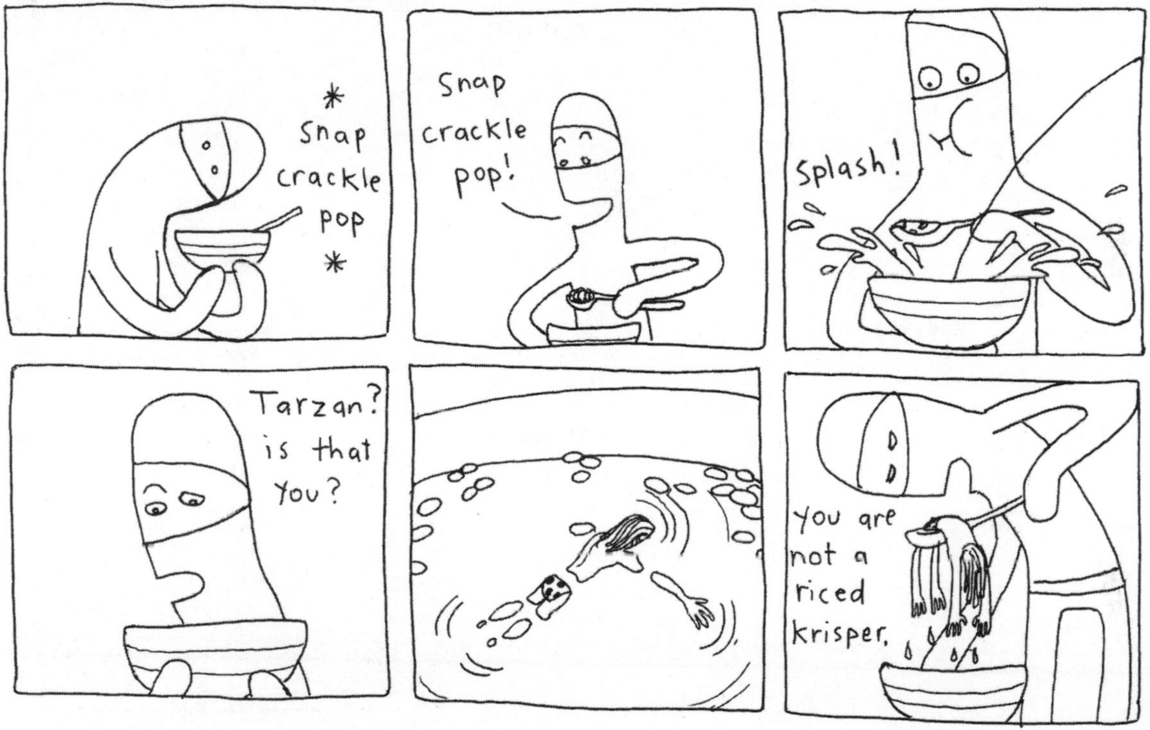
snap crackle pop
Snap crackle pop!
Splash!
Tarzan? is that you?
you are not a riced krisper.

White Ninja slays a dragon

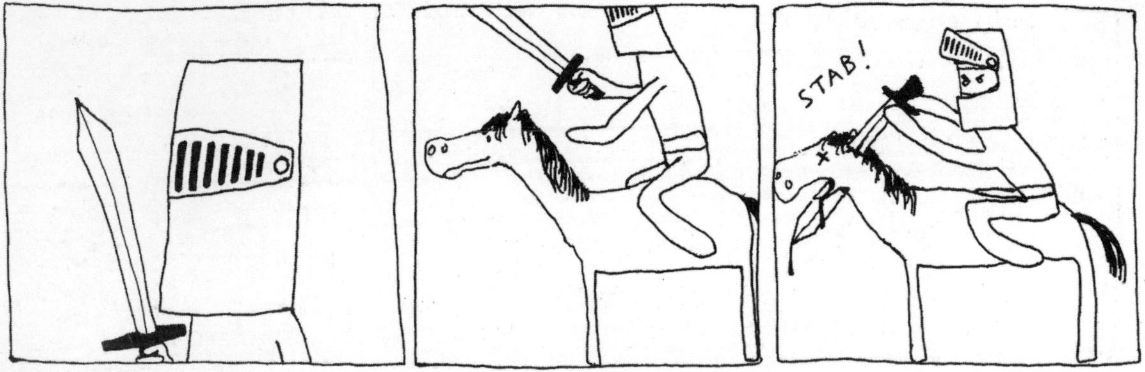
STAB!

White Ninja's New Year's Resolution

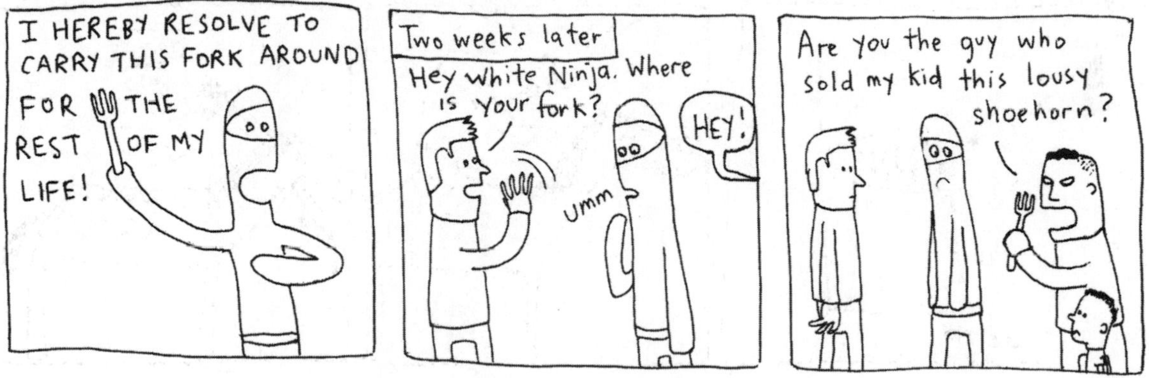
I HEREBY RESOLVE TO CARRY THIS FORK AROUND FOR THE REST OF MY LIFE!
Two weeks later
Hey White Ninja. Where is your fork?
Umm
HEY!
Are you the guy who sold my kid this lousy shoehorn?

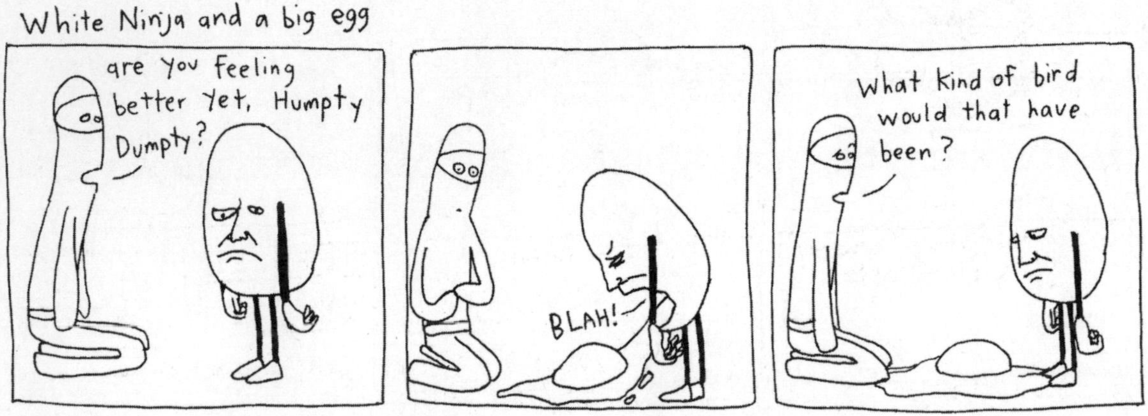
White Ninja and a big egg
are you feeling better yet, Humpty Dumpty?
BLAH!
What kind of bird would that have been?

White Ninja and the no nonsense sandwich

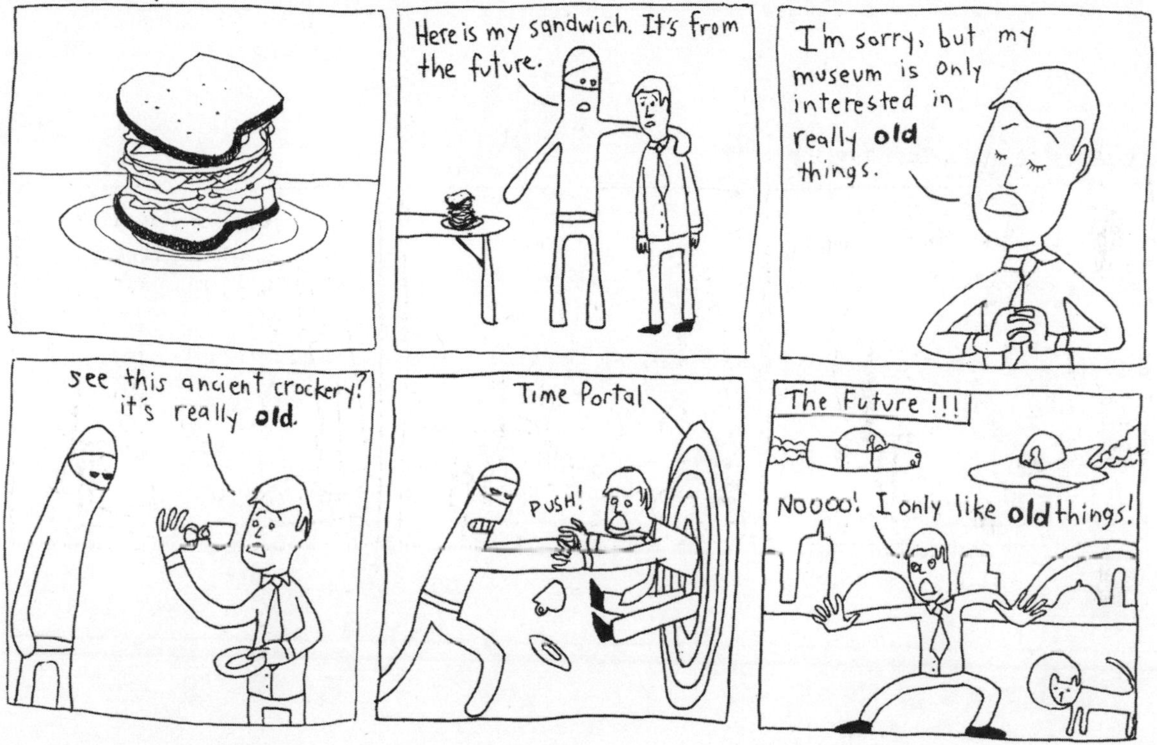
Here is my sandwich. It's from the future.
I'm sorry, but my museum is only interested in really old things.
see this ancient crockery? it's really old.
Time Portal
PUSH!
The Future !!!
NOOOO! I only like old things!

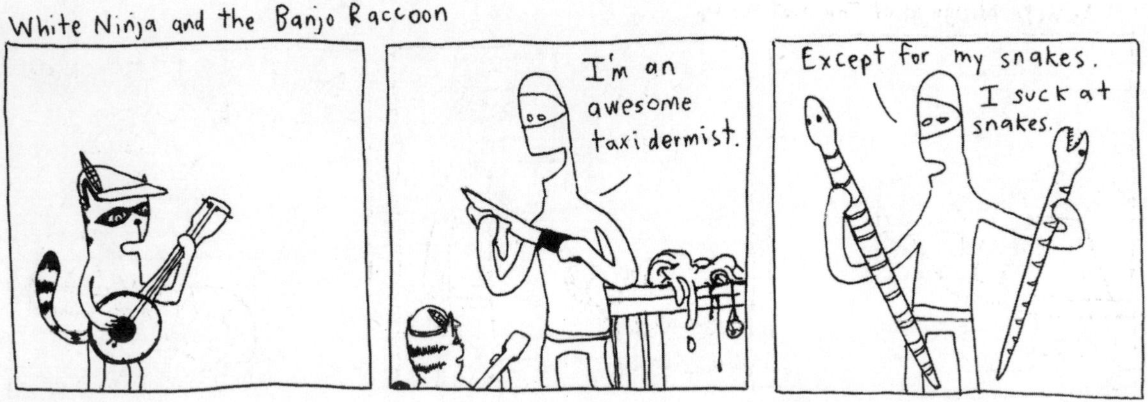
White Ninja and the Banjo Raccoon
I'm an awesome taxidermist.
Except for my snakes.
I suck at snakes.

White Ninja and the fat turtle

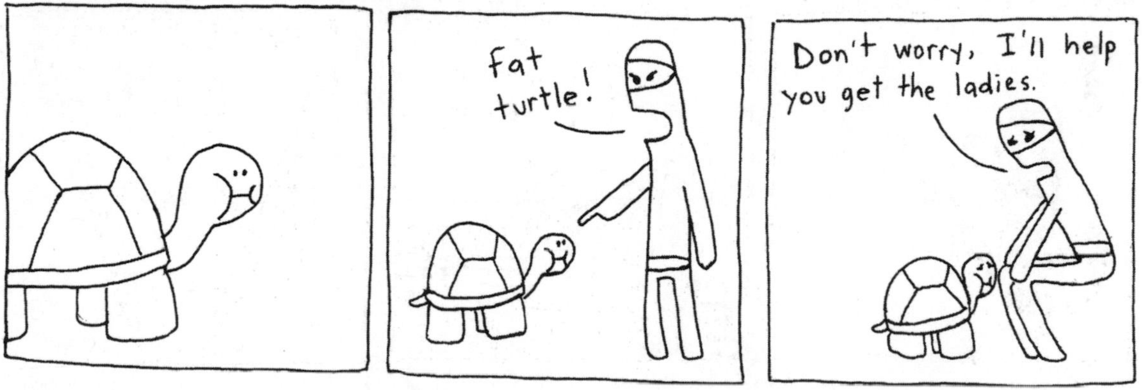
Fat turtle!
Don't worry, I'll help you get the ladies.

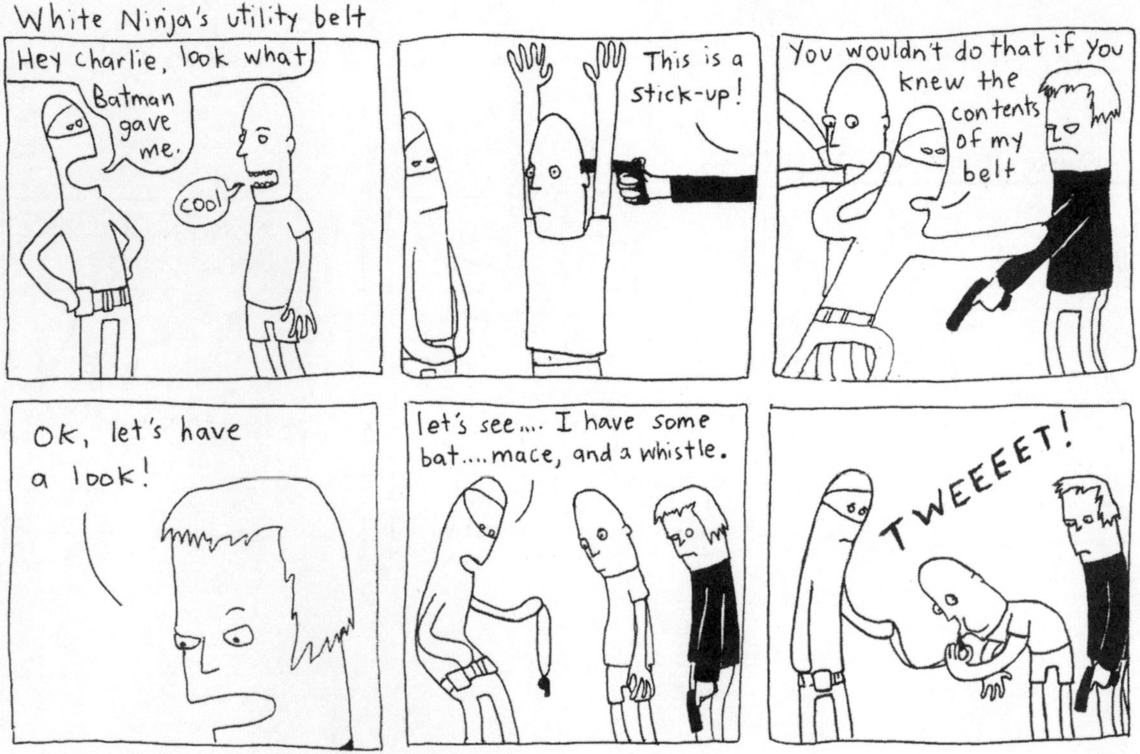
White Ninja's utility belt
Hey Charlie, look what Batman gave me.
cool
This is a stick-up!
You wouldn't do that if you knew the contents of my belt
Ok, let's have a look!
let's see.... I have some bat....mace, and a whistle.
TWEEEET!

White Ninja drinks poison.

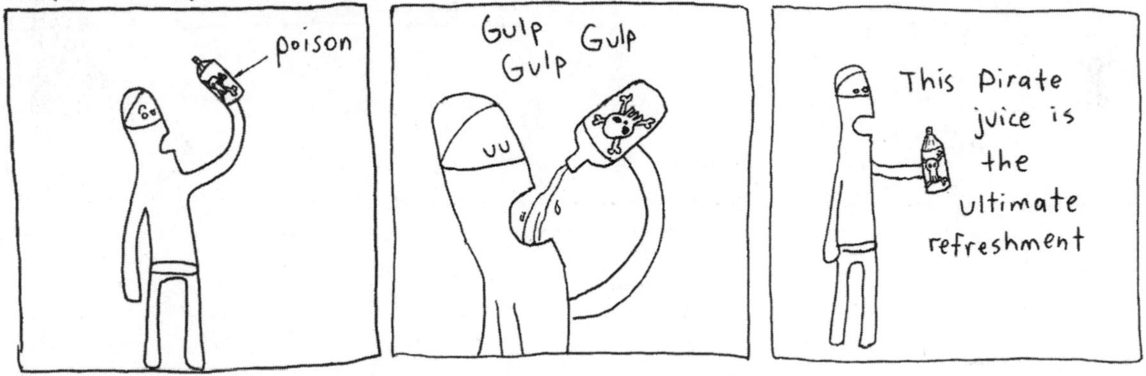
poison
Gulp Gulp Gulp
This pirate juice is the ultimate refreshment

White Ninja and the chinese pug

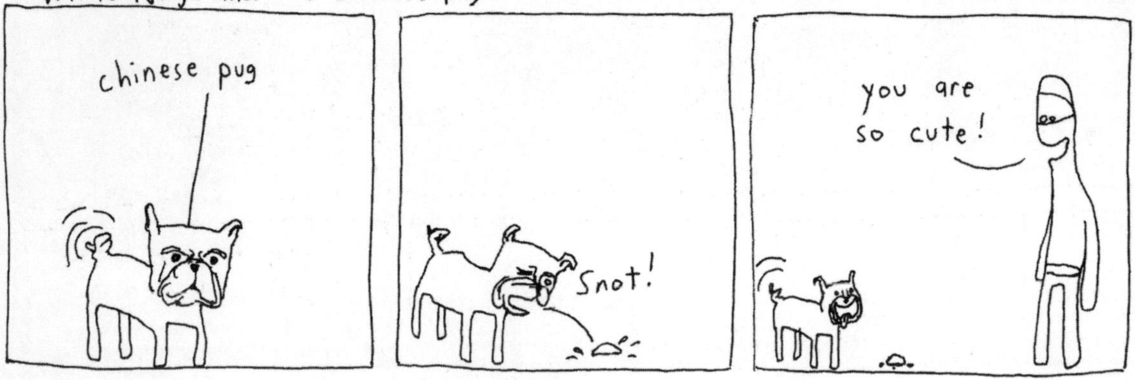
chinese pug
Snot!
you are so cute!

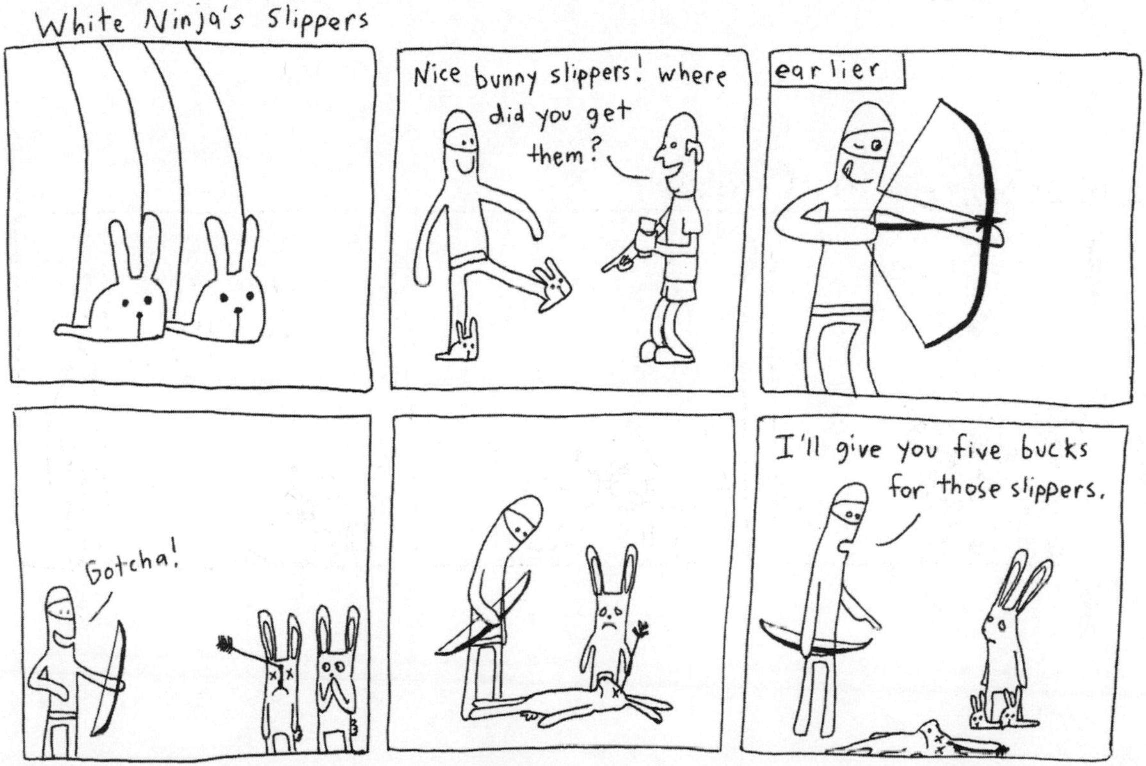

White Ninja's Slippers
Nice bunny slippers! where did you get them?
earlier
Gotcha!
I'll give you five bucks for those slippers.

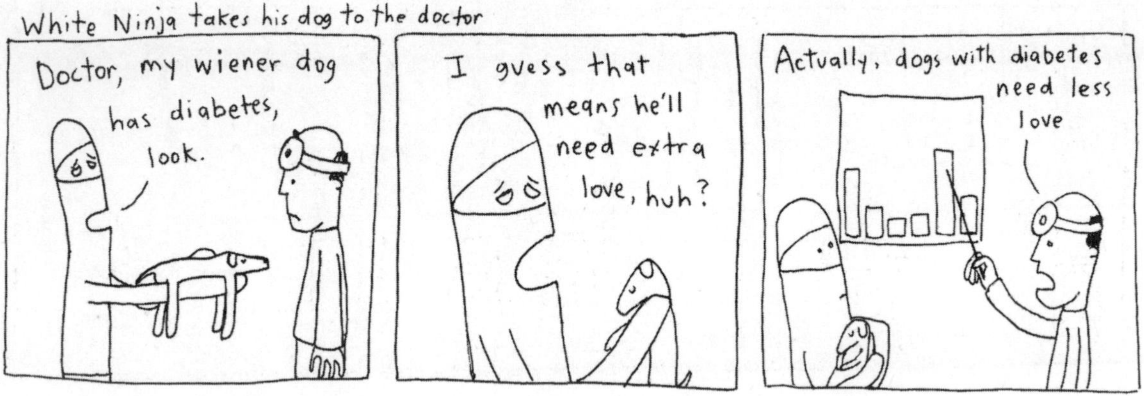
White Ninja takes his dog to the doctor
Doctor, my wiener dog has diabetes, look.
I guess that means he'll need extra love, huh?
Actually, dogs with diabetes need less love

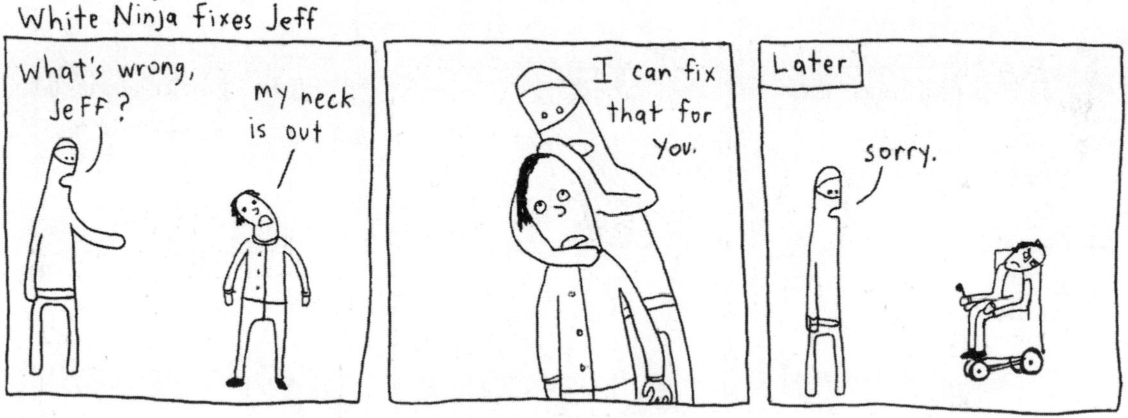
White Ninja fixes Jeff
What's wrong, Jeff?
My neck is out
I can fix that for you.
Later
sorry.

White Ninja and a lobster

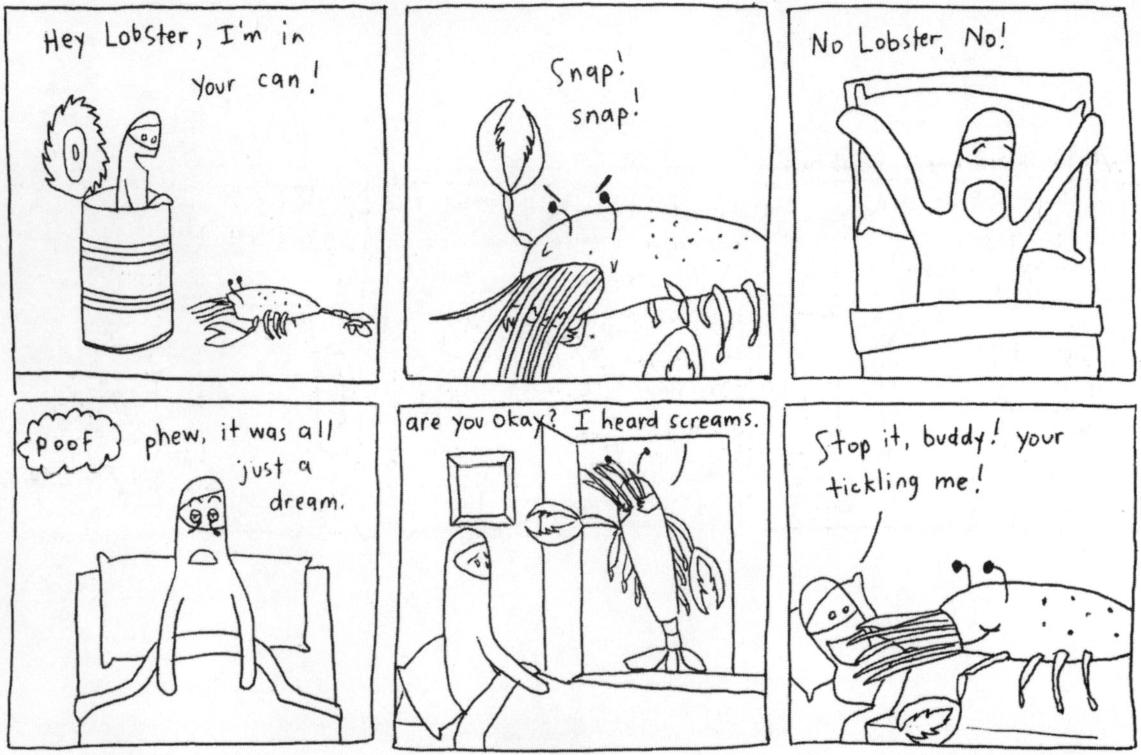

White Ninja needs breakfast

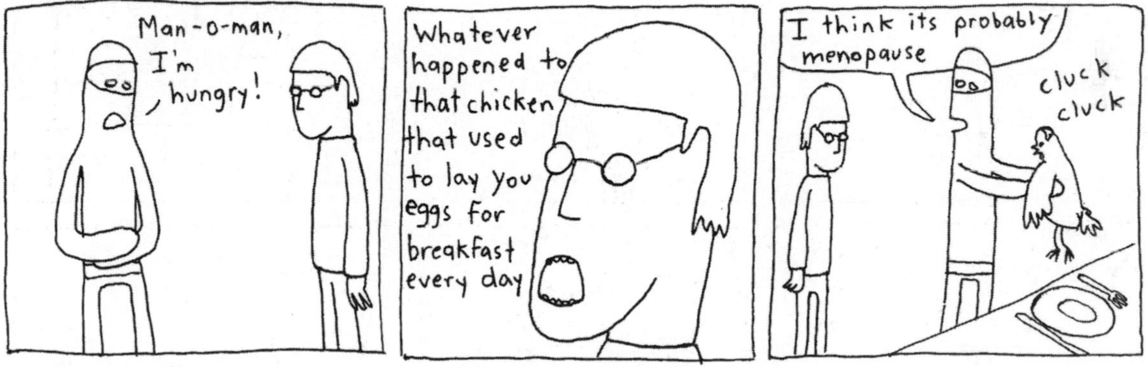
Man-o-man, I'm hungry!
Whatever happened to that chicken that used to lay you eggs for breakfast every day
I think its probably menopause
cluck cluck

White Ninja in: Munga Munga

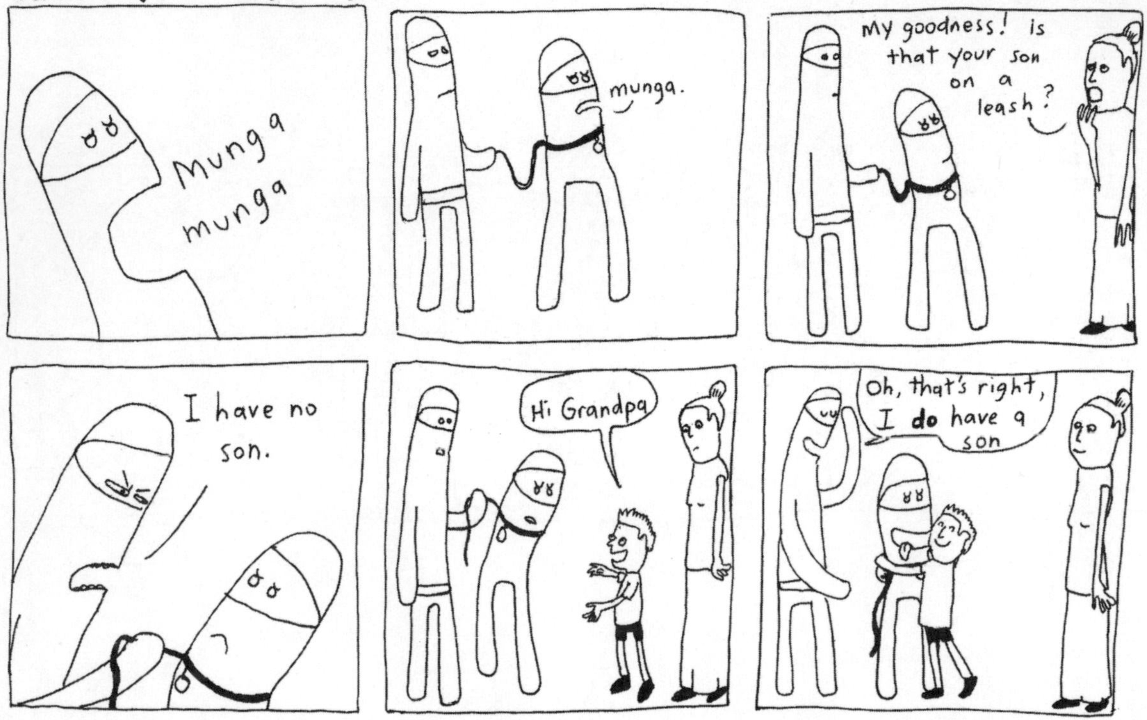
Munga munga
munga.
My goodness! is that your son on a leash?
I have no son.
Hi Grandpa
Oh, that's right, I **do** have a son

White Ninja throws a pie

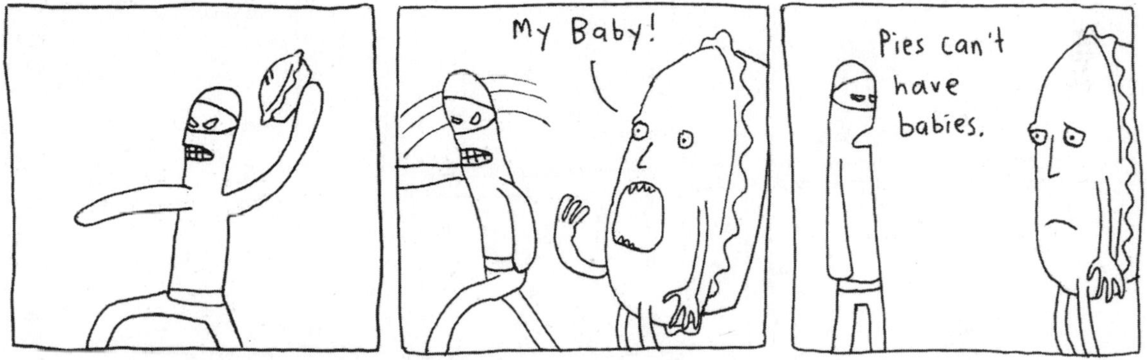
My Baby!
Pies can't have babies.

White Ninja is happy

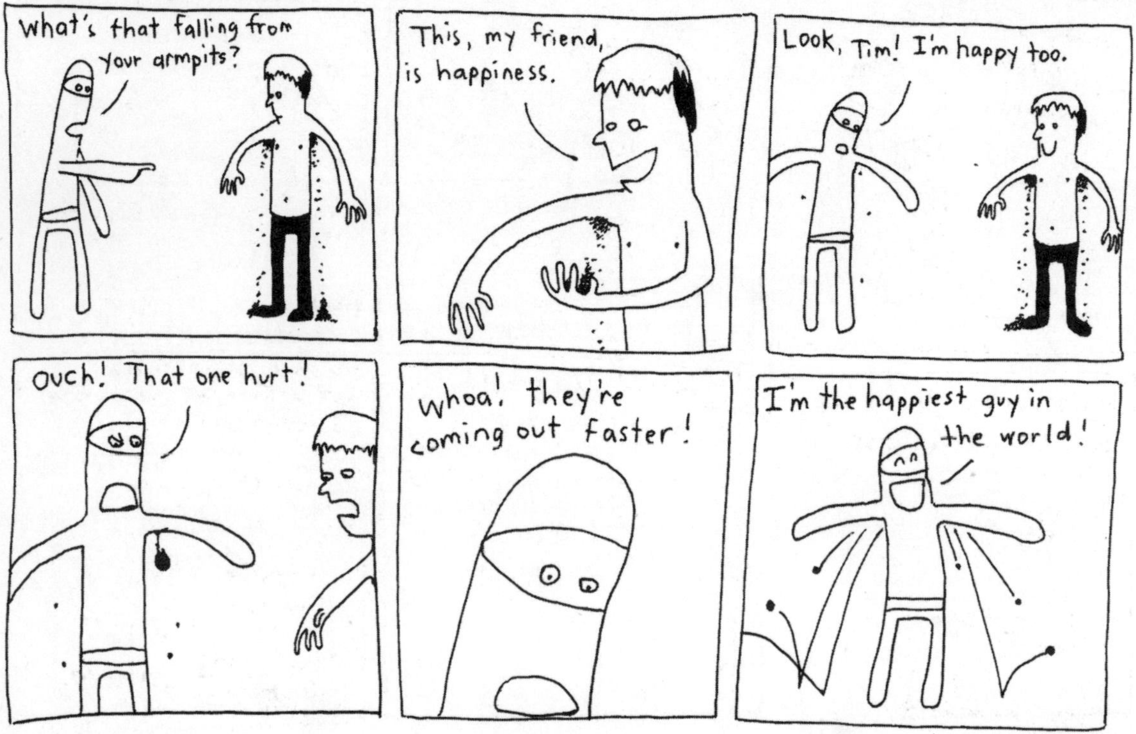
what's that falling from your armpits?
This, my friend, is happiness.
Look, Tim! I'm happy too.
Ouch! That one hurt!
Whoa! they're coming out faster!
I'm the happiest guy in the world!

White Ninja has tea with a giant

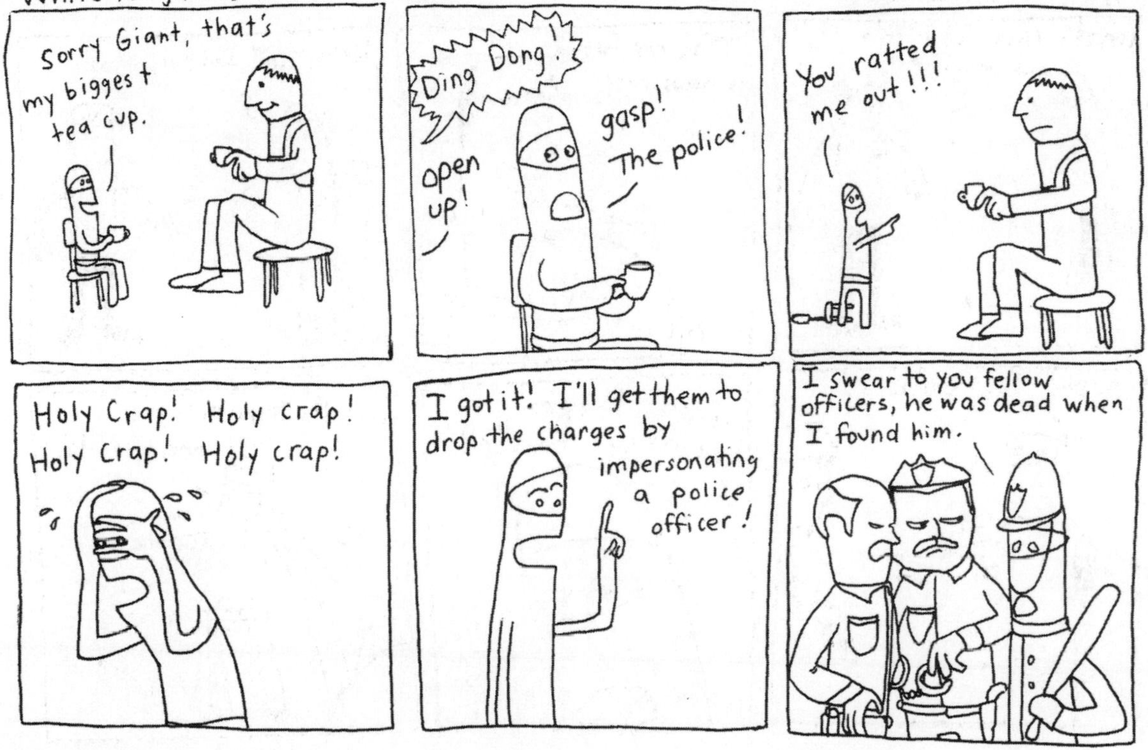
Sorry Giant, that's my biggest tea cup.
Ding Dong!
open up!
gasp! The police!
You ratted me out!!!
Holy Crap! Holy crap! Holy Crap! Holy crap!
I got it! I'll get them to drop the charges by impersonating a police officer!
I swear to you fellow officers, he was dead when I found him.

White Ninja's inconsiderate roommate

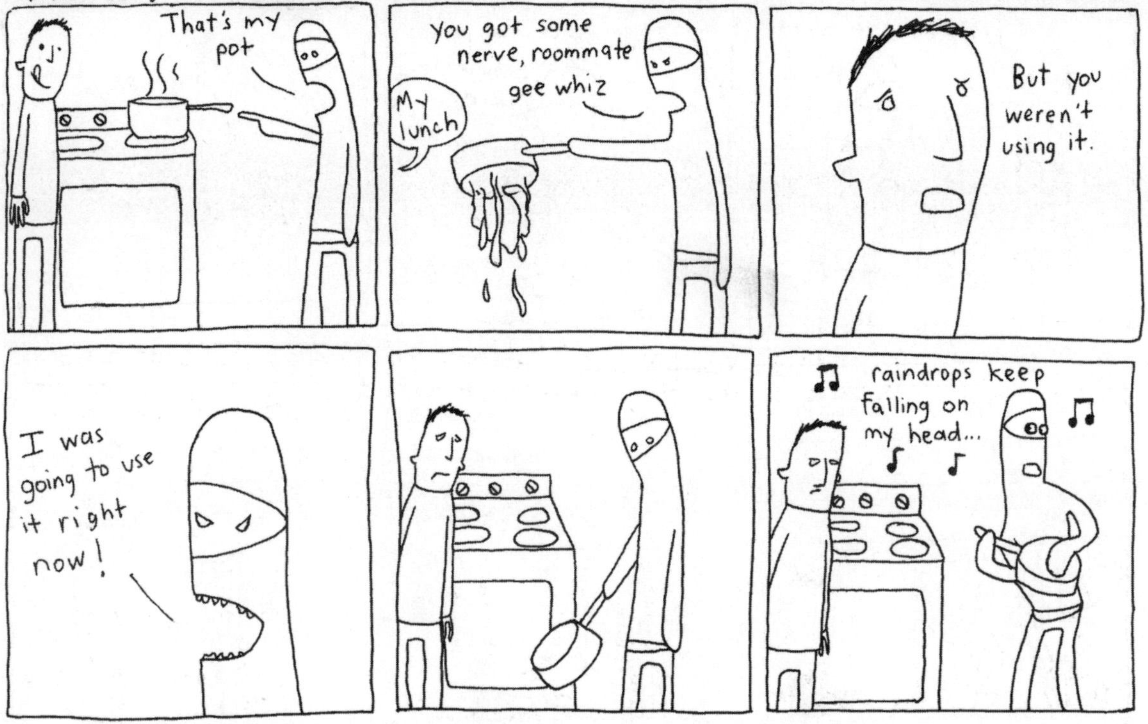
That's my pot
You got some nerve, roommate
gee whiz
My lunch
But you weren't using it.
I was going to use it right now!
raindrops keep falling on my head...

White Ninja is Santa Claus

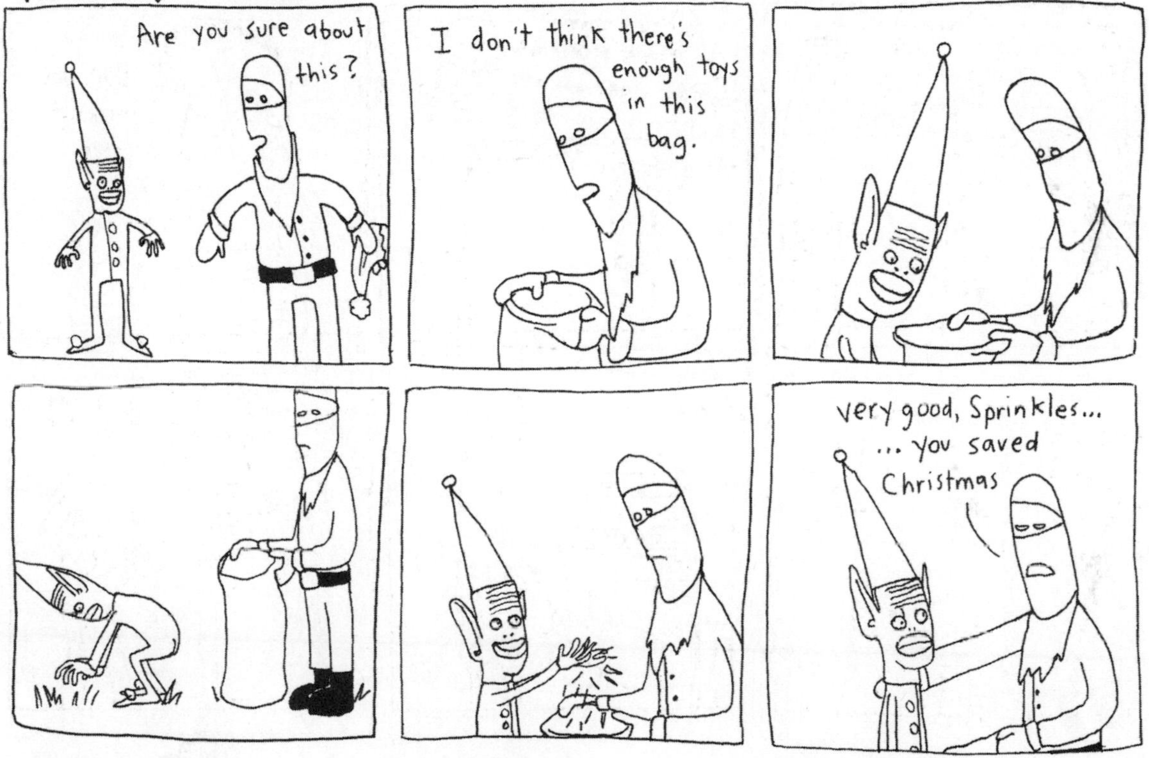

Are you sure about this?
I don't think there's enough toys in this bag.
very good, Sprinkles...
... you saved Christmas

White Ninja wants cosmetic surgery

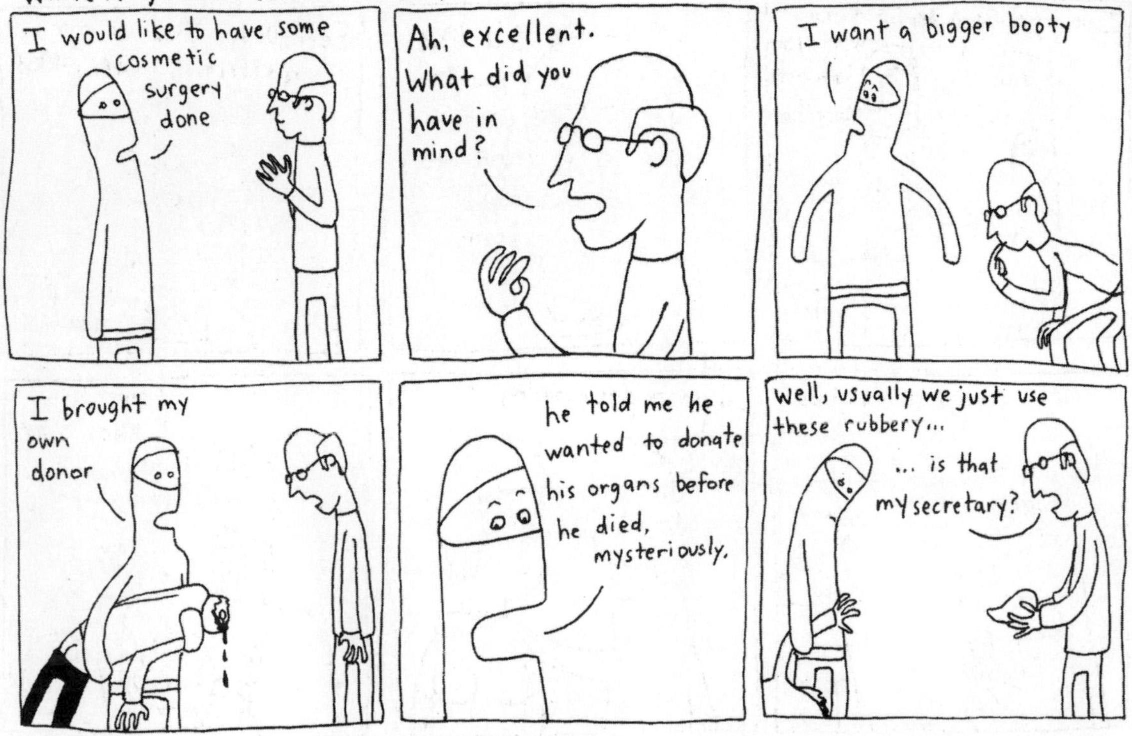
I would like to have some cosmetic surgery done
Ah, excellent. What did you have in mind?
I want a bigger booty
I brought my own donor
he told me he wanted to donate his organs before he died, mysteriously.
well, usually we just use these rubbery...
... is that my secretary?

White Ninja's girlfriend is introduced to his family

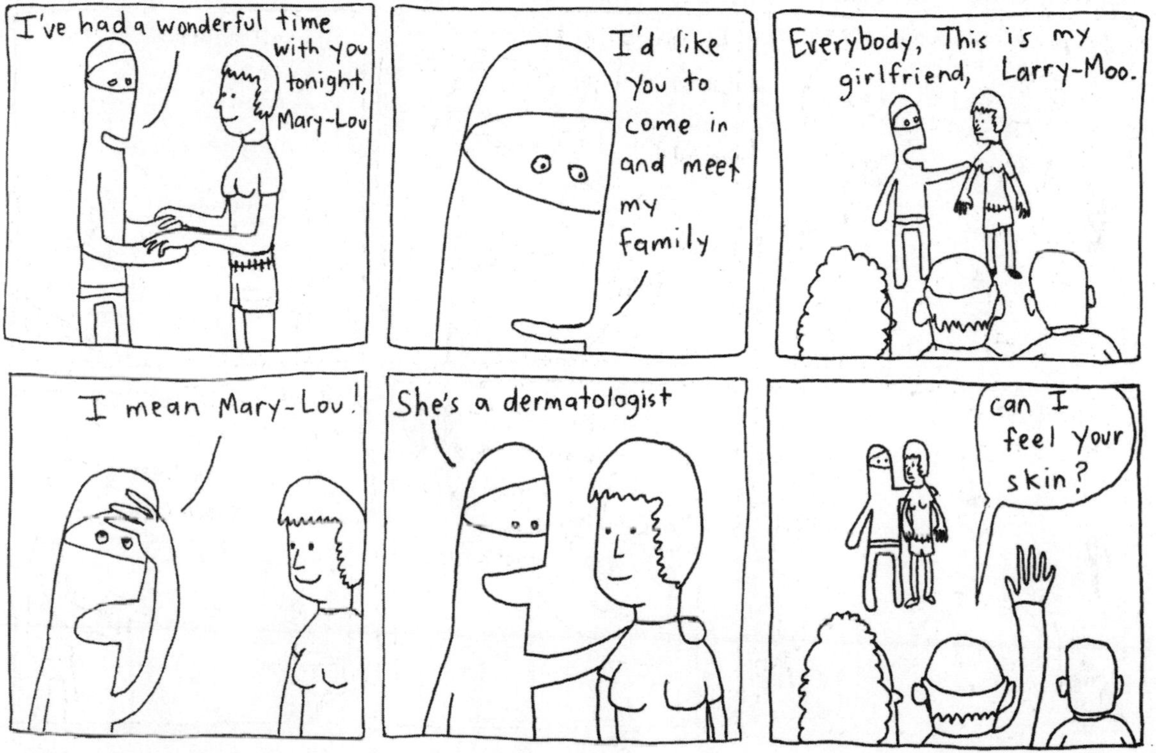
I've had a wonderful time with you tonight, Mary-Lou
I'd like you to come in and meet my family
Everybody, This is my girlfriend, Larry-Moo.
I mean Mary-Lou!
She's a dermatologist
can I feel your skin?

White Ninja enrolls in witch School

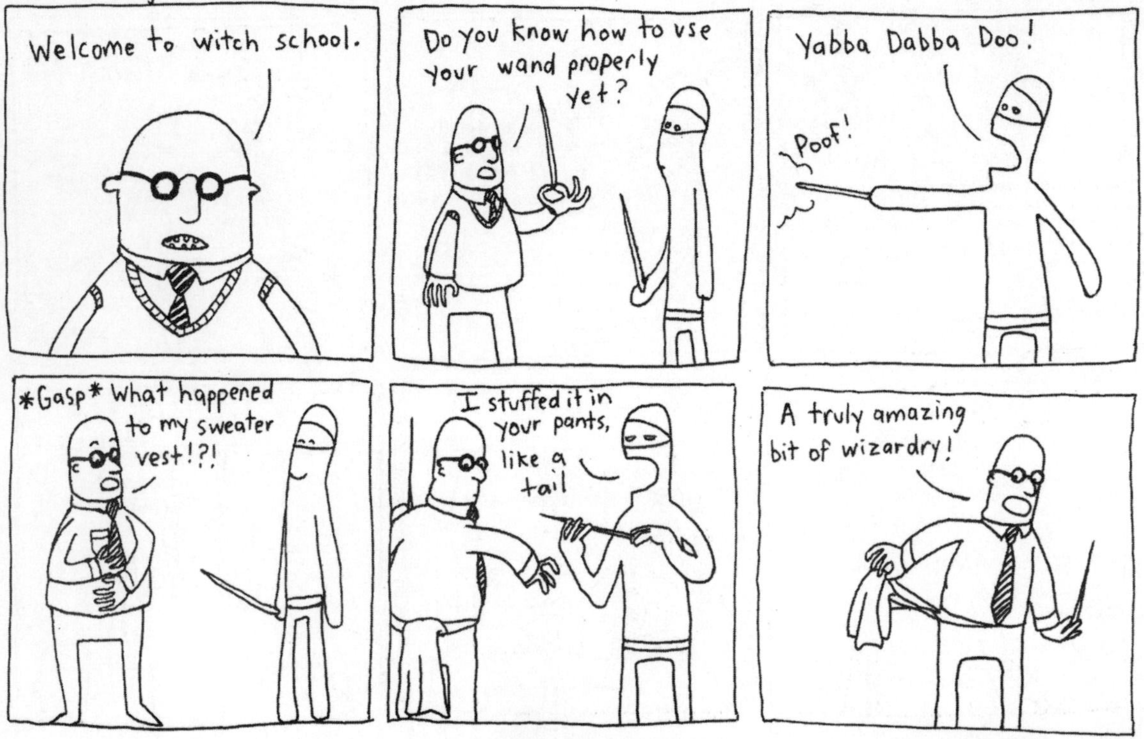
Welcome to witch school.
Do you know how to use your wand properly yet?
Yabba Dabba Doo!
Poof!
Gasp What happened to my sweater vest!?!
I stuffed it in your pants, like a tail
A truly amazing bit of wizardry!

White Ninja hurts a peacock

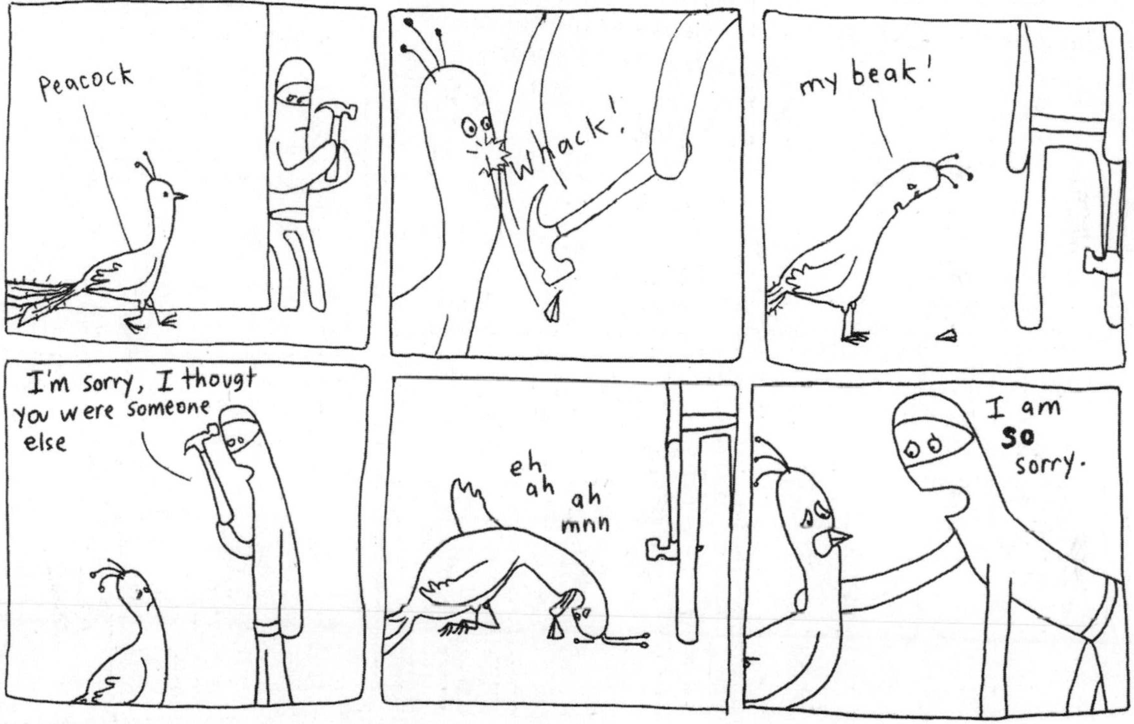
peacock
Whack!
my beak!
I'm sorry, I thougt you were someone else
eh ah ah mnn
I am SO sorry.

White Ninja's monkey

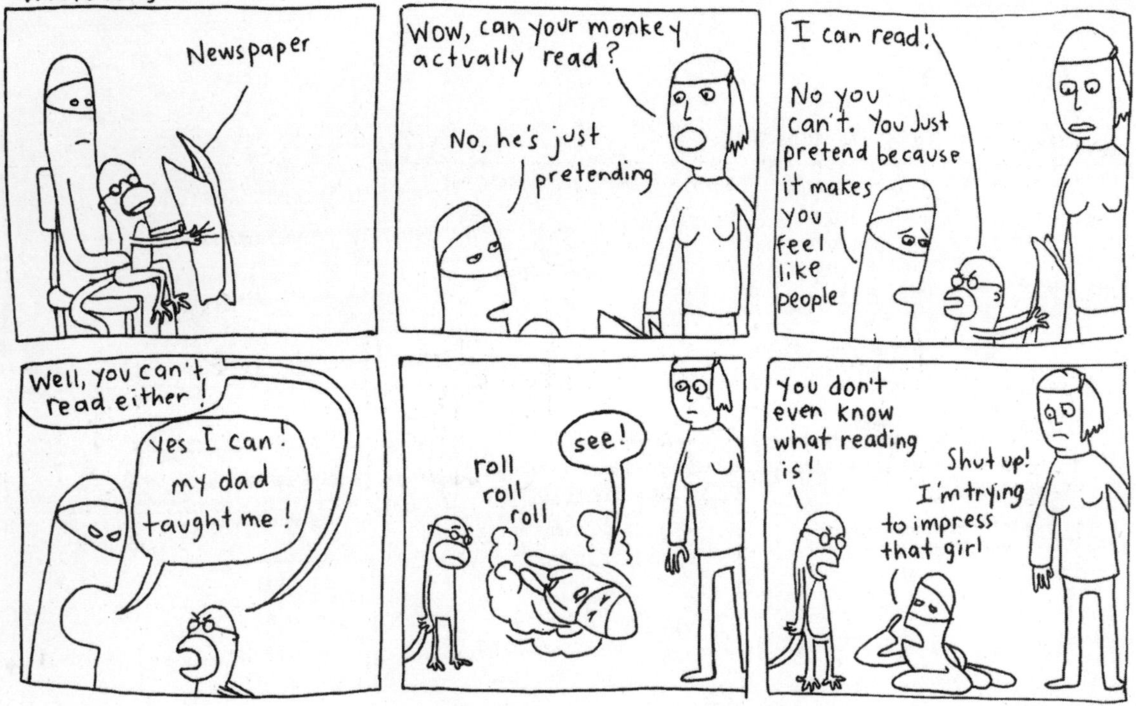

Newspaper
Wow, can your monkey actually read?
No, he's just pretending
I can read!
No you can't. You Just pretend because it makes you feel like people
Well, you can't read either!
yes I can! my dad taught me!
roll roll roll
see!
you don't even know what reading is!
Shut up! I'm trying to impress that girl

White Ninja talks to a potato

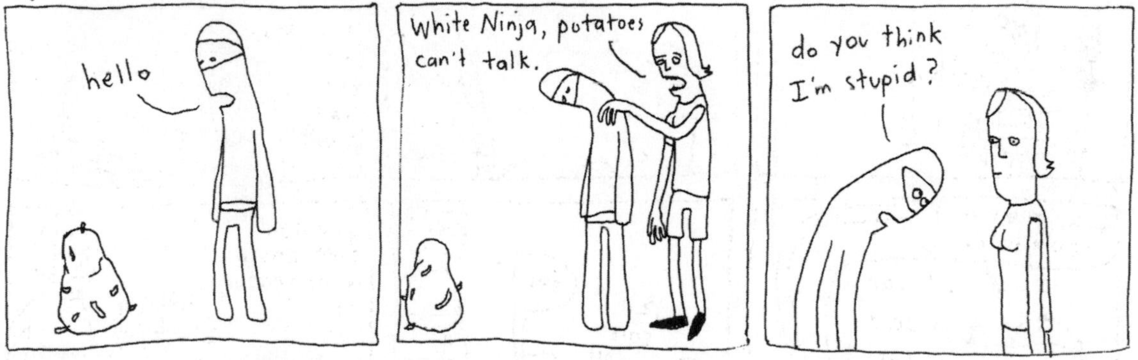
hello
White Ninja, potatoes can't talk.
do you think I'm stupid?

White Ninja's big day
jump
Dear Diary.
Today I jumped
a bump.

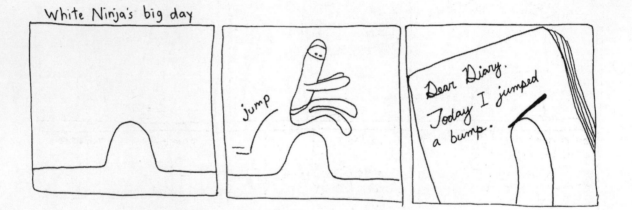

White Ninja stares at a light

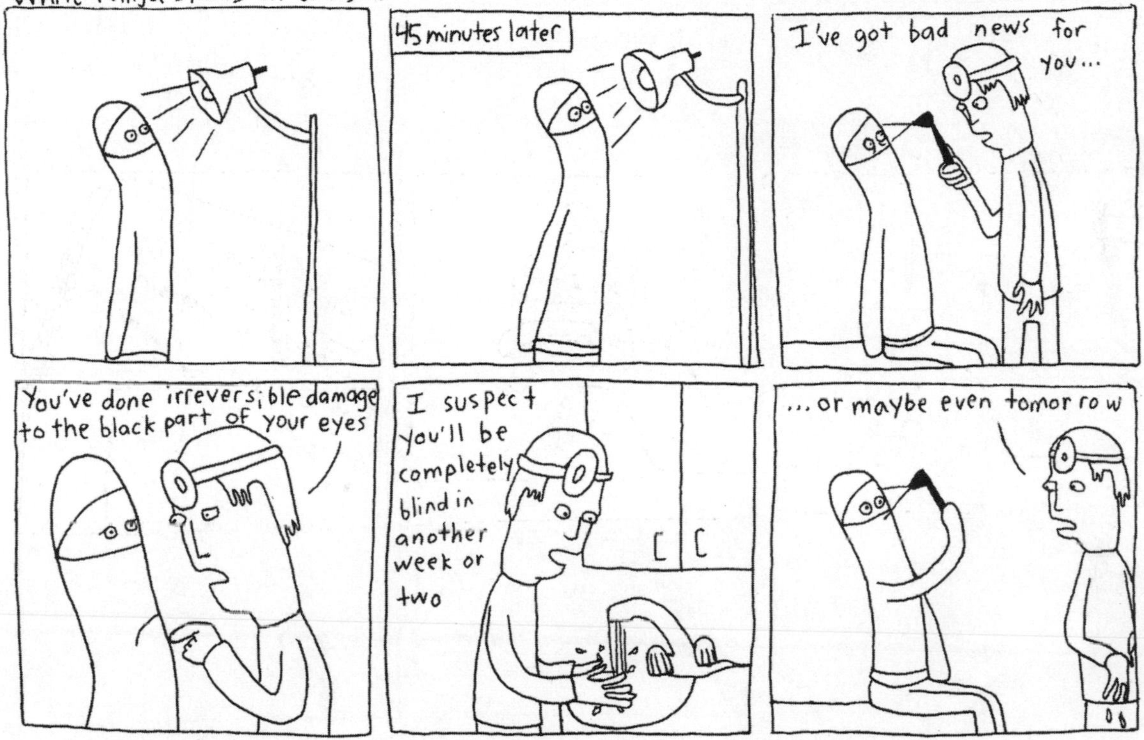
45 minutes later
I've got bad news for you...
You've done irreversible damage to the black part of your eyes
I suspect you'll be completely blind in another week or two
...or maybe even tomorrow

White Ninja has an office job

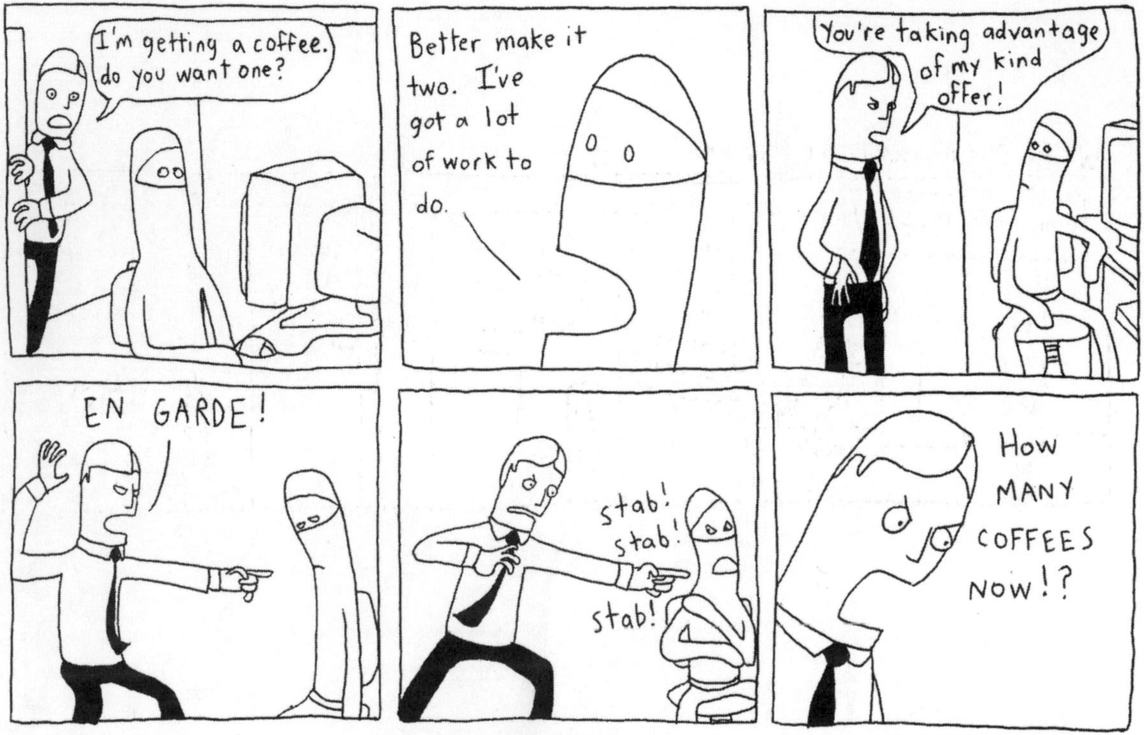

I'm getting a coffee. do you want one?
Better make it two. I've got a lot of work to do.
You're taking advantage of my kind offer!
EN GARDE!
stab! stab! stab!
HOW MANY COFFEES NOW!?

White Ninja goes to the Museum

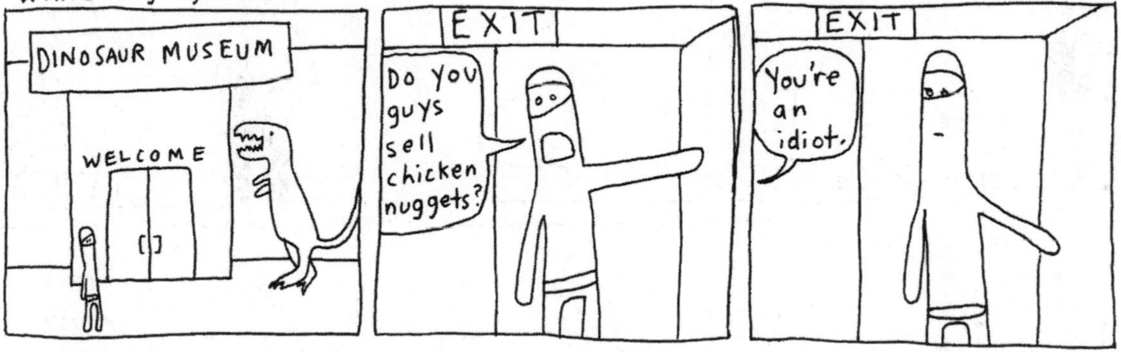
DINOSAUR MUSEUM
WELCOME
EXIT
Do you guys sell chicken nuggets?
EXIT
You're an idiot.

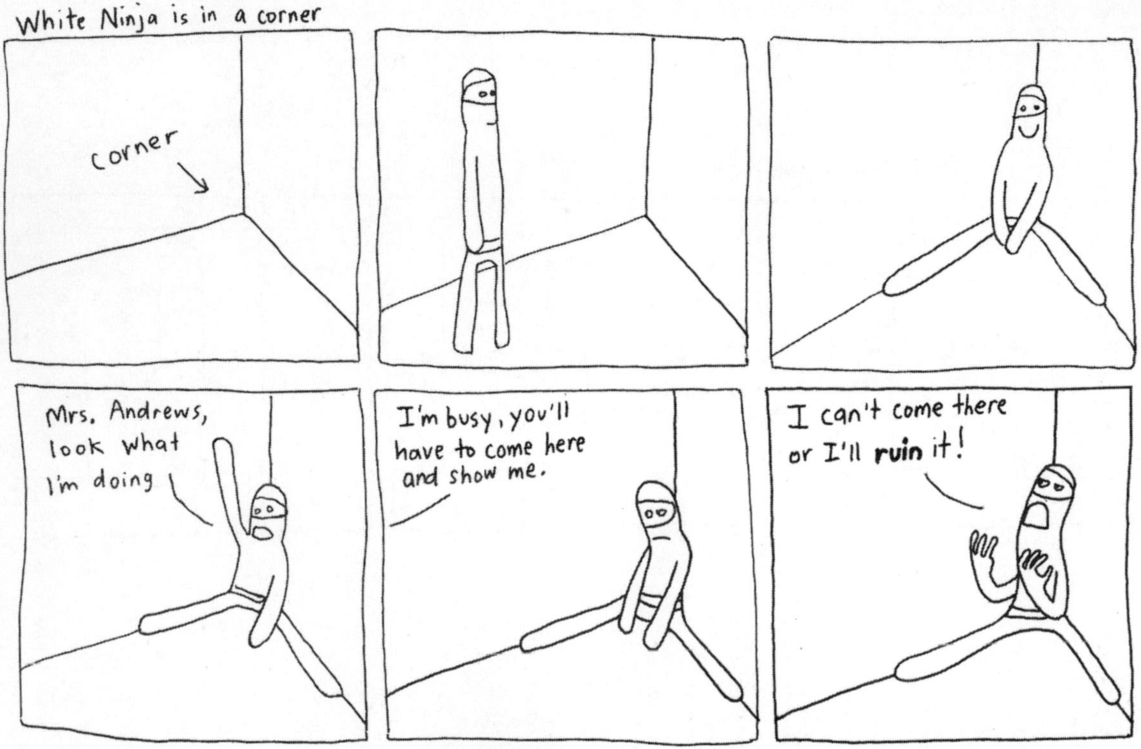
White Ninja is in a corner
corner
Mrs. Andrews, look what I'm doing
I'm busy, you'll have to come here and show me.
I can't come there or I'll **ruin** it!

White Ninja gets dumped

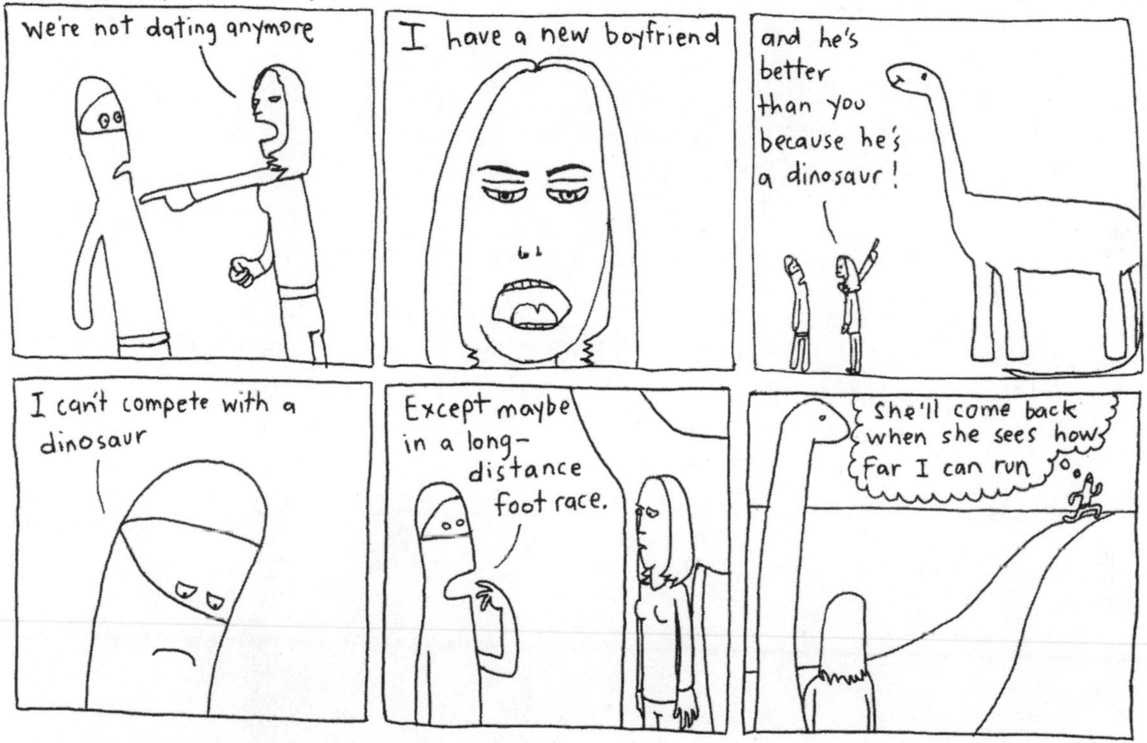

White Ninja is on fire

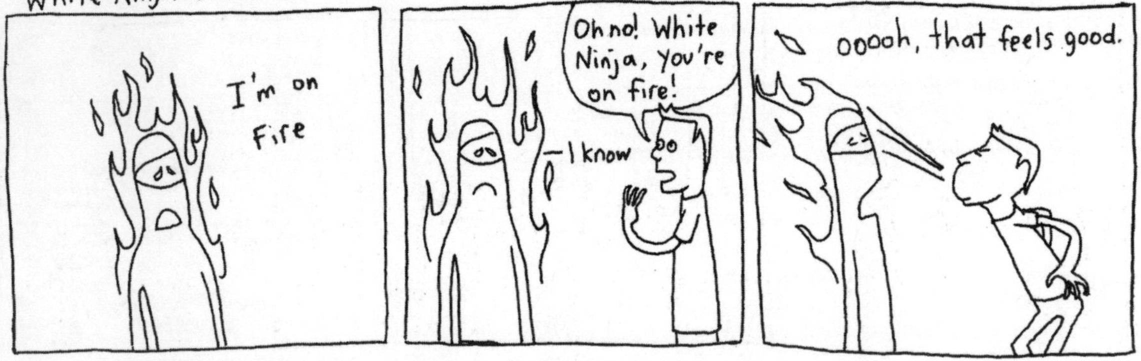

White Ninja makes a Zillion dollars

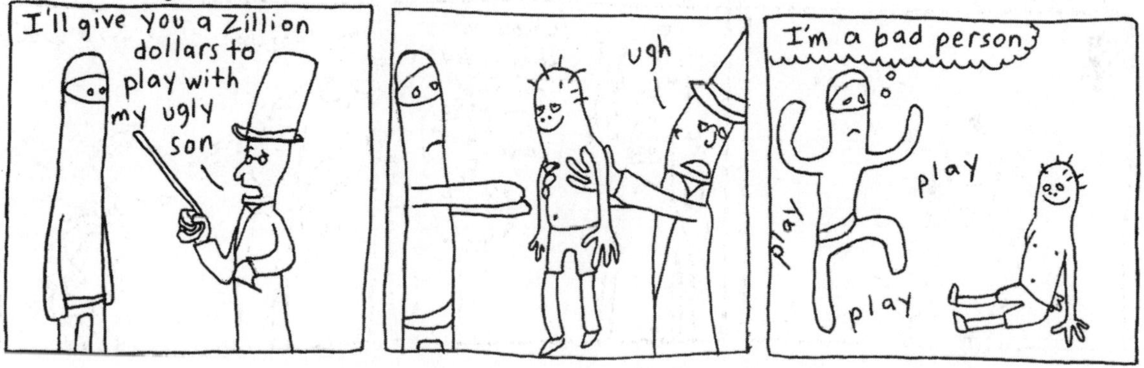
I'll give you a Zillion dollars to play with my ugly son
ugh
I'm a bad person
play
play
play

White Ninja and the boy with wet feet

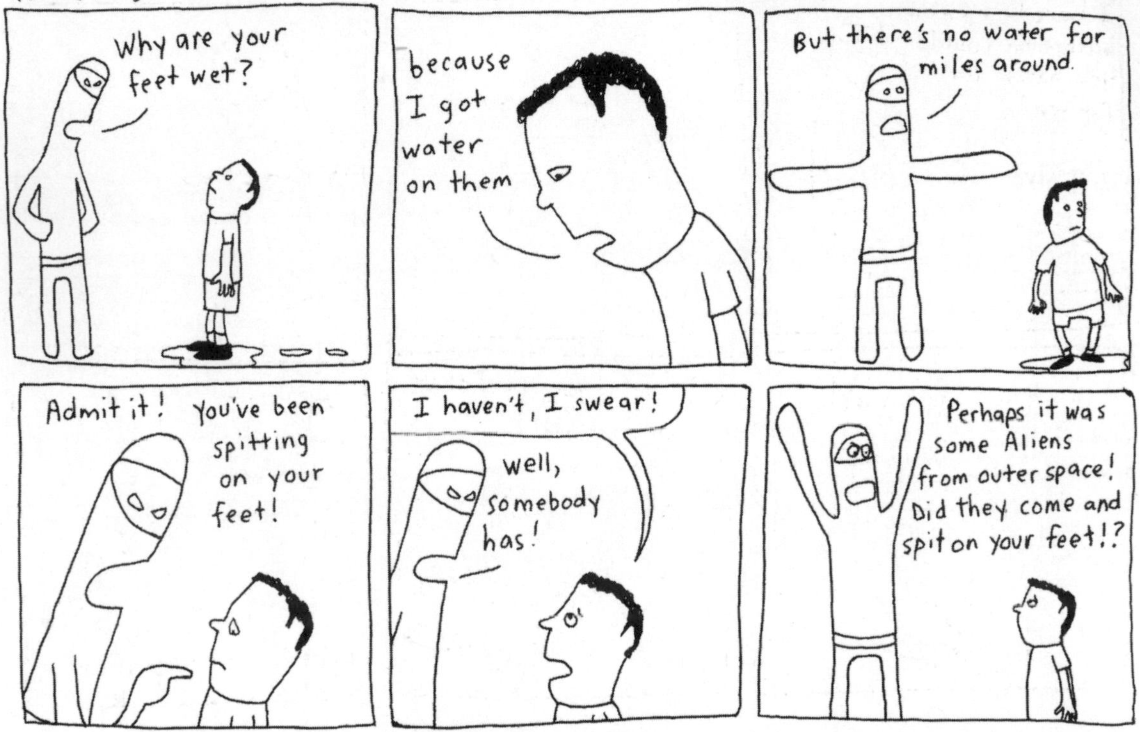
Why are your feet wet?
because I got water on them
But there's no water for miles around.
Admit it! You've been spitting on your feet!
I haven't, I swear!
well, somebody has!
Perhaps it was some Aliens from outer space! Did they come and spit on your feet!?

White Ninja helps a chicken

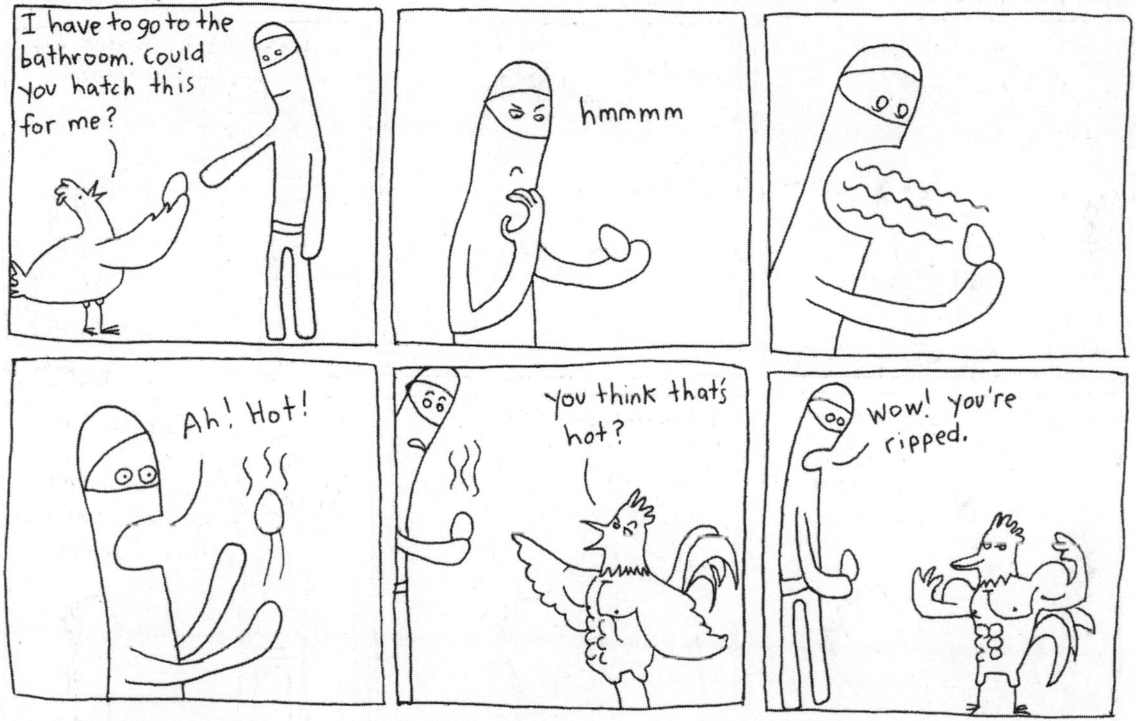
I have to go to the bathroom. Could you hatch this for me?
hmmmm
Ah! Hot!
you think that's hot?
wow! you're ripped.

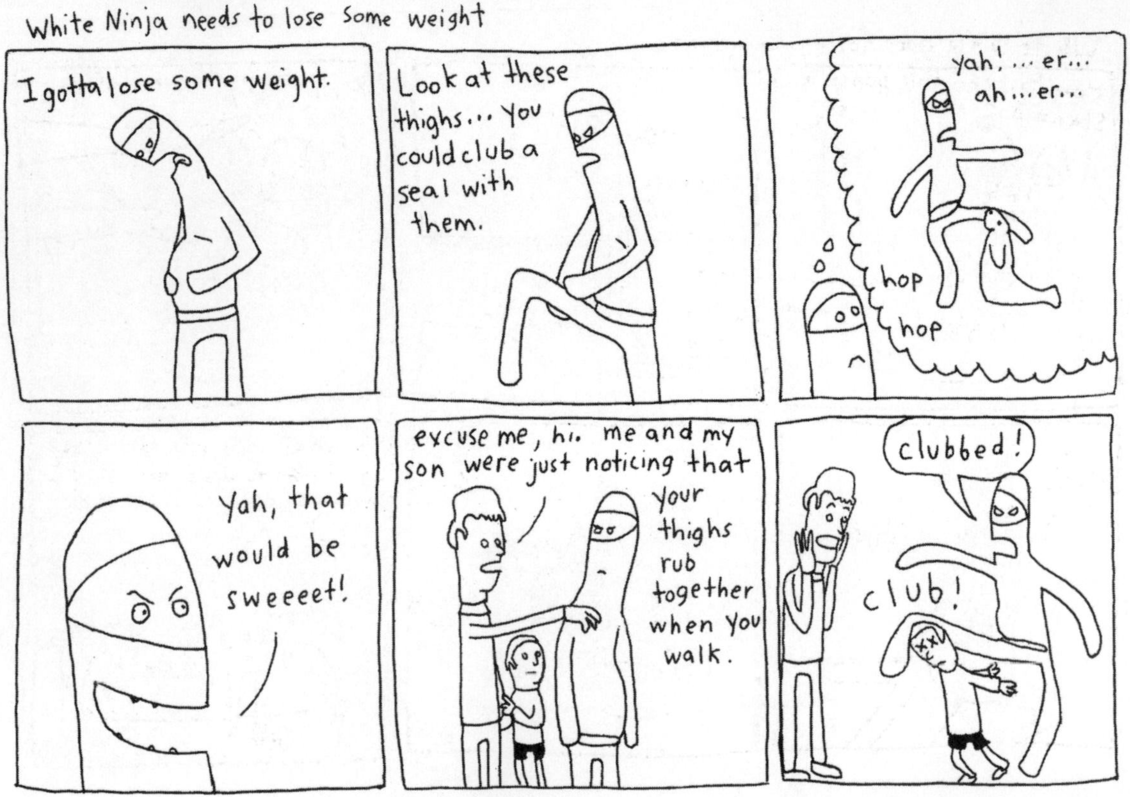
White Ninja needs to lose some weight
I gotta lose some weight.
Look at these thighs... You could club a seal with them.
yah! ...er... ah...er...
hop
hop
Yah, that would be sweeeet!
excuse me, hi. me and my son were just noticing that your thighs rub together when you walk.
clubbed!
club!

White Ninja goes for a sleigh ride

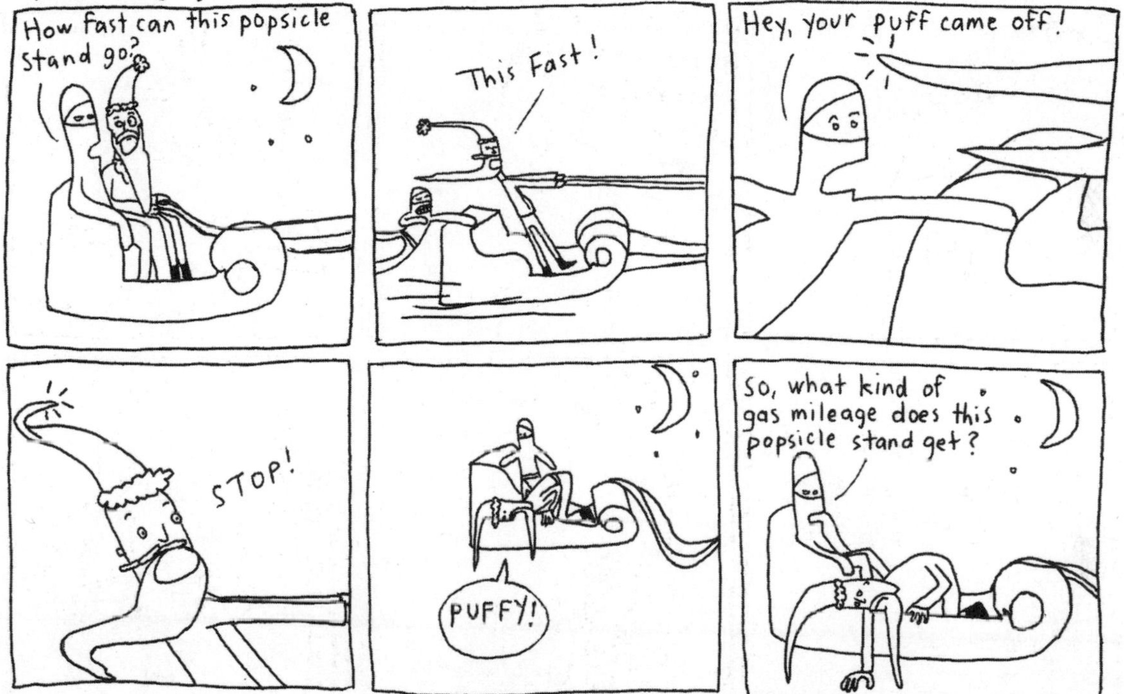

White Ninja : the camel

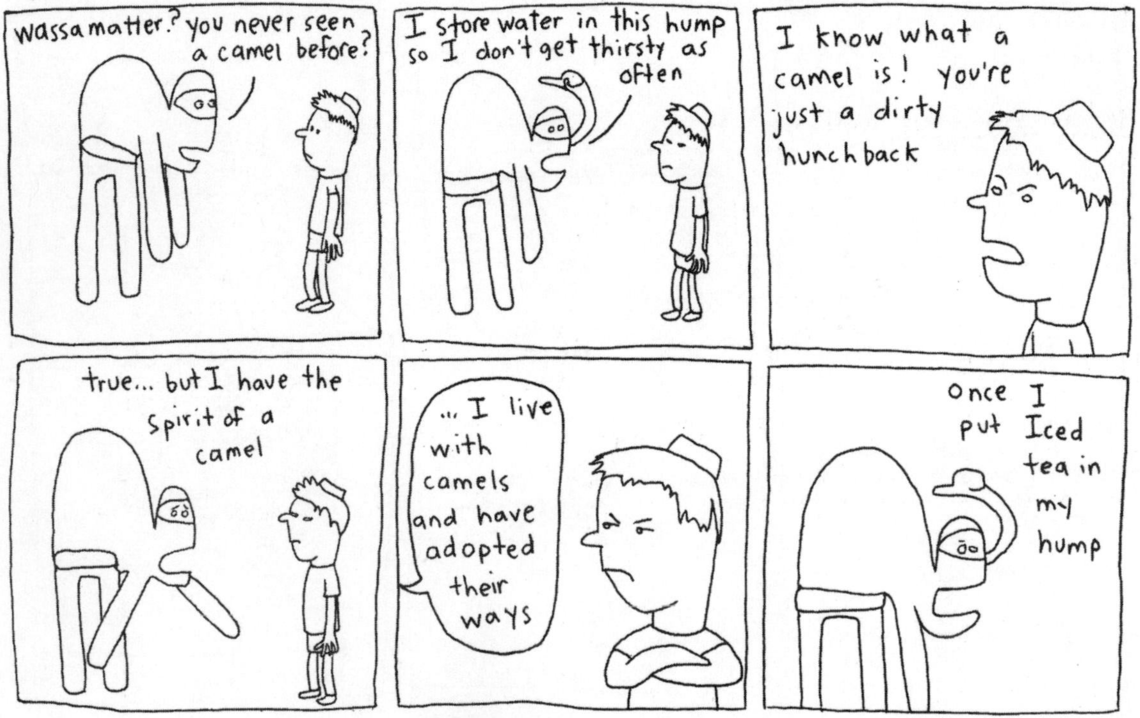

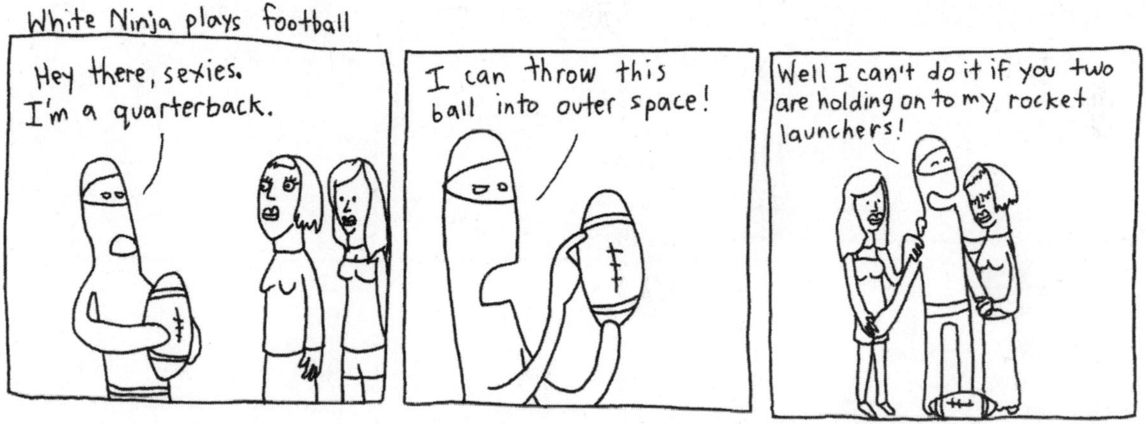
White Ninja plays football
Hey there, sexies. I'm a quarterback.
I can throw this ball into outer space!
Well I can't do it if you two are holding on to my rocket launchers!

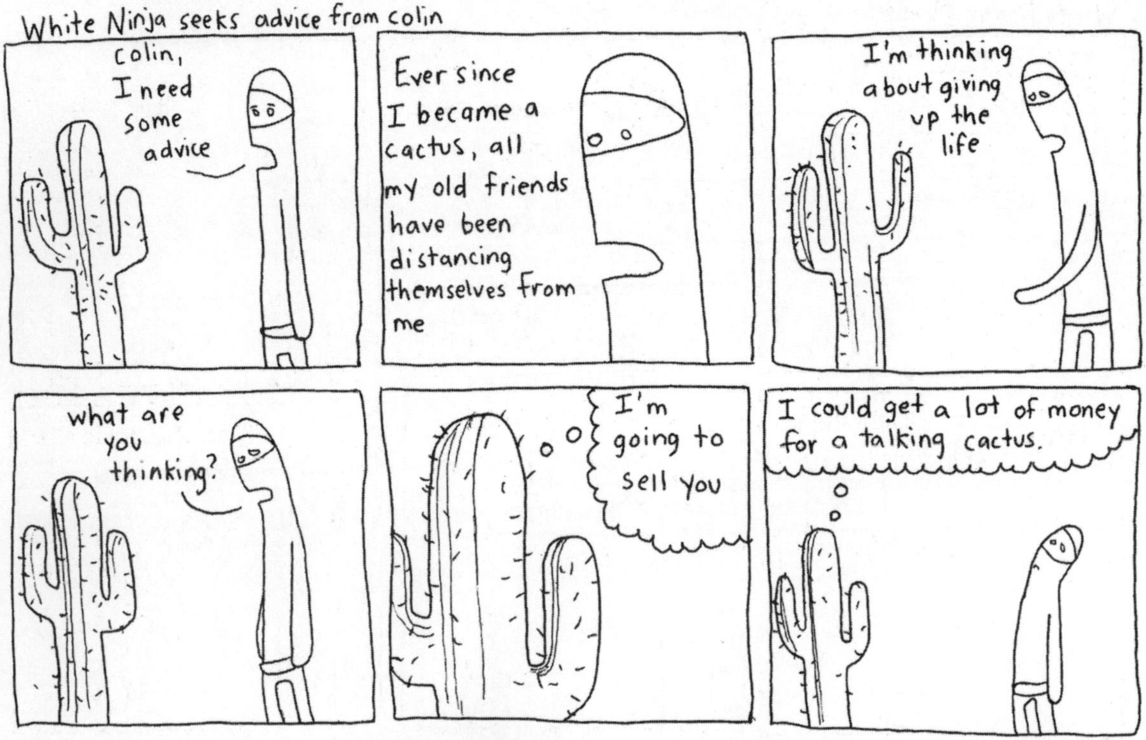
White Ninja seeks advice from colin
colin, I need some advice
Ever since I became a cactus, all my old friends have been distancing themselves from me
I'm thinking about giving up the life
what are you thinking?
I'm going to sell you
I could get a lot of money for a talking cactus.

White Ninja Moniters a guy's health

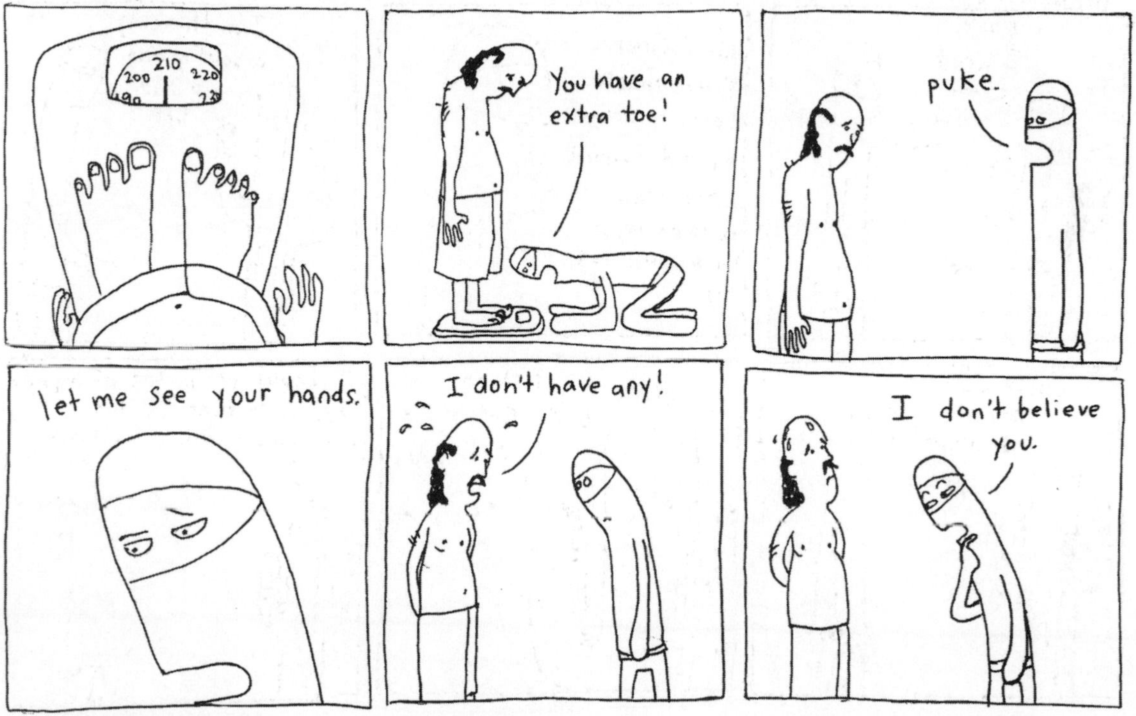
200
210
220
You have an extra toe!
puke.
let me see your hands.
I don't have any!
I don't believe you.

White Ninja in : First Words

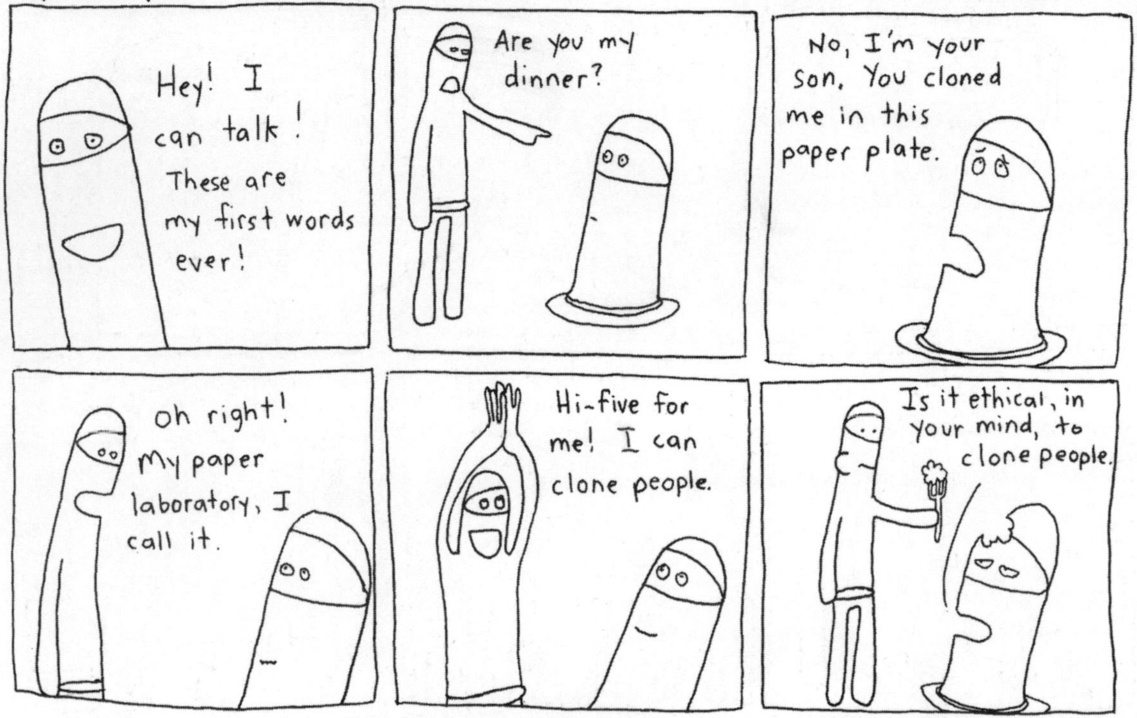

White Ninja puts a wiffle ball on a pylon

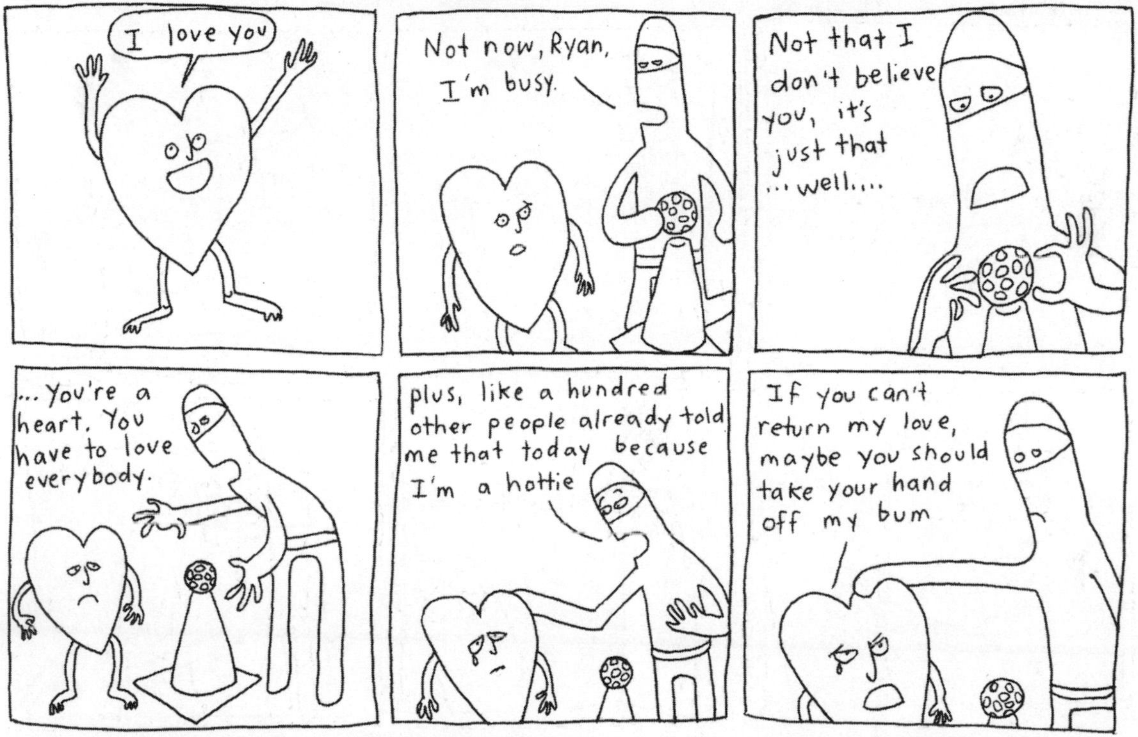
I love you
Not now, Ryan, I'm busy.
Not that I don't believe you, it's just that ... well....
... You're a heart. You have to love everybody.
plus, like a hundred other people already told me that today because I'm a hottie
If you can't return my love, maybe you should take your hand off my bum

White Ninja pet pet pets a kitty

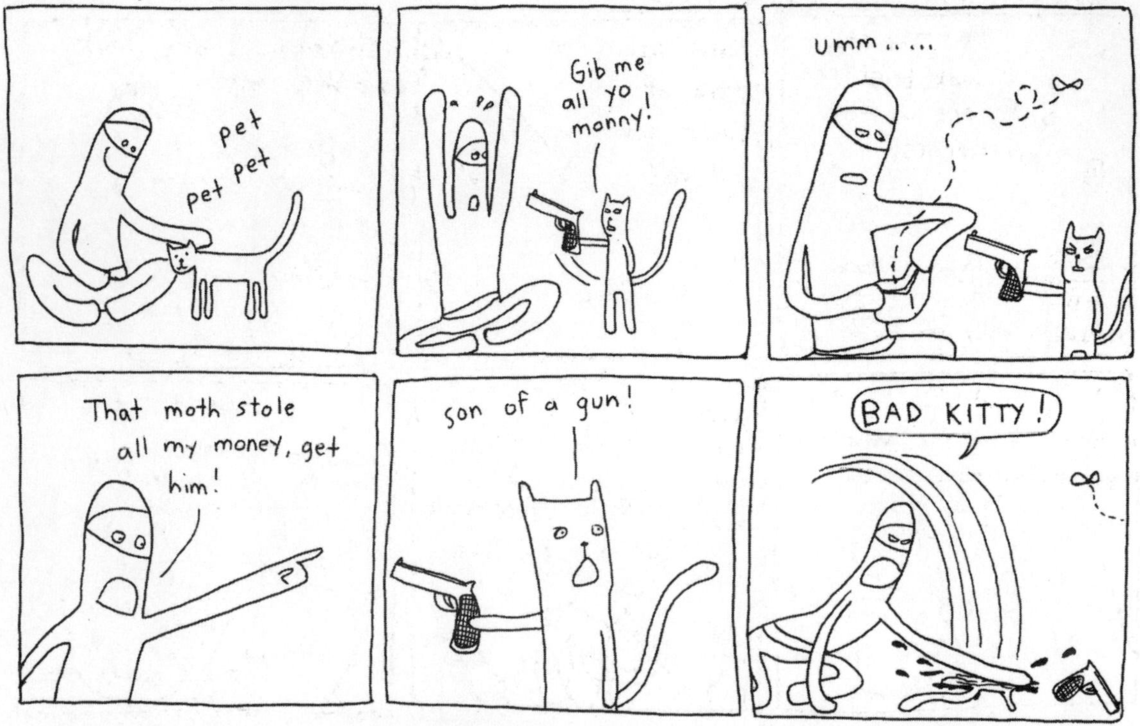
pet
pet pet
pet
Gib me all yo monny!
umm.....
That moth stole all my money, get him!
son of a gun!
BAD KITTY!

White Ninja goes camping with a guy

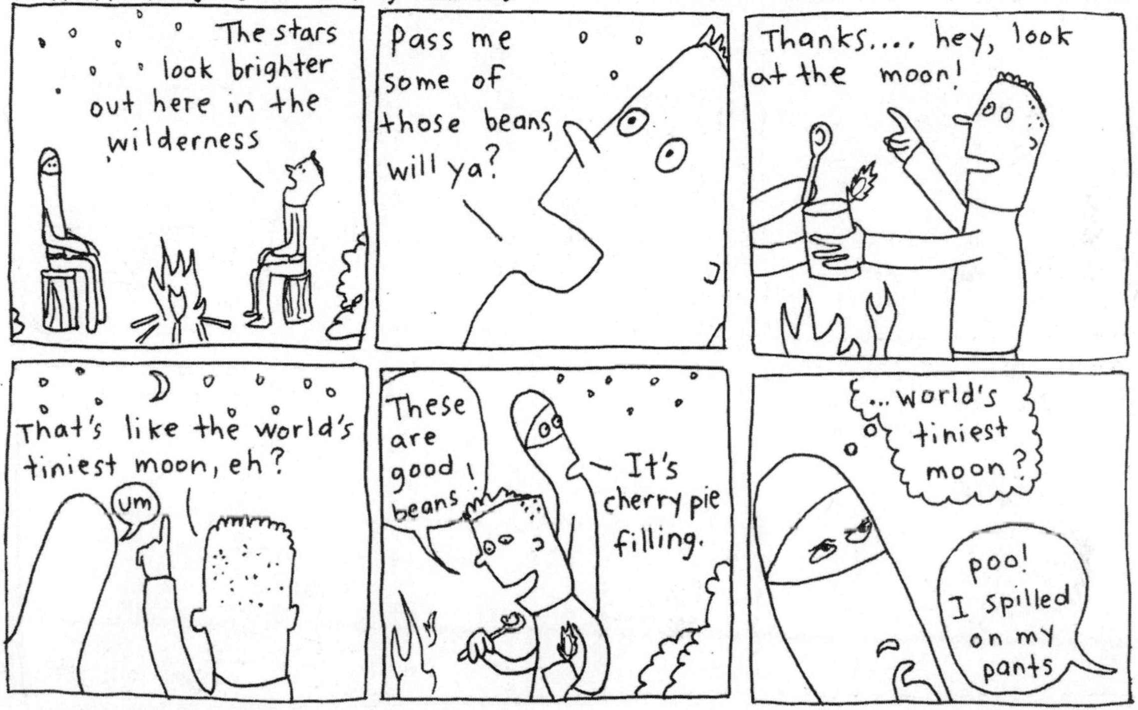

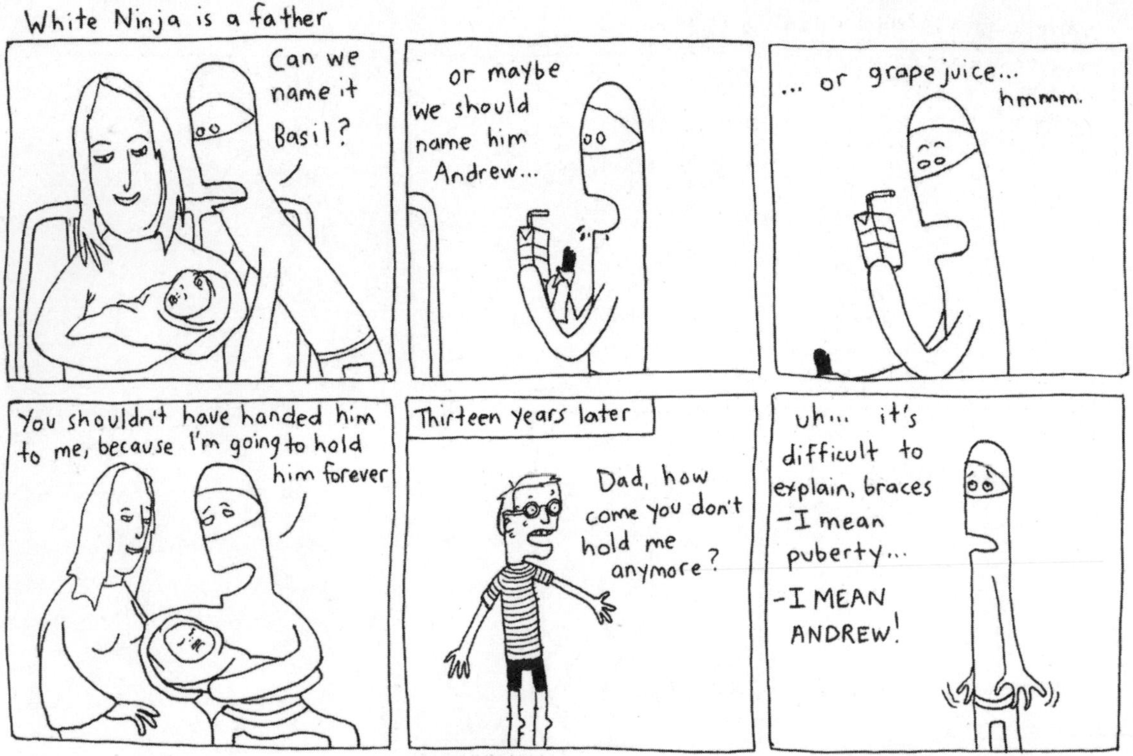
White Ninja is a father
Can we name it Basil?
or maybe we should name him Andrew...
... or grape juice... hmmm.
You shouldn't have handed him to me, because I'm going to hold him forever
Thirteen years later
Dad, how come you don't hold me anymore?
uh... it's difficult to explain, braces -I mean puberty... -I MEAN ANDREW!

White Ninja ponders the meaning of life

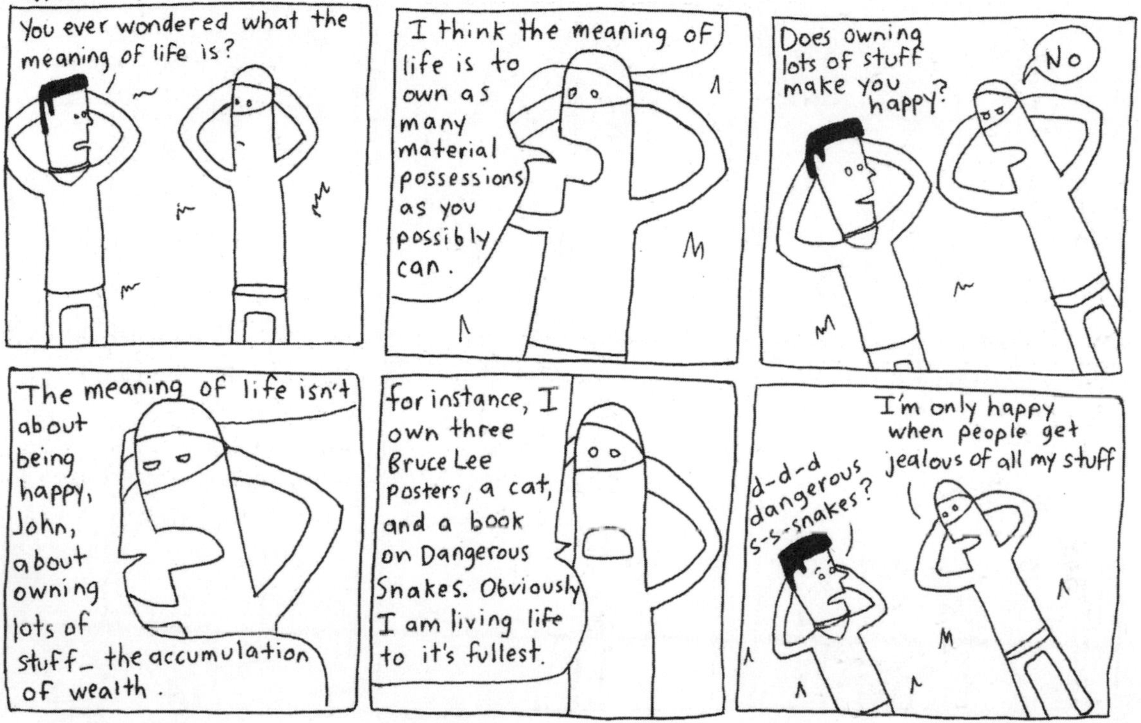

You ever wondered what the meaning of life is?
I think the meaning of life is to own as many material possessions as you possibly can.
Does owning lots of stuff make you happy?
No
The meaning of life isn't about being happy, John, about owning lots of stuff_ the accumulation of wealth.
for instance, I own three Bruce Lee posters, a cat, and a book on Dangerous Snakes. Obviously I am living life to it's fullest.
d-d-d dangerous s-s-snakes?
I'm only happy when people get jealous of all my stuff

White Ninja is a space man

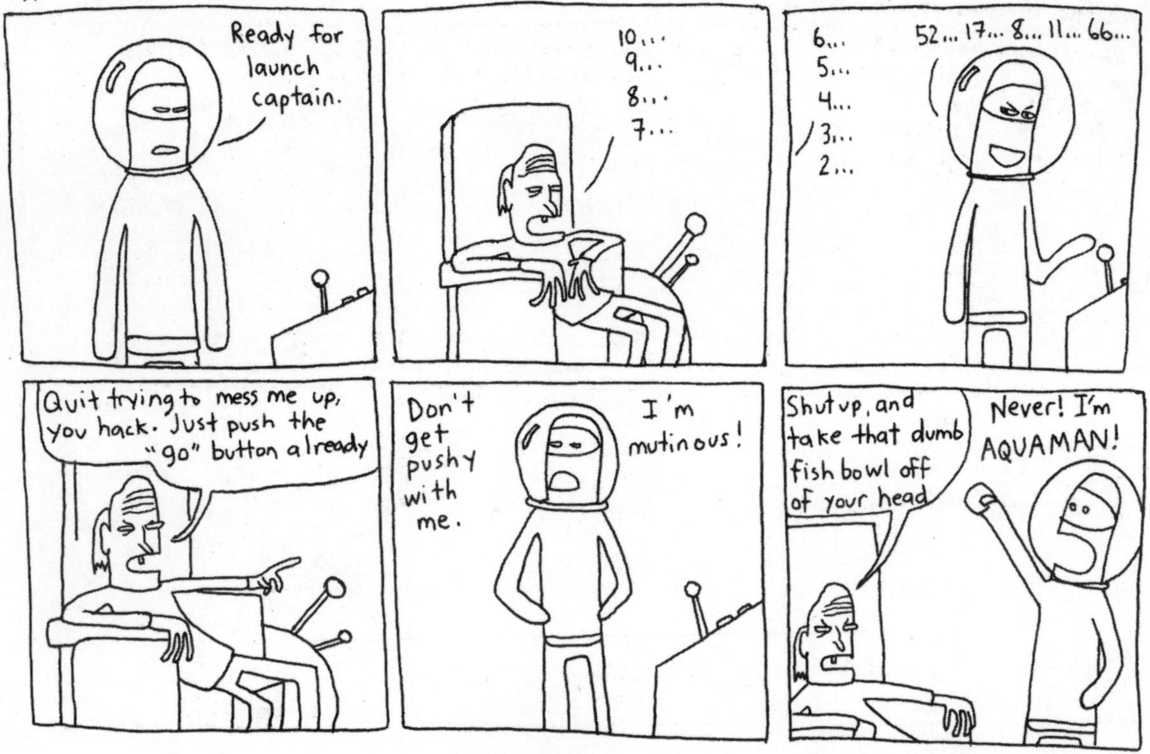
Ready for launch captain.
10... 9... 8... 7...
6... 5... 4... 3... 2...
52... 17... 8... 11... 66...
Quit trying to mess me up, you hack. Just push the "go" button already
Don't get pushy with me.
I'm mutinous!
Shutup, and take that dumb fish bowl off of your head
Never! I'm AQUAMAN!

White Ninja's leg is not broken

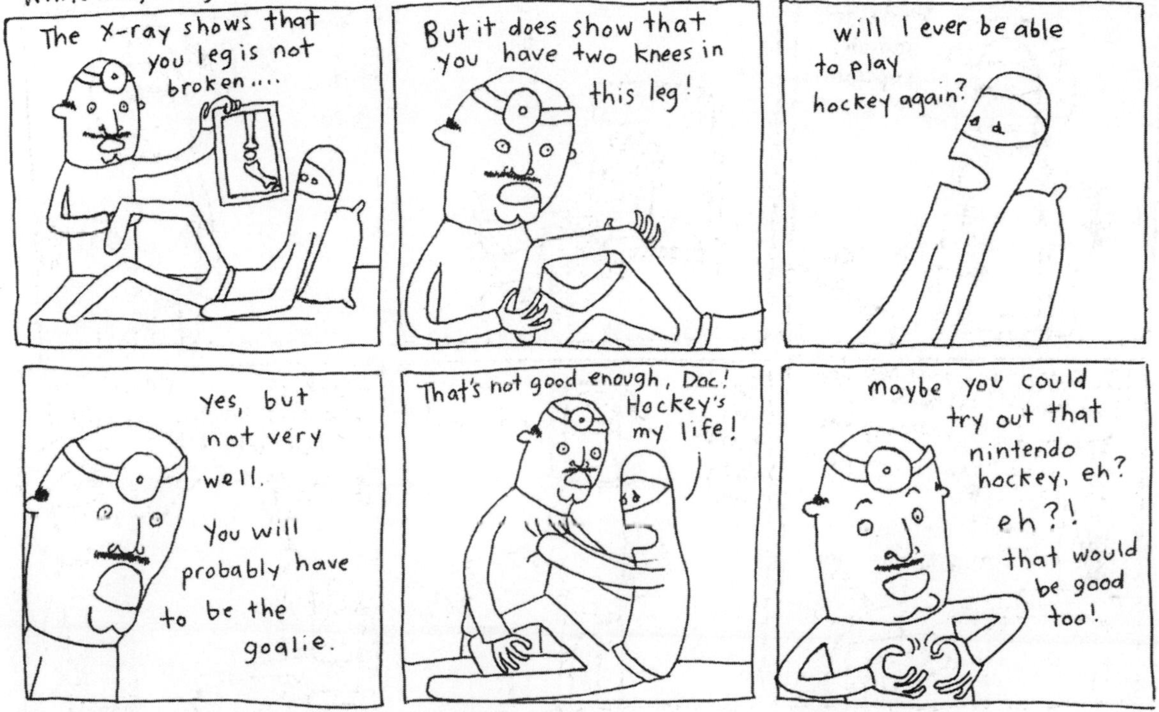
The X-ray shows that you leg is not broken....
But it does show that you have two knees in this leg!
will I ever be able to play hockey again?
yes, but not very well.
You will probably have to be the goalie.
That's not good enough, Doc! Hockey's my life!
maybe you could try out that nintendo hockey, eh?
eh?!
that would be good too!

White Ninja has a happy birthday

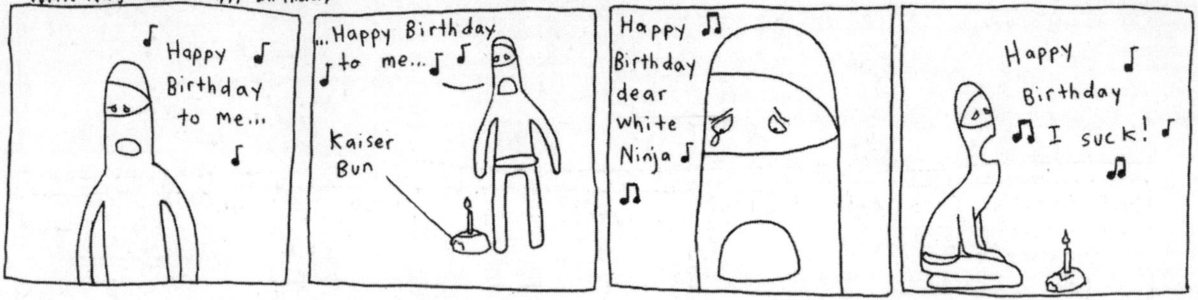
Happy Birthday to me...
...Happy Birthday to me...
Kaiser Bun
Happy Birthday dear white Ninja
Happy Birthday I suck!

White Ninja's armpit pants

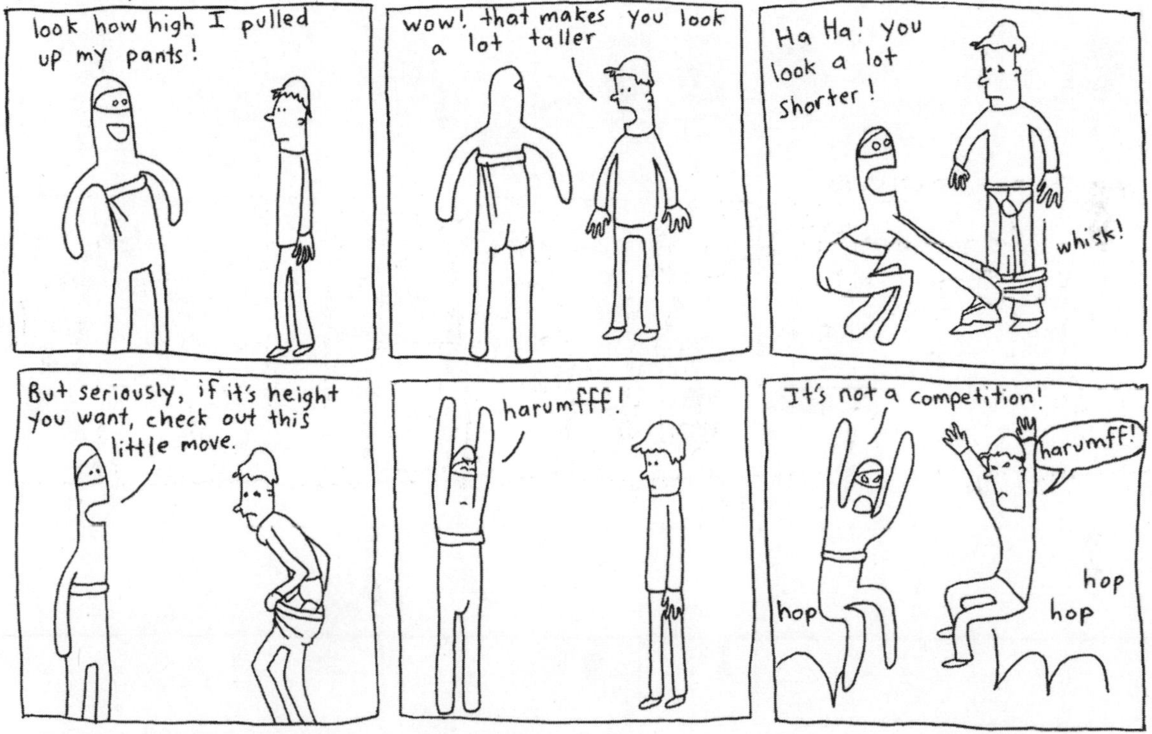
look how high I pulled up my pants!
wow! that makes you look a lot taller
Ha Ha! you look a lot shorter!
whisk!
But seriously, if it's height you want, check out this little move.
harumfff!
It's not a competition!
harumff!
hop
hop
hop

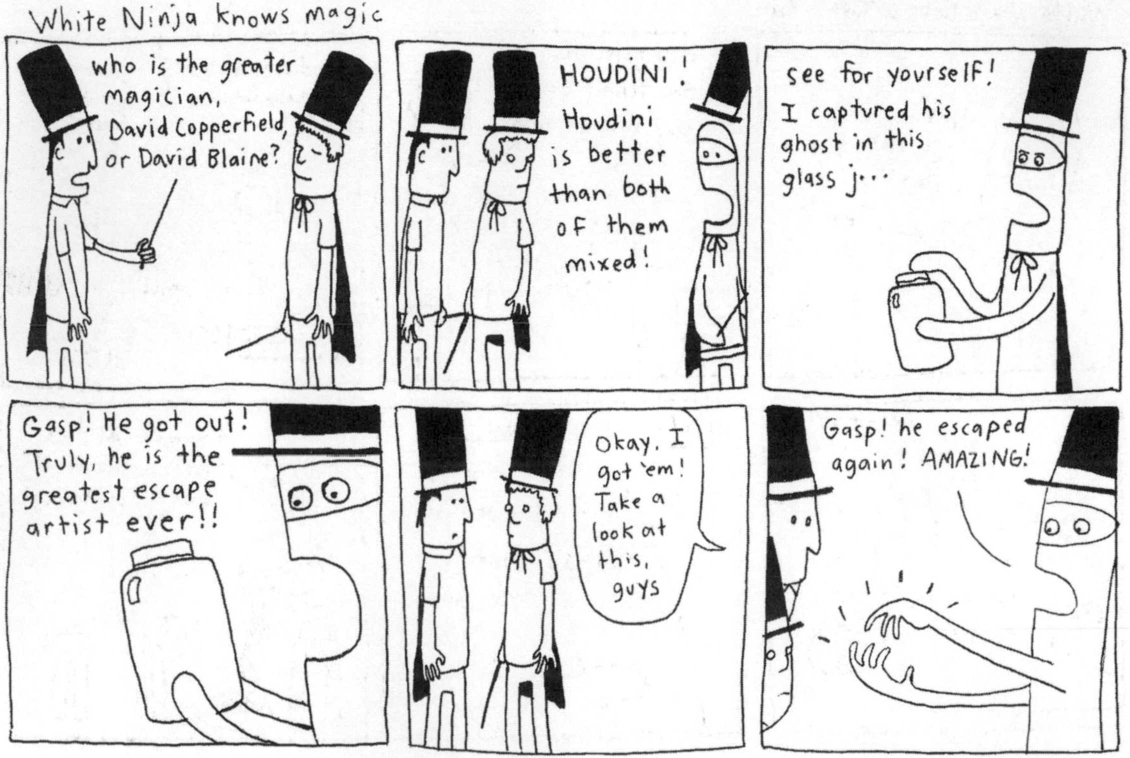
White Ninja knows magic
who is the greater magician, David Copperfield, or David Blaine?
HOUDINI!
Houdini is better than both of them mixed!
see for yourself! I captured his ghost in this glass j...
Gasp! He got out! Truly, he is the greatest escape artist ever!!
Okay. I got 'em! Take a look at this, guys
Gasp! he escaped again! AMAZING!

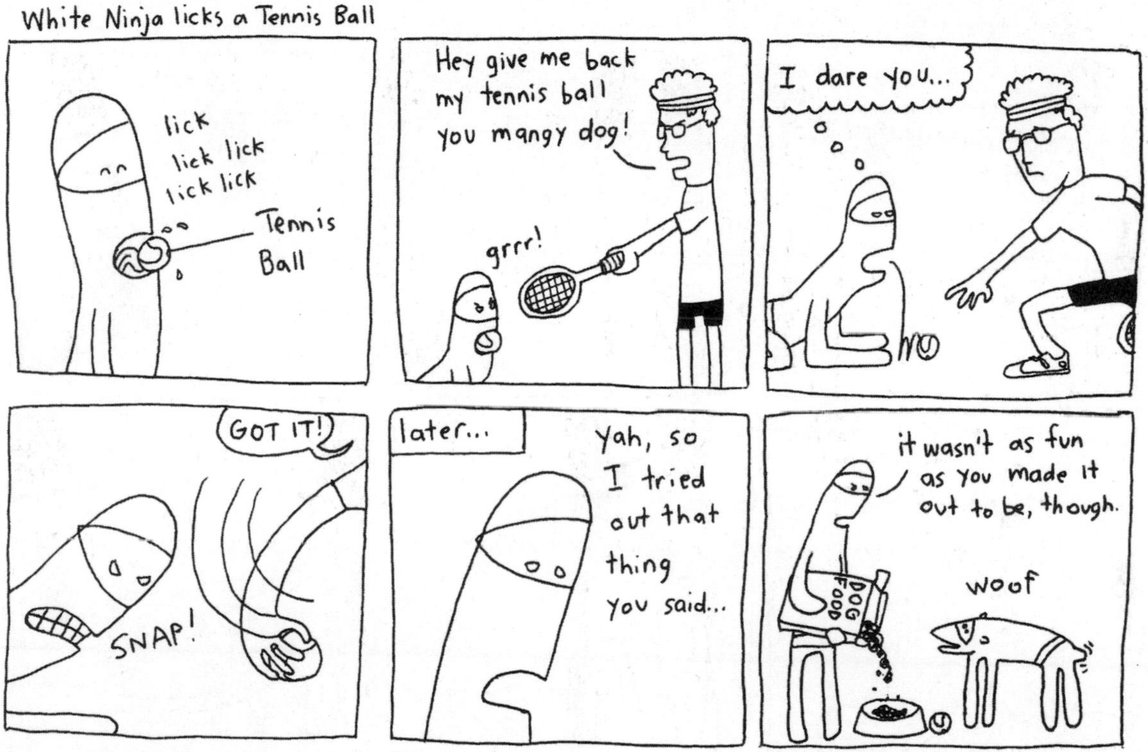
White Ninja licks a Tennis Ball
lick
lick lick
lick lick
Tennis Ball
Hey give me back my tennis ball you mangy dog!
grrr!
I dare you...
GOT IT!
SNAP!
later...
Yah, so I tried out that thing you said...
it wasn't as fun as you made it out to be, though.
DOG FOOD
woof

White Ninja befriends a small child

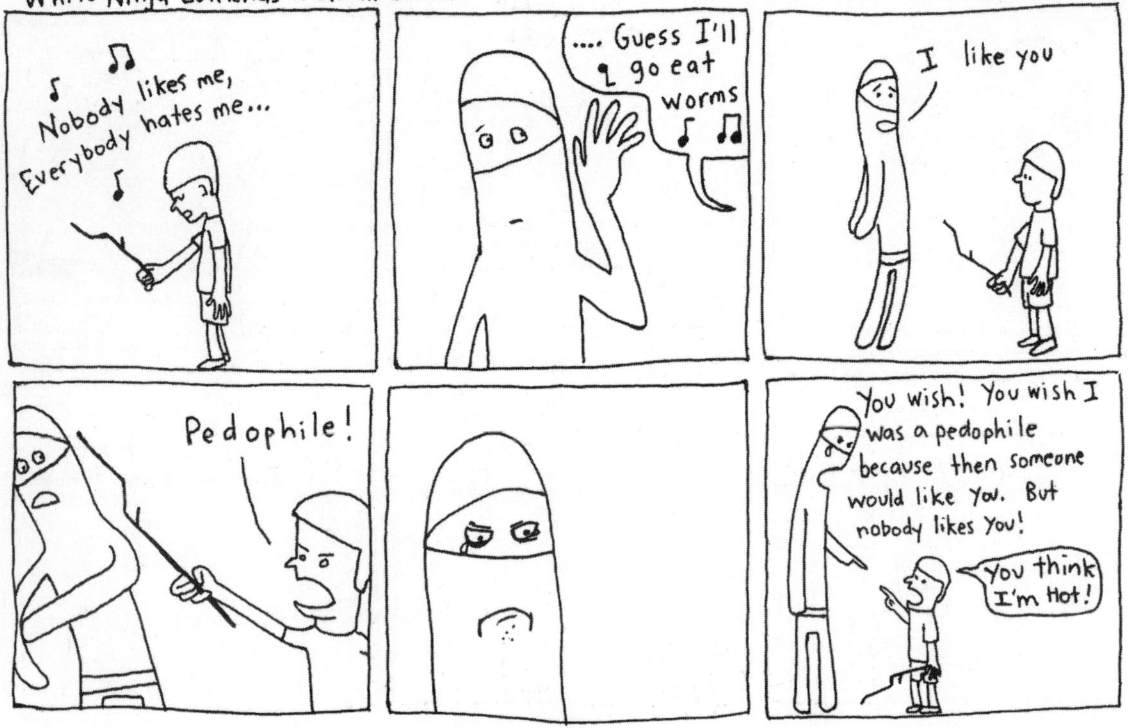

Nobody likes me, Everybody hates me...
.... Guess I'll go eat worms
I like you
Pedophile!
You wish! You wish I was a pedophile because then someone would like You. But nobody likes You!
You think I'm Hot!

White Ninja Knows Everything

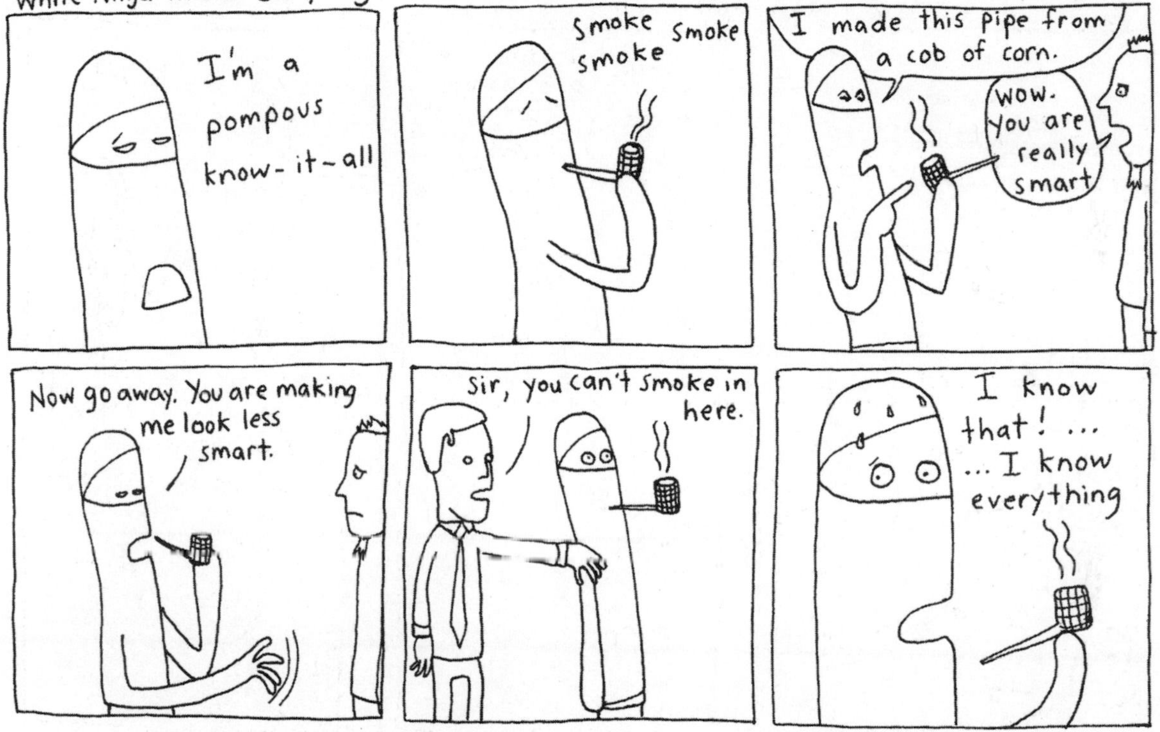

I'm a pompous know-it-all
Smoke Smoke smoke
I made this pipe from a cob of corn.
Wow. You are really smart
Now go away. You are making me look less smart.
Sir, you can't smoke in here.
I know that! ... ... I know everything

White Ninja and the monk

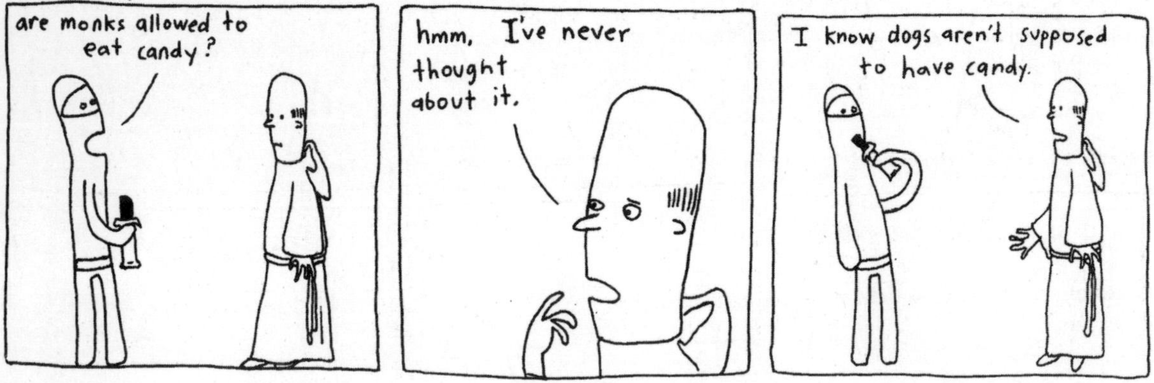
are monks allowed to eat candy?
hmm, I've never thought about it.
I know dogs aren't supposed to have candy.

White Ninja's pig

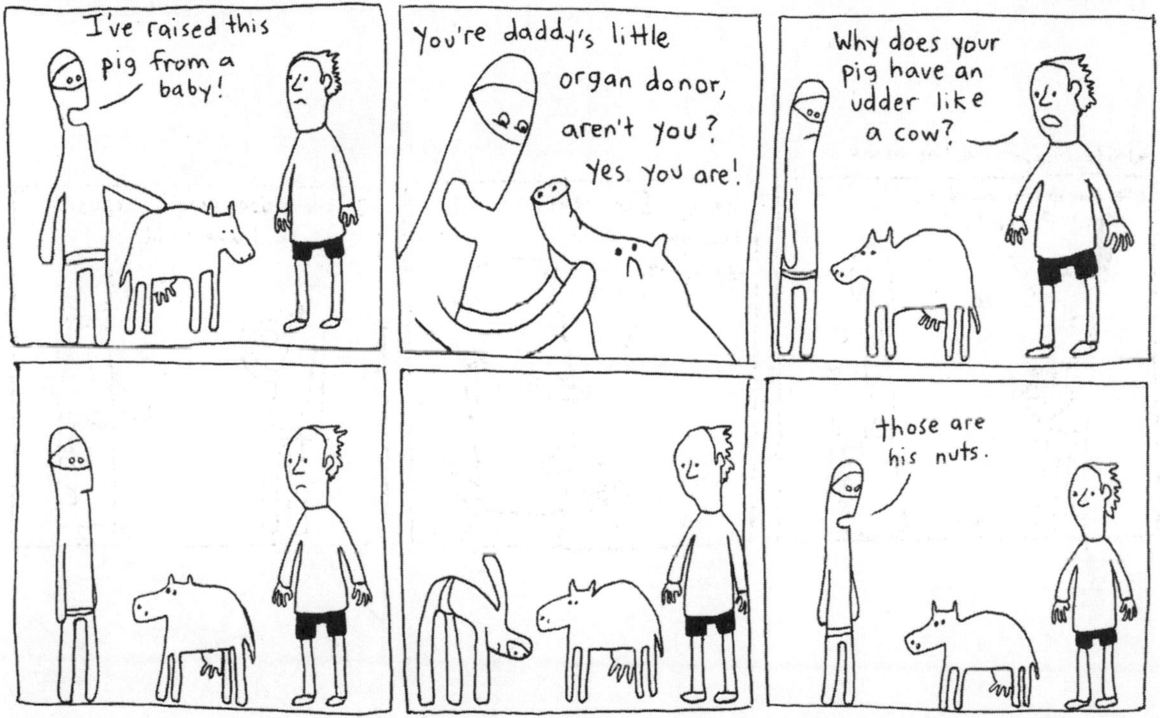
I've raised this pig from a baby!
You're daddy's little organ donor, aren't you? Yes you are!
Why does your pig have an udder like a cow?
those are his nuts.

White Ninja and the mystery gotch

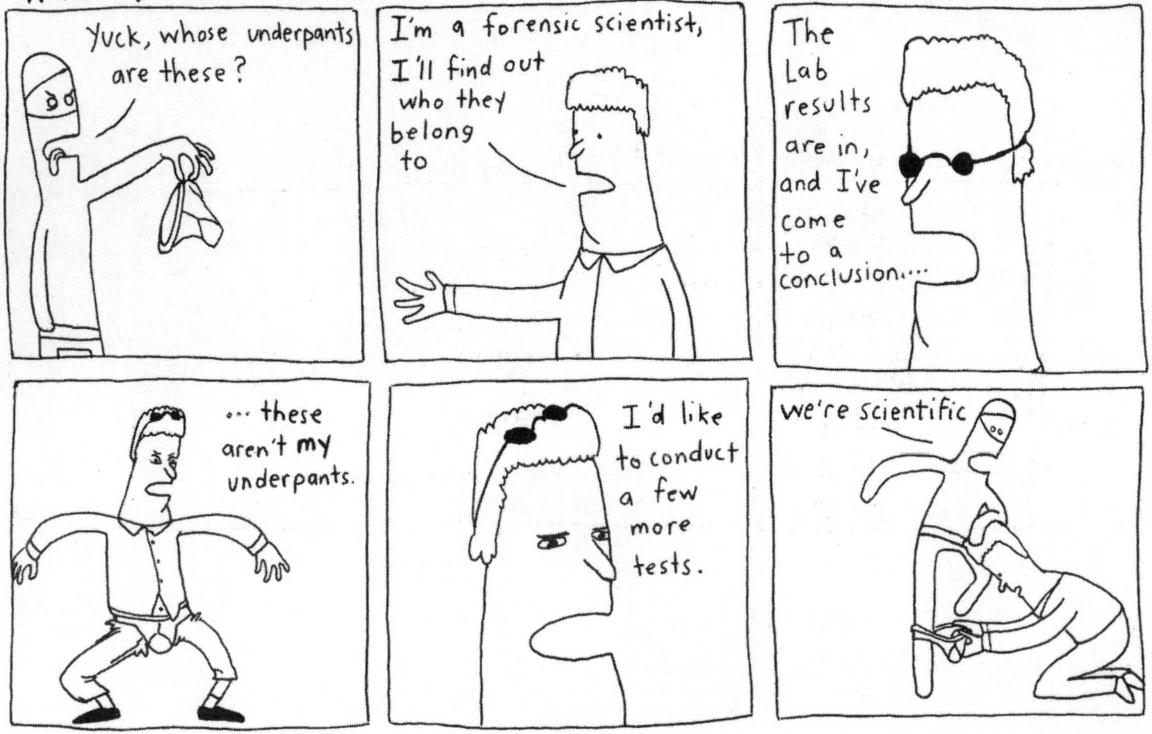
Yuck, whose underpants are these?
I'm a forensic scientist, I'll find out who they belong to
The Lab results are in, and I've come to a conclusion....
... these aren't my underpants.
I'd like to conduct a few more tests.
we're scientific

White Ninja is concerned about Tom's outfit.

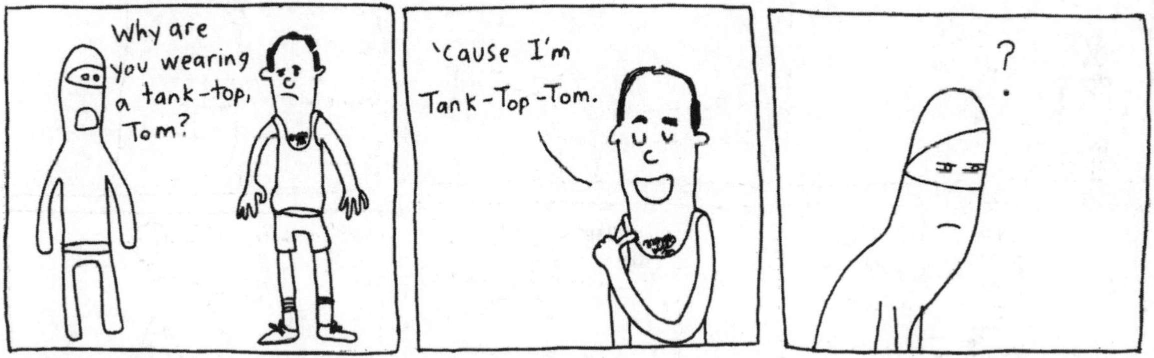
Why are you wearing a tank-top, Tom?
'cause I'm Tank-Top-Tom.
?

White Ninja gets sucky service

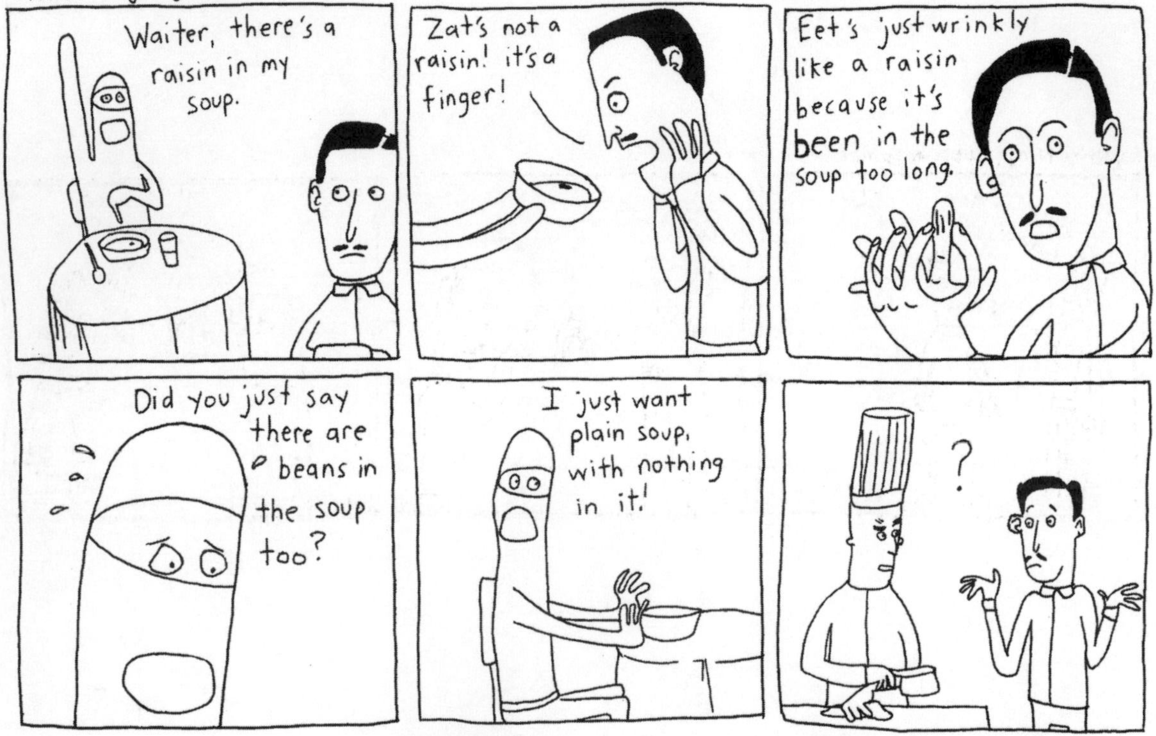
Waiter, there's a raisin in my soup.
Zat's not a raisin! it's a finger!
Eet's just wrinkly like a raisin because it's been in the soup too long.
Did you just say there are beans in the soup too?
I just want plain soup. with nothing in it!
?

White Ninja spots a Spider

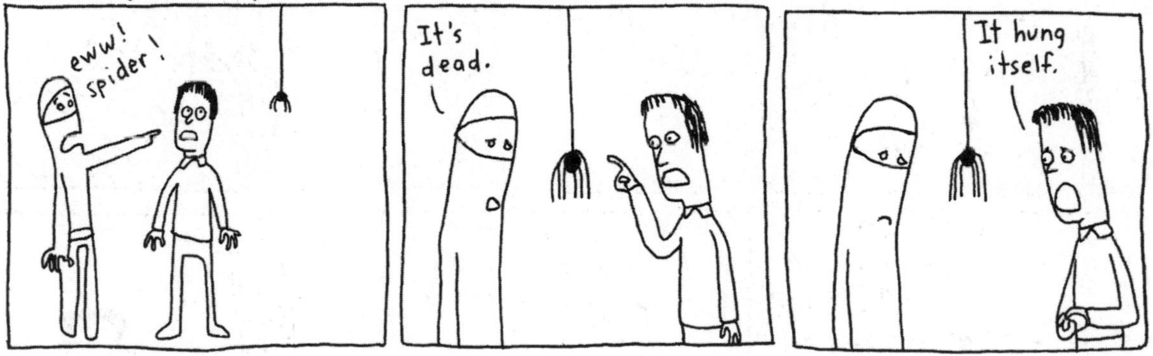
eww! spider!
It's dead.
It hung itself.

White Ninja and the new student

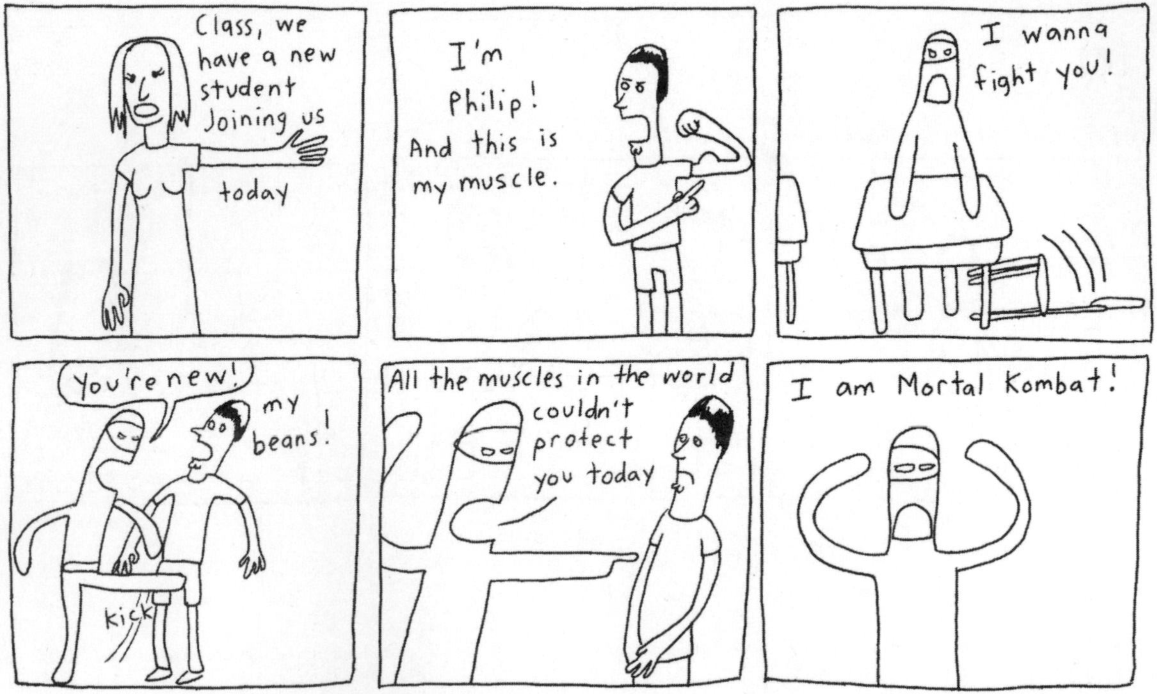
Class, we have a new student Joining us today
I'm Philip! And this is my muscle.
I wanna fight you!
You're new!
kick
my beans!
All the muscles in the world couldn't protect you today
I am Mortal Kombat!

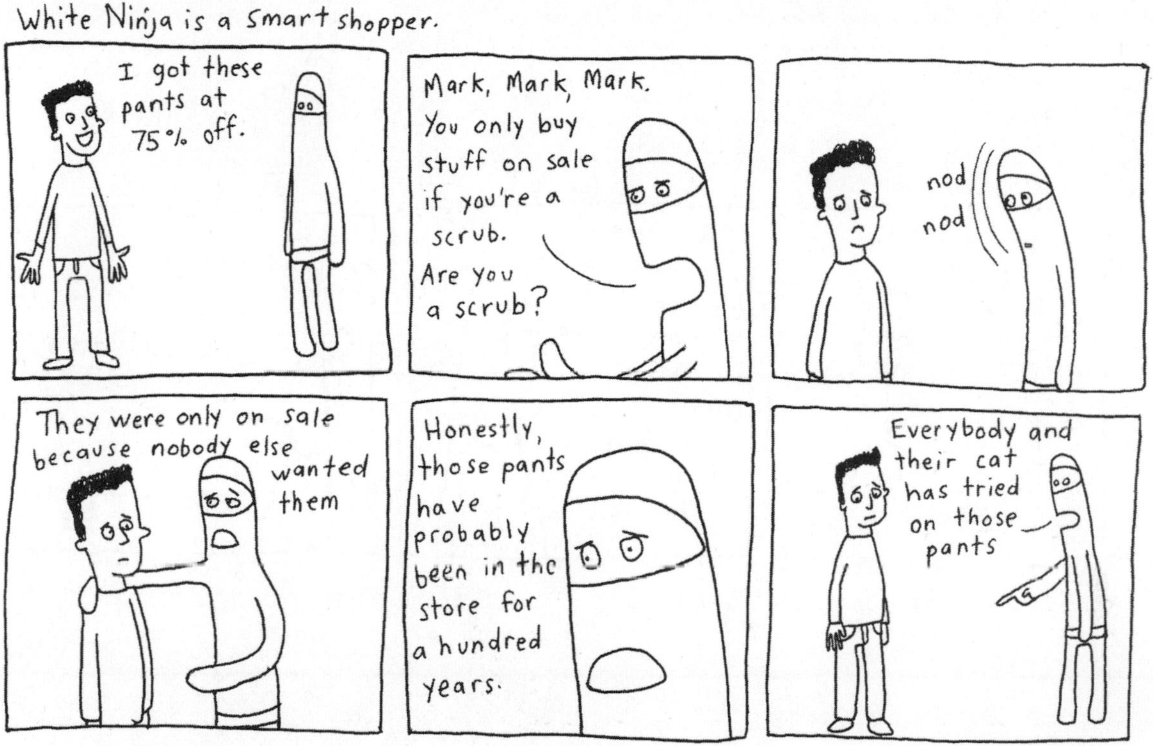
White Ninja is a smart shopper.
I got these pants at 75% off.
Mark, Mark, Mark.
You only buy stuff on sale if you're a scrub.
Are you a scrub?
nod nod
They were only on sale because nobody else wanted them
Honestly, those pants have probably been in the store for a hundred years.
Everybody and their cat has tried on those pants

White Ninja's bed time story

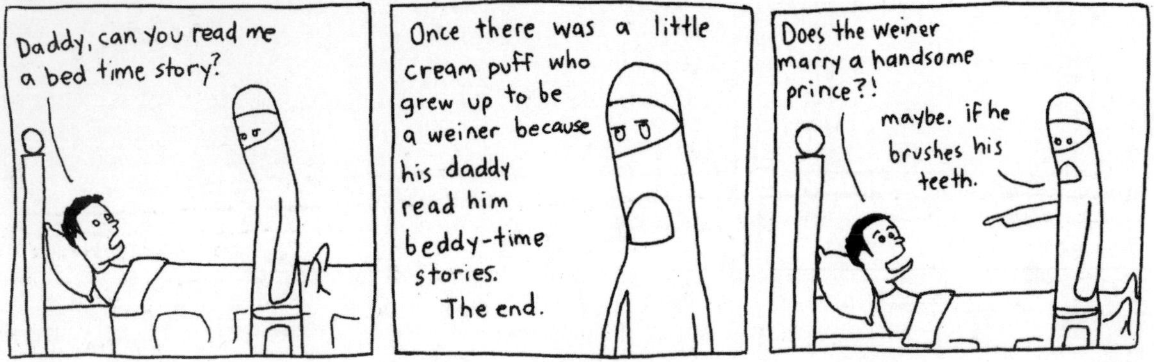
Daddy, can you read me a bed time story?
Once there was a little cream puff who grew up to be a weiner because his daddy read him beddy-time stories. The end.
Does the weiner marry a handsome prince?!
maybe. if he brushes his teeth.

White Ninja knows what a good tattoo looks like

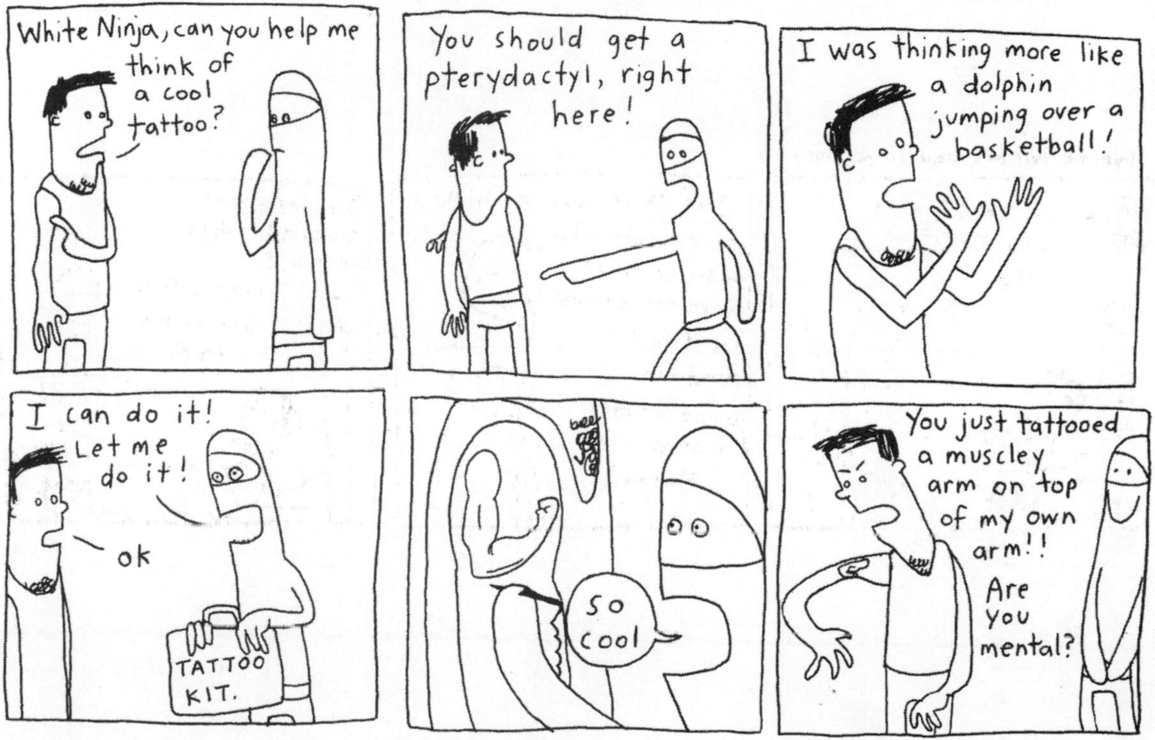
White Ninja, can you help me think of a cool tattoo?
You should get a pterydactyl, right here!
I was thinking more like a dolphin jumping over a basketball!
I can do it! Let me do it!
ok
TATTOO KIT.
So cool
You just tattooed a muscley arm on top of my own arm!! Are you mental?

White Ninja has a big fish

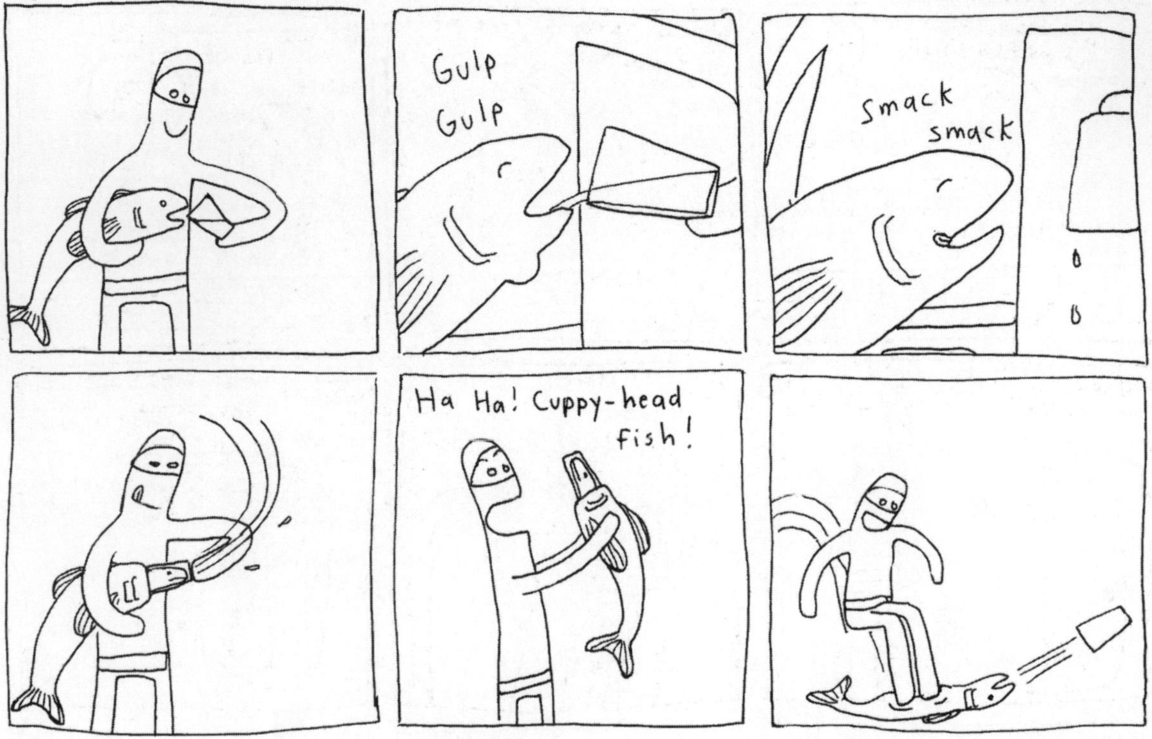
Gulp
Gulp
Smack
smack
Ha Ha! Cuppy-head fish!

White Ninja and the Martian

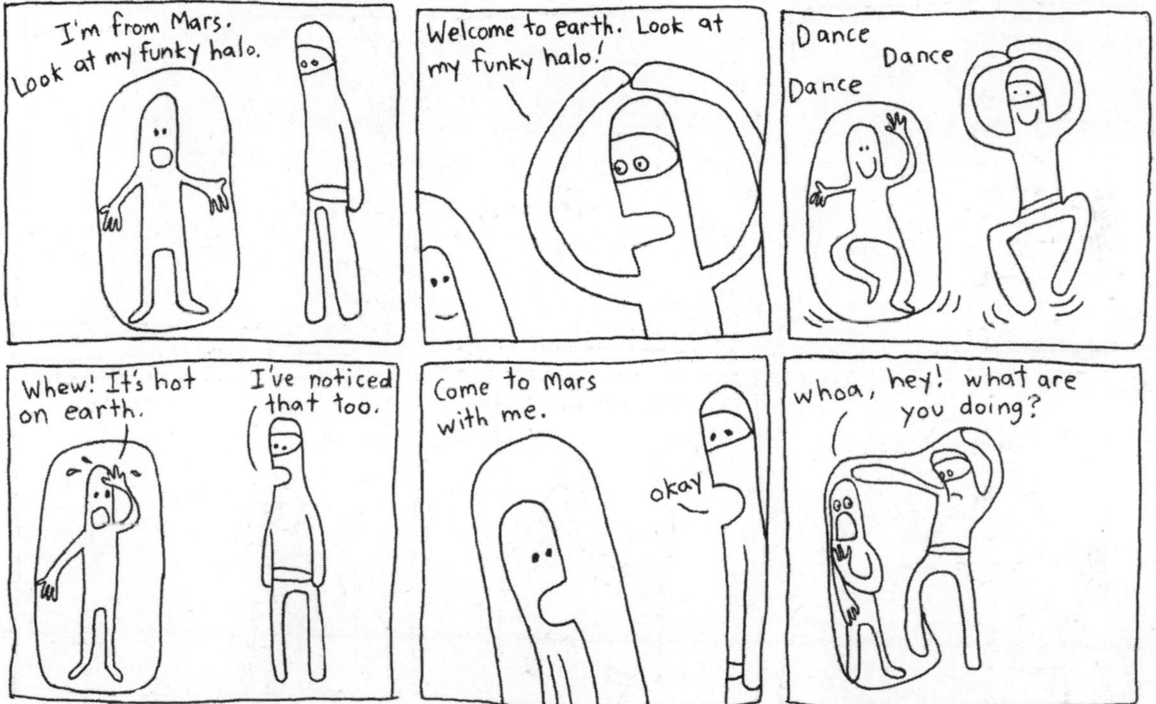

I'm from Mars.
Look at my funky halo.
Welcome to earth. Look at my funky halo!
Dance
Dance
Dance
Whew! It's hot on earth.
I've noticed that too.
Come to Mars with me.
okay
whoa,
hey! what are you doing?

White Ninja goes shoeshopping

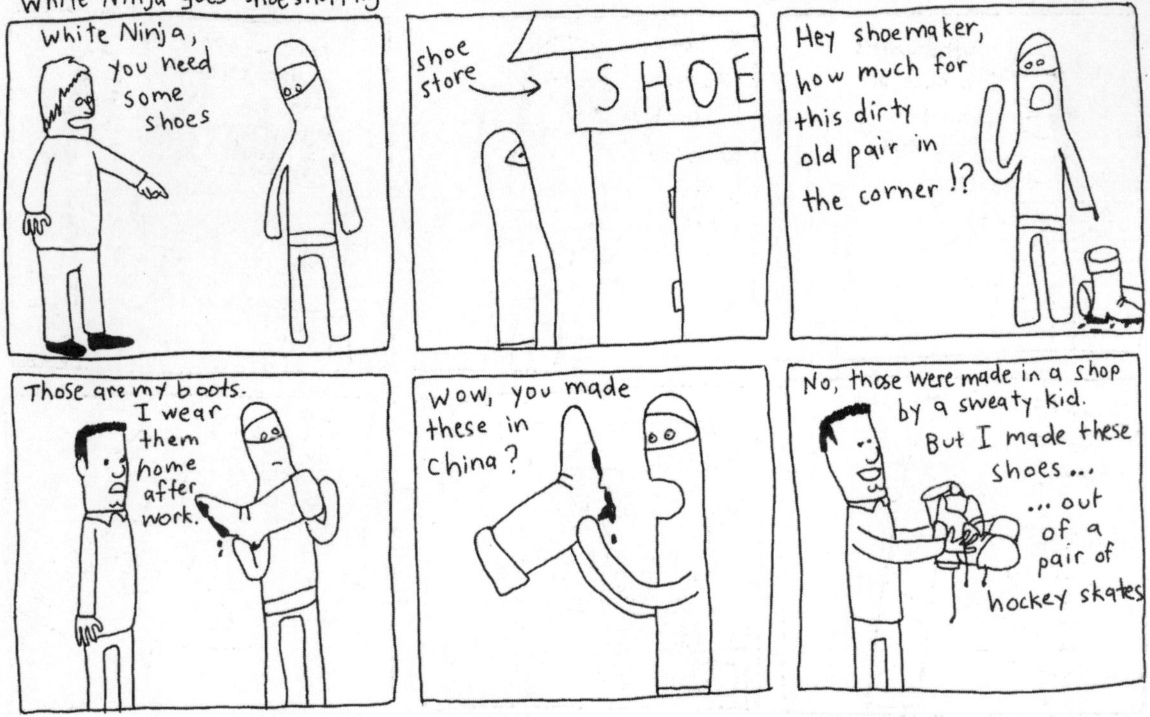
White Ninja, you need some shoes
shoe store
SHOE
Hey shoemaker, how much for this dirty old pair in the corner !?
Those are my boots.
I wear them home after work.
Wow, you made these in China?
No, those were made in a shop by a sweaty kid.
But I made these shoes...
...out of a pair of hockey skates

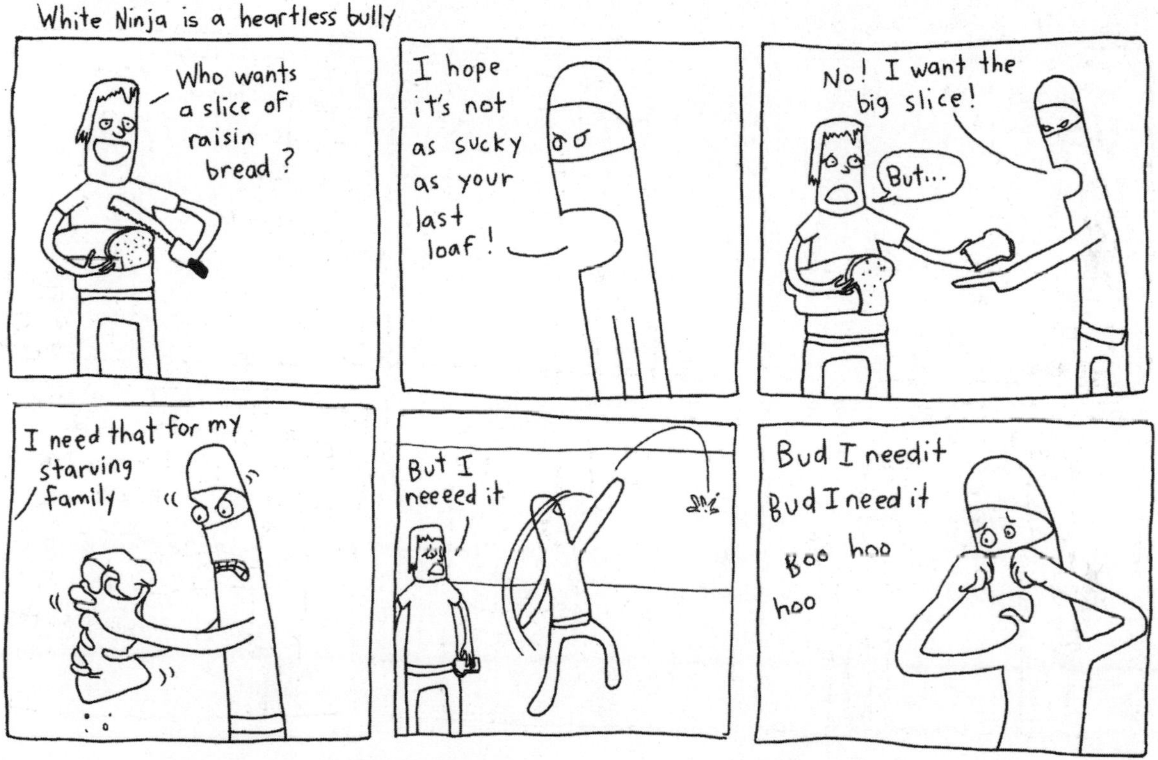
White Ninja is a heartless bully
Who wants a slice of raisin bread?
I hope it's not as sucky as your last loaf!
No! I want the big slice!
But...
I need that for my starving family
But I neeeed it
Bud I needit
Bud I need it
Boo hoo
hoo

White Ninja writes a book

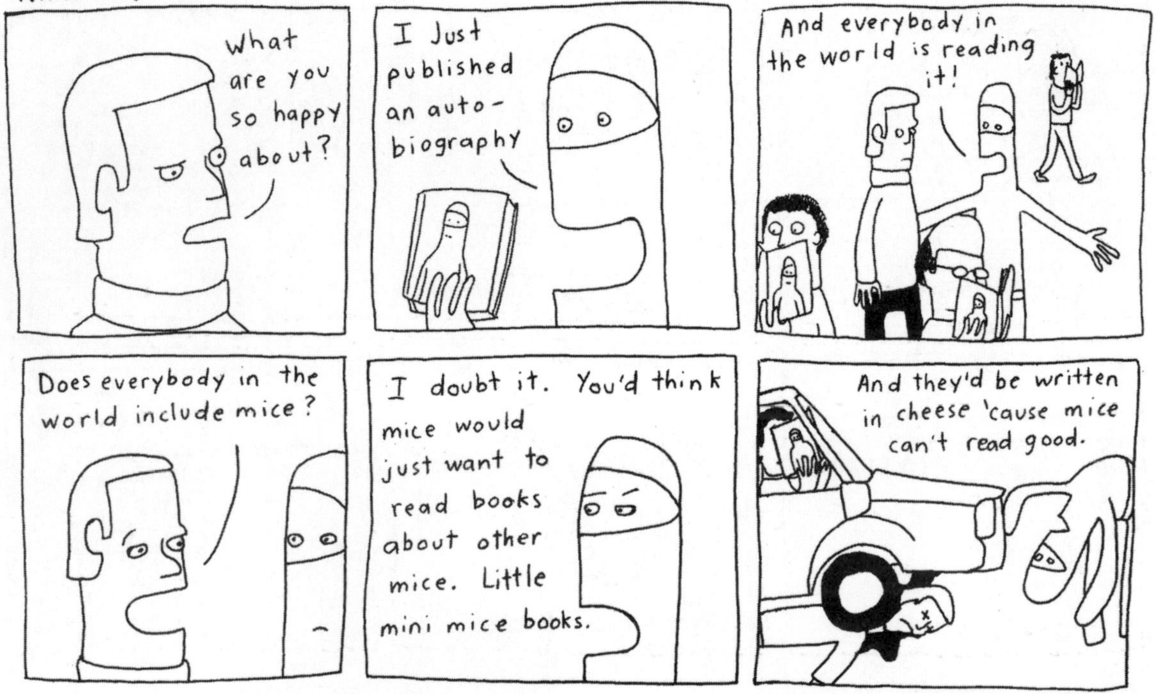

White Ninja's wig

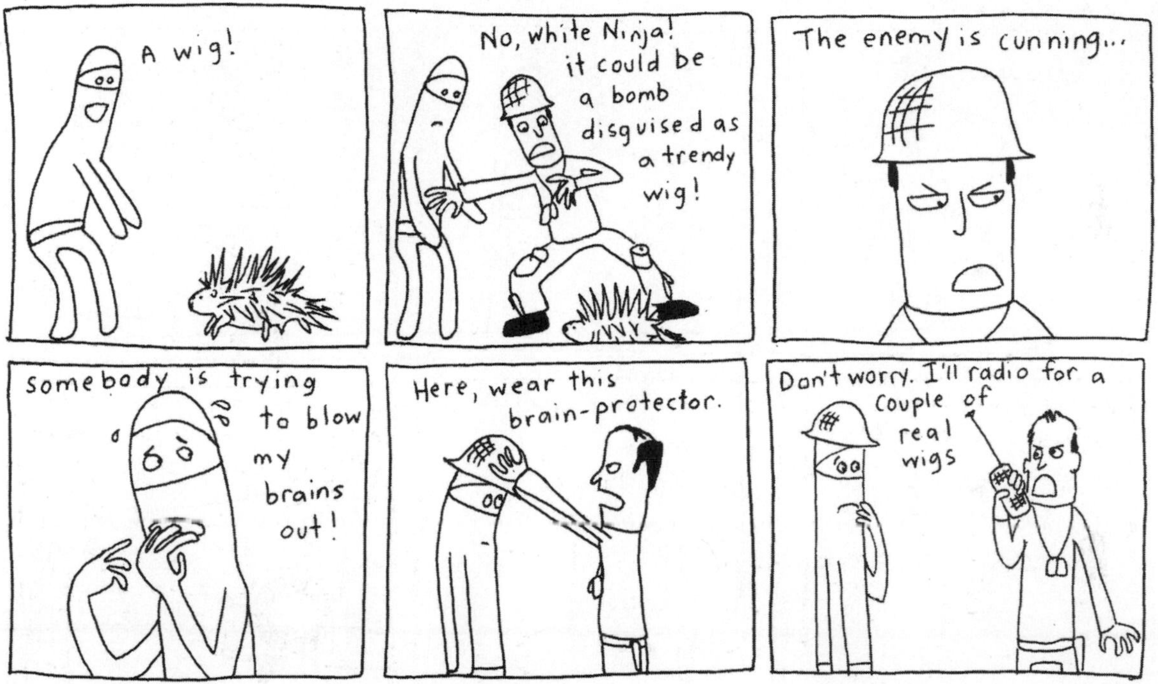
A wig!
No, white Ninja! it could be a bomb disguised as a trendy wig!
The enemy is cunning...
Somebody is trying to blow my brains out!
Here, wear this brain-protector.
Don't worry. I'll radio for a couple of real wigs

White Ninja is bothered by a turtle

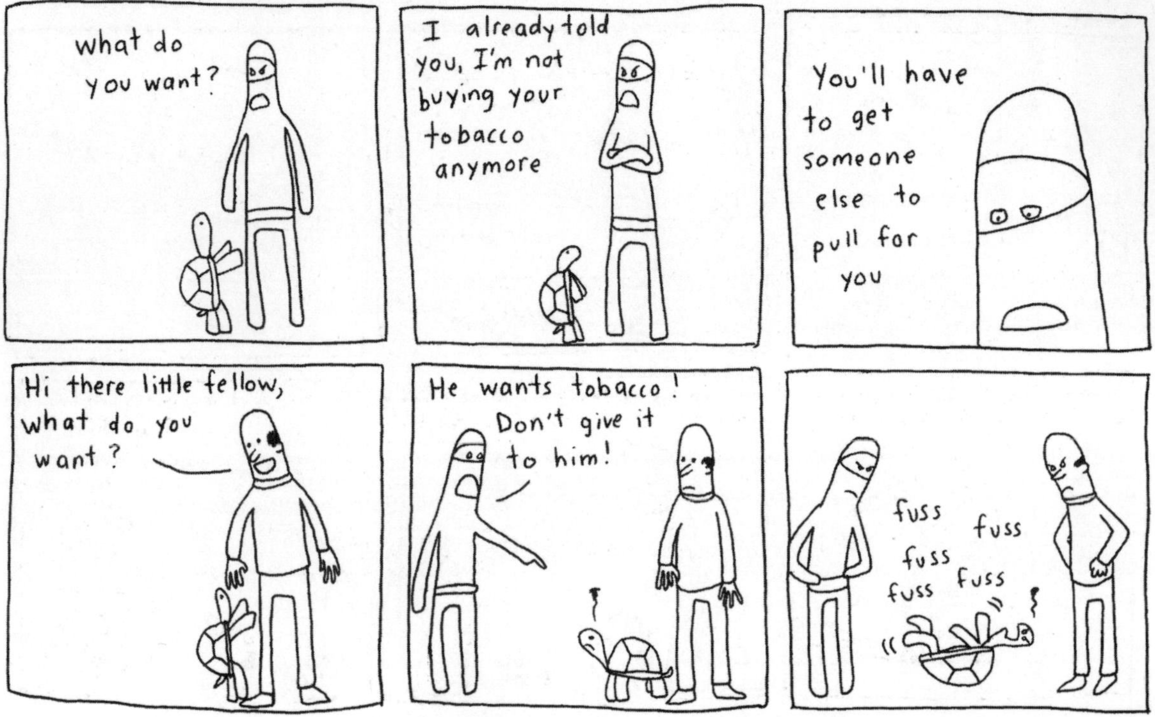
what do you want?
I already told you, I'm not buying your tobacco anymore
You'll have to get someone else to pull for you
Hi there little fellow, what do you want?
He wants tobacco! Don't give it to him!
fuss fuss fuss fuss fuss

White Ninja and the big moth

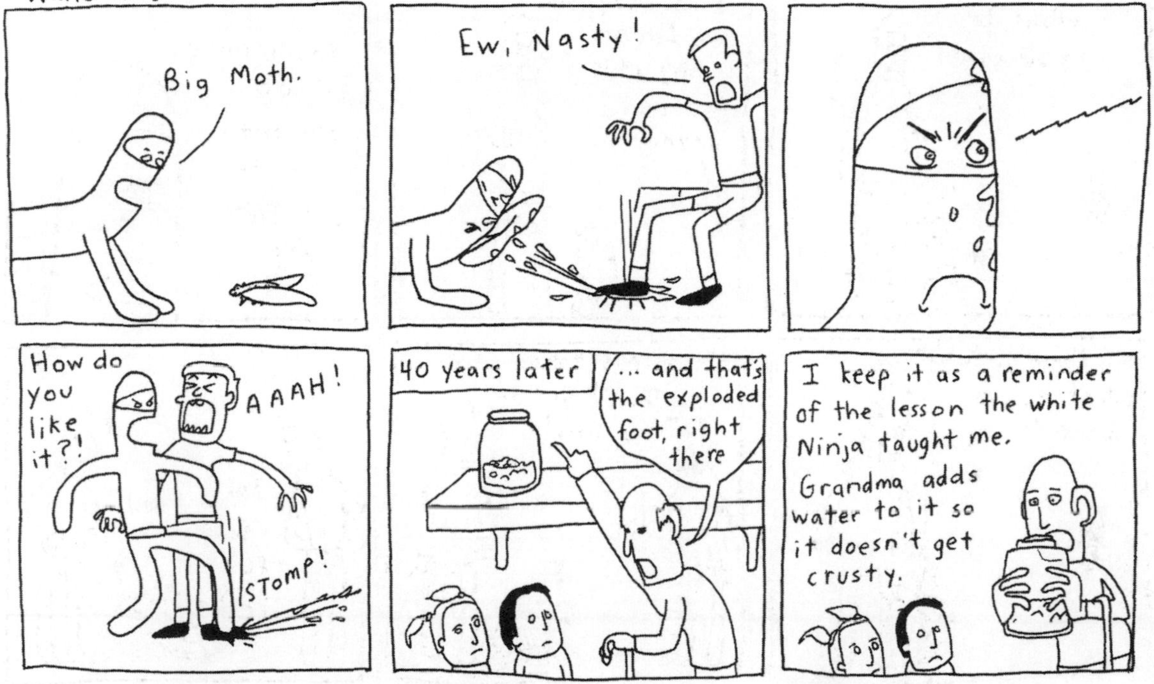
Big Moth.
Ew, Nasty!
How do you like it?!
AAAH!
STOMP!
40 years later
... and that's the exploded foot, right there
I keep it as a reminder of the lesson the white Ninja taught me.
Grandma adds water to it so it doesn't get crusty.

White Ninja's stupid cousin

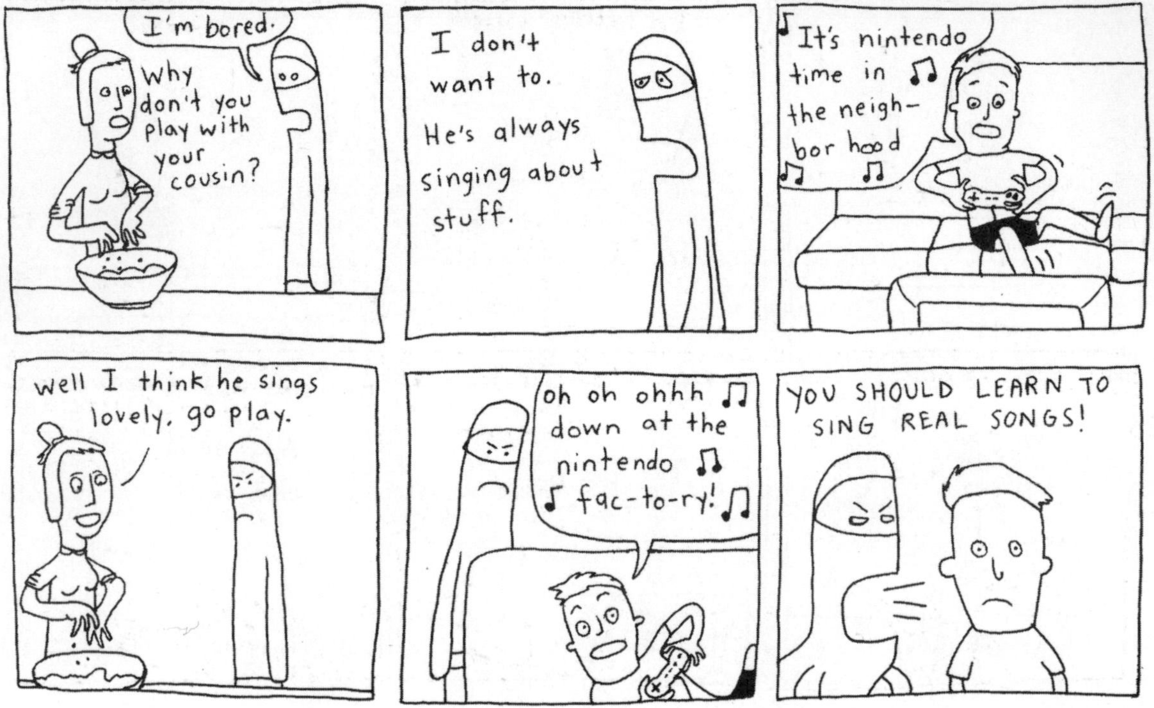

White Ninja and the rabbits

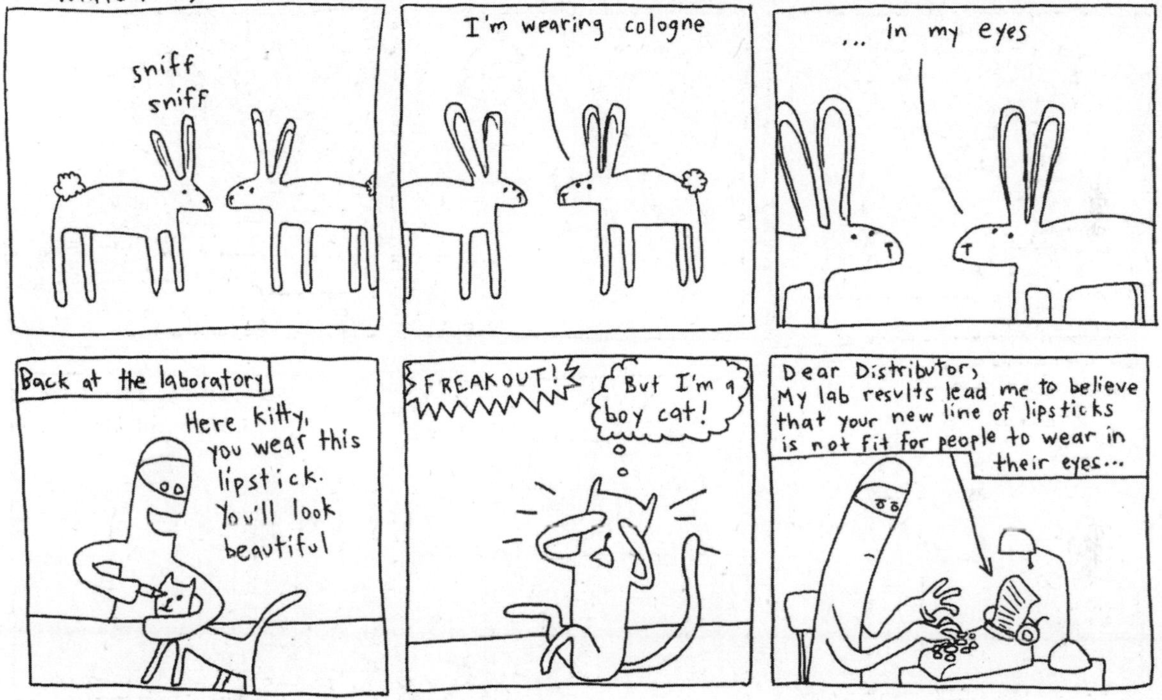
sniff
sniff
I'm wearing cologne
... in my eyes
Back at the laboratory
Here kitty, you wear this lipstick. You'll look beautiful
FREAKOUT!
But I'm a boy cat!
Dear Distributor,
My lab results lead me to believe that your new line of lipsticks is not fit for people to wear in their eyes...

White ninja dresses like a flower

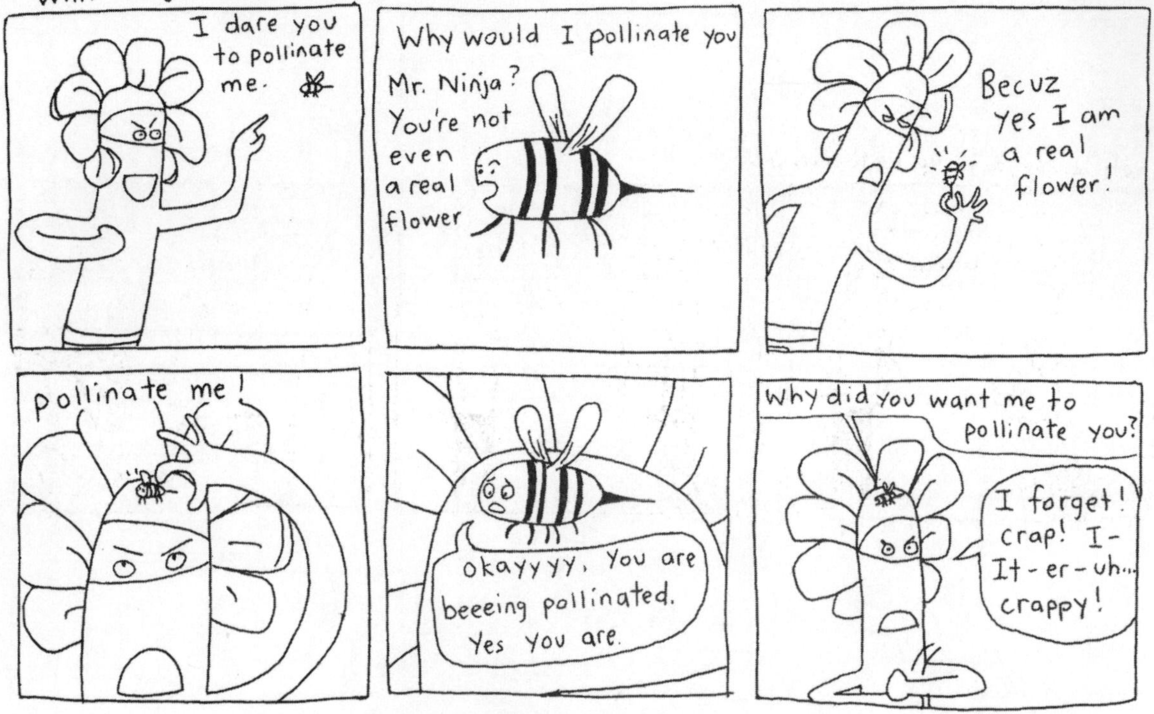
I dare you to pollinate me.
Why would I pollinate you Mr. Ninja? You're not even a real flower
Becuz yes I am a real flower!
pollinate me!
okayyyy, You are beeeing pollinated. Yes You are.
Why did you want me to pollinate you?
I forget! crap! I- It-er-uh... crappy!

White Ninja is up to Something

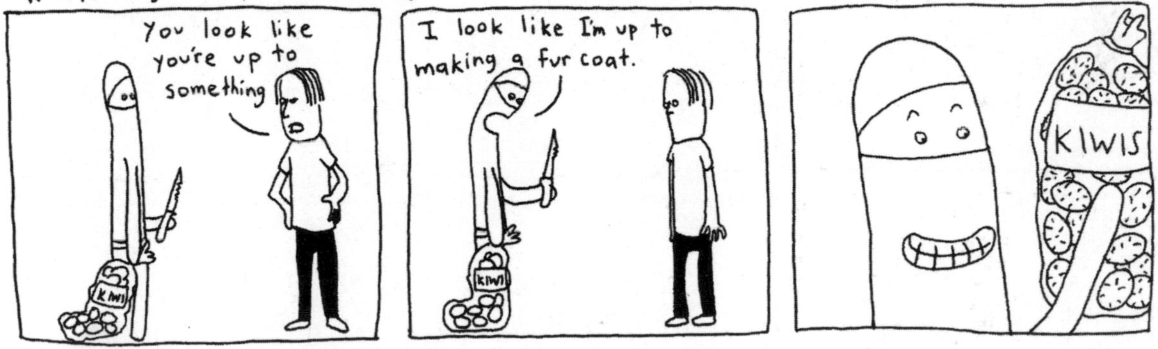
You look like you're up to something
KIWI
I look like I'm up to making a fur coat.
KIWI
KIWIS

White Ninja in: Hottie Alert

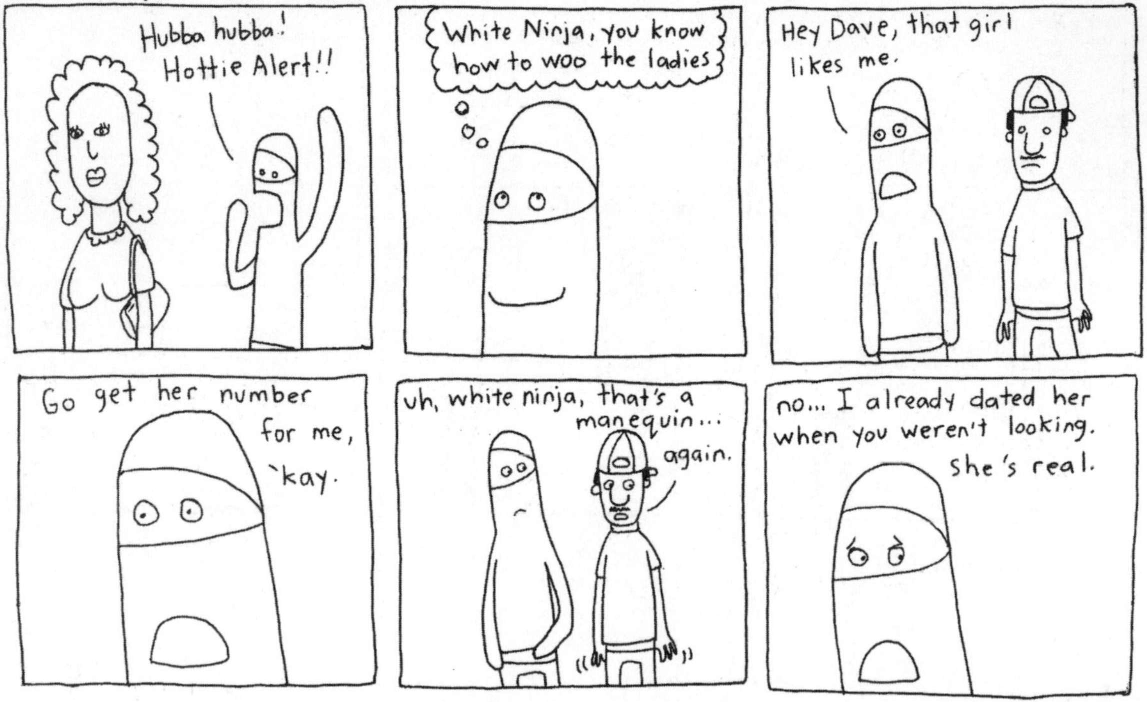
Hubba hubba! Hottie Alert!!
White Ninja, you know how to woo the ladies
Hey Dave, that girl likes me.
Go get her number for me, `kay.
uh, white ninja, that's a manequin... again.
no... I already dated her when you weren't looking. She's real.

White Ninja changes for the better

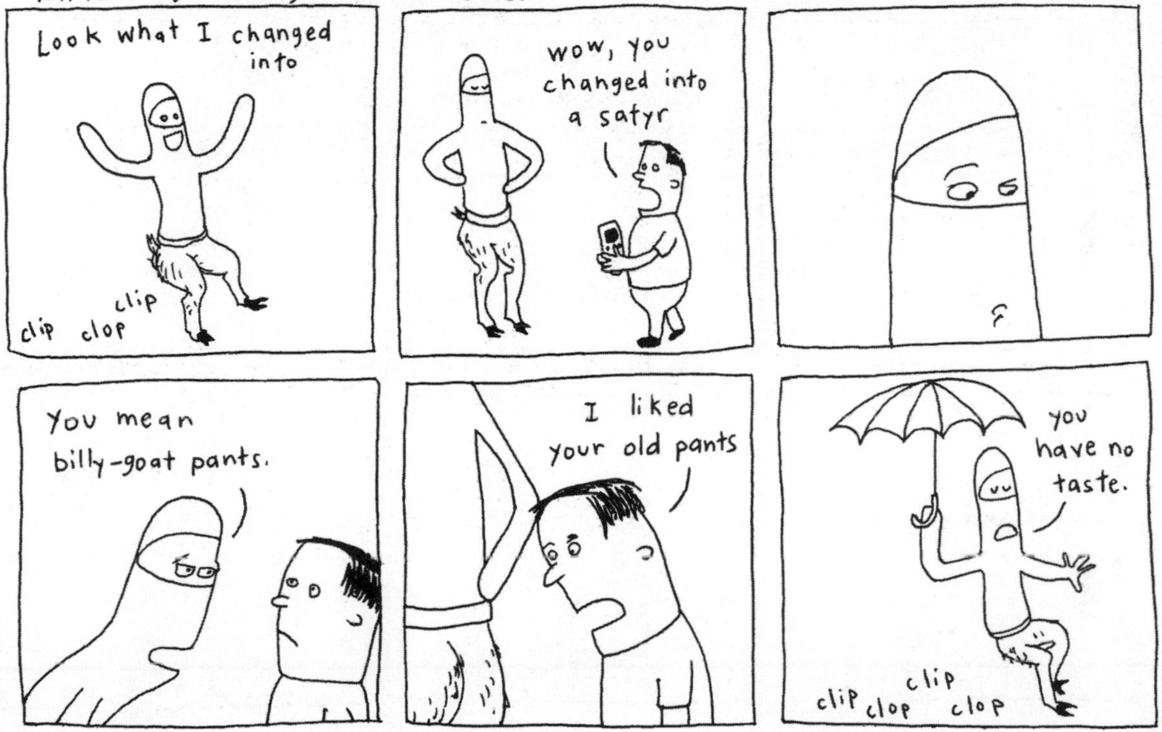
Look what I changed into
clip clop clip
wow, you changed into a satyr
You mean billy-goat pants.
I liked your old pants
you have no taste.
clip clop clip clop

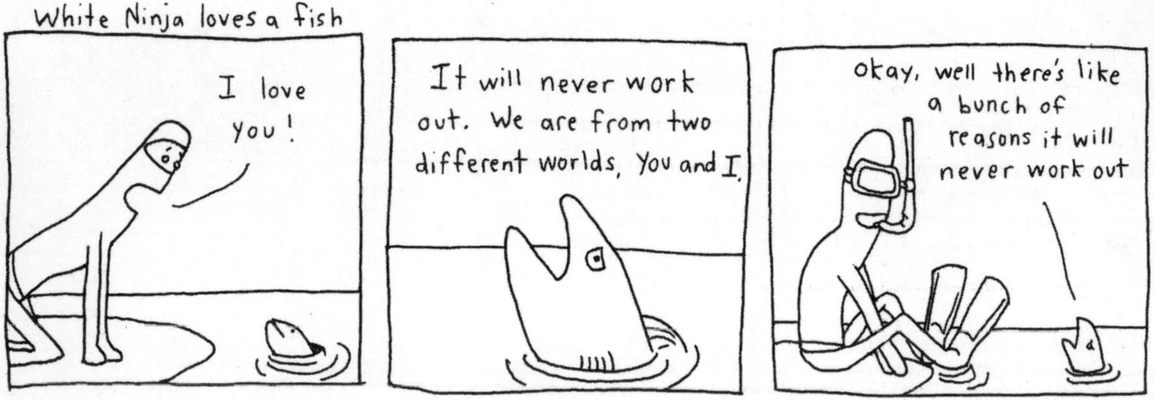
White Ninja loves a fish
I love you!
It will never work out. We are from two different worlds, you and I.
Okay, well there's like a bunch of reasons it will never work out

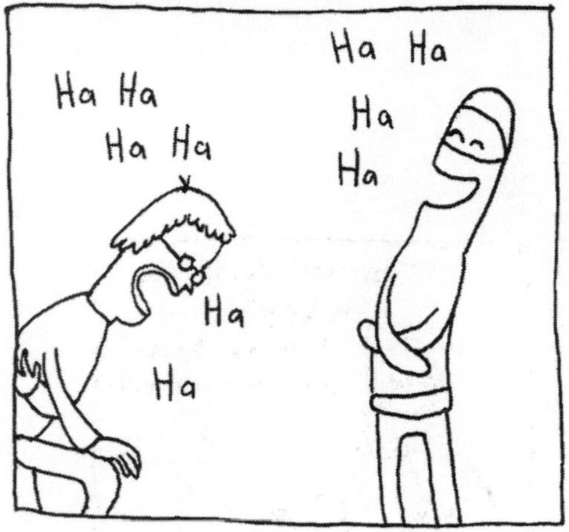
Ha Ha
Ha Ha
Ha Ha
Ha
Ha
Ha
Ha

BONUS COMICS

The following eight comic strips were never published on the tragically spectacular website whiteninjacomics.com. The reason: Kent didn't think they were funny enough. The reason they are appearing in this book: Scott thinks they totally were funny enough. Enjoy.

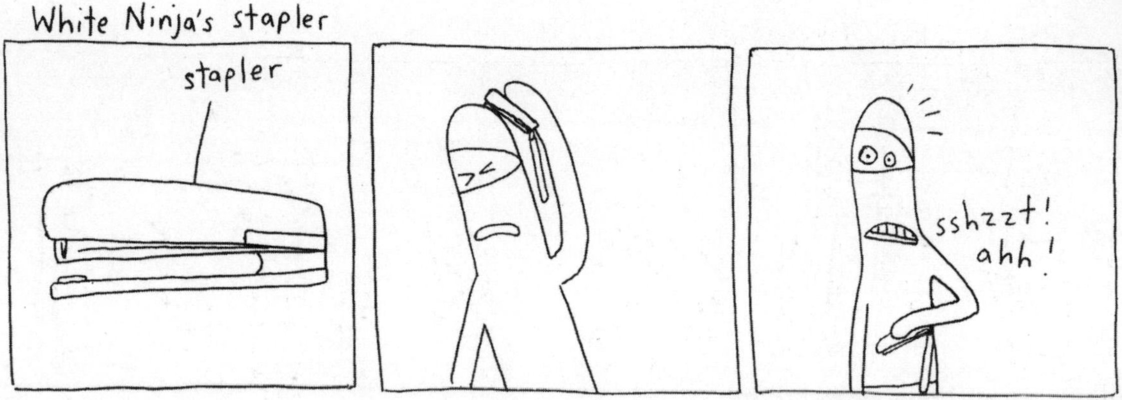
White Ninja's stapler
stapler
sshzzt!
ahh!

White Ninja has a quick wit

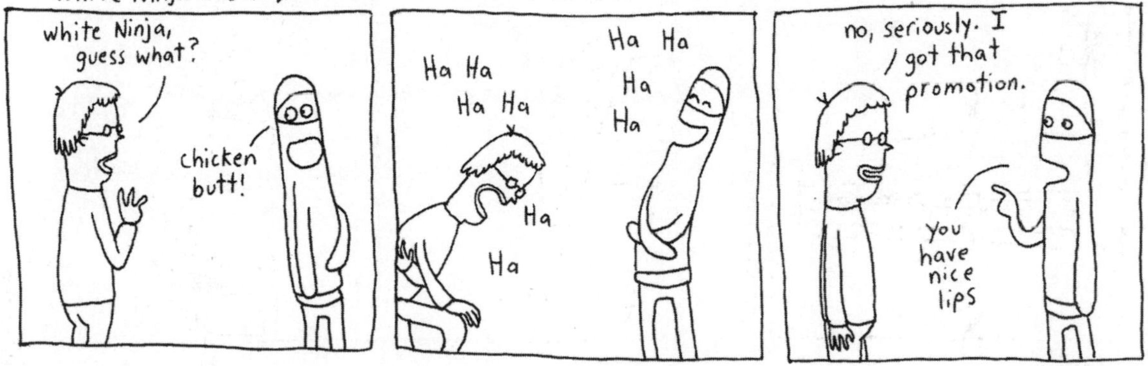
white Ninja, guess what?
chicken butt!
Ha Ha
Ha Ha
Ha
Ha
Ha Ha
Ha
Ha
no, seriously. I got that promotion.
You have nice lips

White Ninja's wet socks

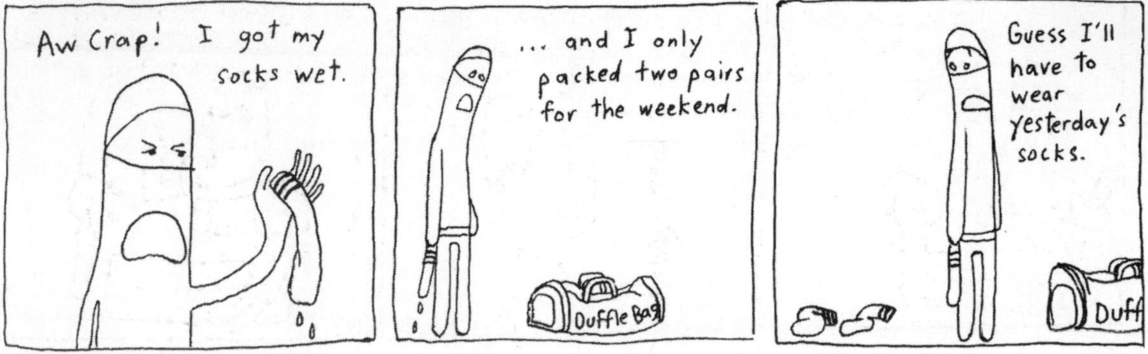
Aw Crap! I got my socks wet.
... and I only packed two pairs for the weekend.
Duffle Bag
Guess I'll have to wear yesterday's socks.
Duff

White Ninja is proud of his son

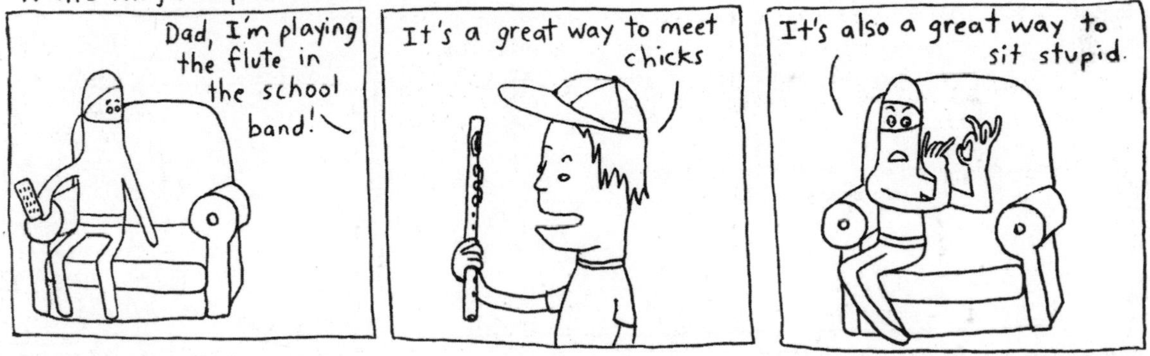
Dad, I'm playing the flute in the school band!
It's a great way to meet chicks
It's also a great way to sit stupid.

White Ninja eats lunch at work

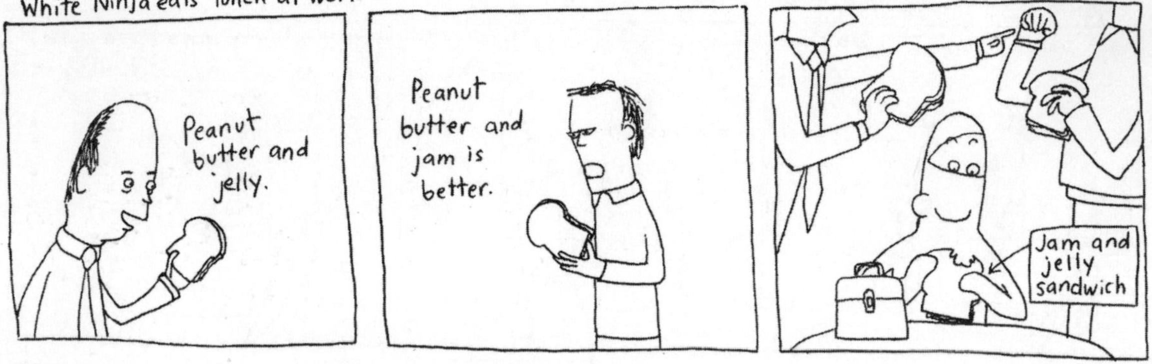
Peanut butter and jelly.
Peanut butter and jam is better.
Jam and jelly sandwich

White Ninja boards a pirate vessel

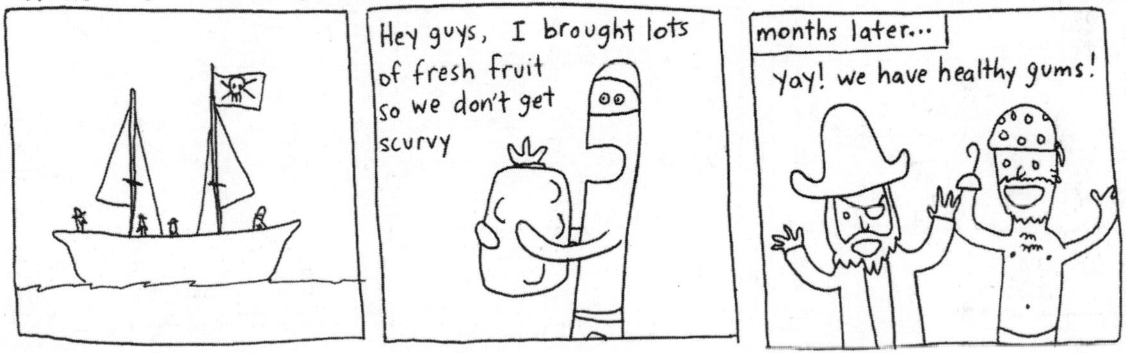
Hey guys, I brought lots of fresh fruit so we don't get scurvy
months later...
Yay! we have healthy gums!

White Ninja plays floor hockey

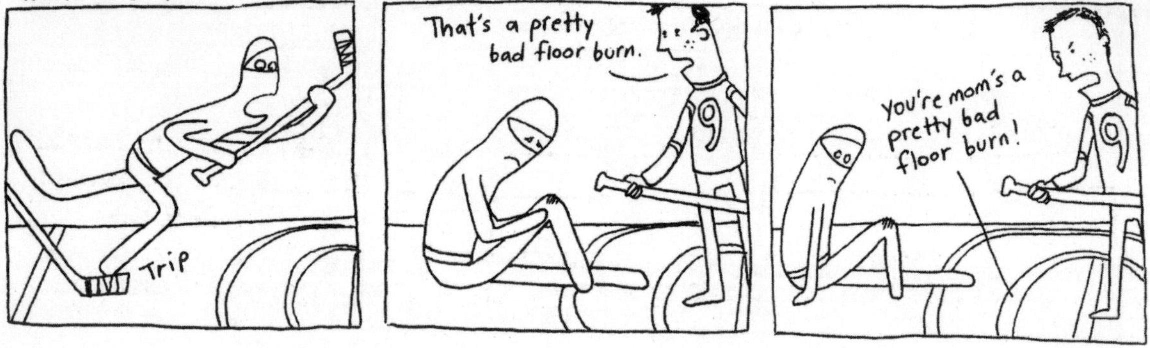
Trip
That's a pretty bad floor burn.
You're mom's a pretty bad floor burn!

White Ninja in the sun

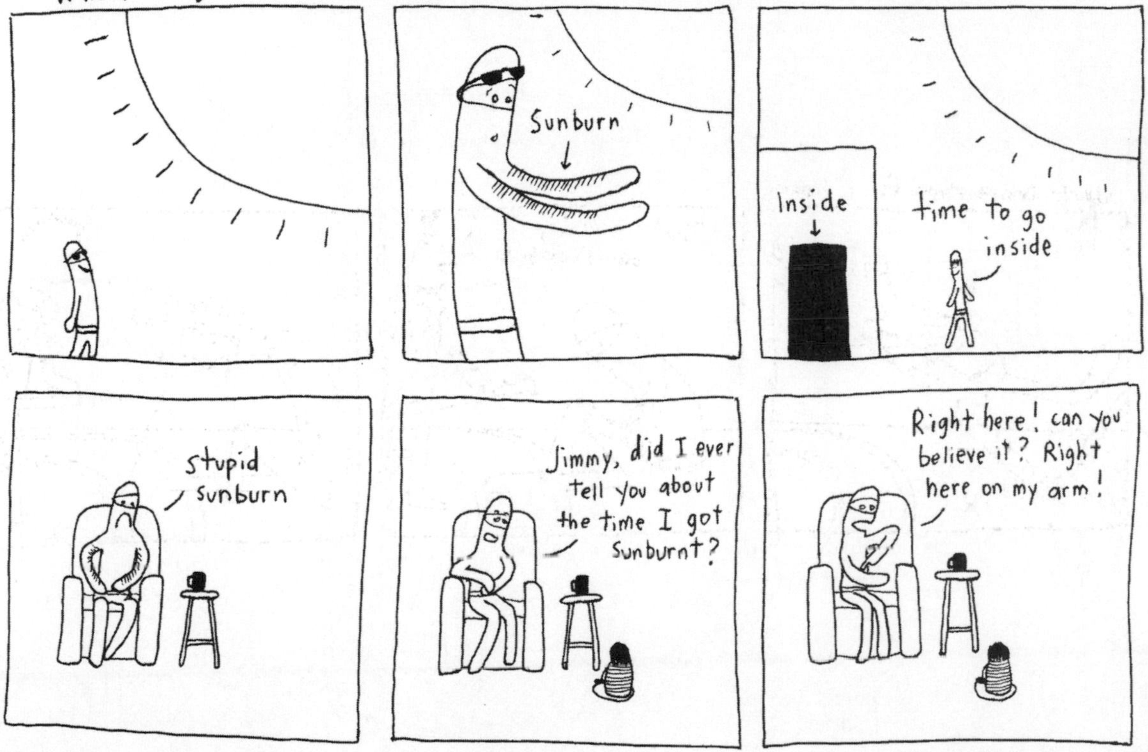
Sunburn
Inside
time to go inside
stupid sunburn
Jimmy, did I ever tell you about the time I got Sunburnt?
Right here! can you believe it? Right here on my arm!

ORINGINAL WHITE NINJA SKETCHES

In the initial development of White Ninja, we drew up a number of versions of the character before we got it just right. Here are a few of the sketches that didn't make the cut for one reason or another

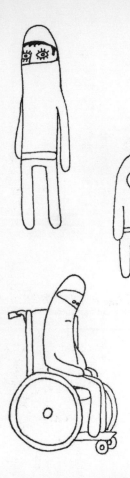

THE ORIGIN OF WHITE NINJA

Like every great comic book super hero, White Ninja has a fascinating story about how he attained his super-human powers. In fact, White Ninja has many stories. Over the past seven years, Kent and I have been questioned repeatedly about the origin of White Ninja. Though many inquirers may have been wondering about the development of the character from a concept to a comic, Kent and I always chose to ignore any intimations that might lead us down that road and instead gave a detailed history of White Ninja's life before becoming a comic book super hero. In our attempts to make an exciting, unique story for the interviewer, however, the origin story tended to change (in small details) from week to week. Allow us to share with you a few examples of origin stories, and you will see what has irked comic book historians and White Ninja enthusiasts for years.

Origin story #1
This origin story was given in our very first interview ever for our hometown University Newspaper. When asked to explain the origin of White Ninja, having never before thought about such a stupid question, we managed to pull this gem off the top of our heads:

Scott: *He was the son of a wealthy business tycoon.*
Kent: *From the future!*
Scott: *Yah, and he escaped to the present through a time portal in his linen closet.*
Kent: *To start a rock and roll band.*
Scott: *But then his band was killed.*
Kent: *By Aslan!!!*
Scott: *Then he spent the next five years trying to avenge the death of his rock band.*
Kent: *But he hit his head and got amnesia.*
Scott: *So he wandered the streets for a couple of weeks.*
Kent: *And then one day he fell into a vat of ooze.*

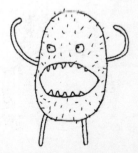

I'm a werewolf!

Scott: *And then he morphed into a half-man, half-ninja!!! And now he is a comic super-hero.*

Or so it was recorded anyways.

Origin story #2
Shortly after our first origin story was recorded, we published a White Ninja comic called "The Origin of White Ninja" – a tell-all six panel story about White Ninja's acquisition of Ninja Powers. In it – and you can see for yourself because it is included in this book – a nerdy boy with glasses (and no hands, apparently) stumbles upon a leaky canister of ooze. In this story, the boy, named Matthew, drinks the ooze and immediately morphs into a ninja. Note: he does not fall into the ooze as is explained in the previous story. This story also has the addition of a crime-fighting partner, for as soon as the morphing is complete, a pickle floats by whom White Ninja claims as his pickle sidekick. This Batman and Robin-esque relationship lasted only one comic as the pickle has never again appeared in a White Ninja strip. Still, the pickle has magically attained somewhat of a legend status and is probably the most recognized of all characters to appear in the White Ninja adventures.

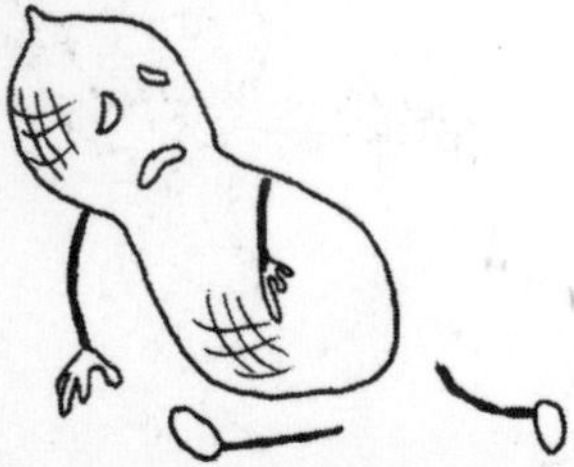

Origin story #3
To give you an example of how far the origin story of White Ninja has strayed from the earliest records, here is our latest version of White Ninja's foundation, given in an on-line interview:

Scott: *Ok, the really REAL origin of White Ninja goes like this: A young Japanese couple consummated their arranged marriage, out of obligation, resulting in a child that no one really cared too much about.*
Kent: *Years of neglect turned the child into a hideous caterpillar. But one day, the caterpillar convinced a princess to kiss him, claiming he would turn into a handsome prince. He didn't, but finally 'getting some' inspired him to change*

his glum perspective on life.
Scott: *He spun a cocoon around his body, preparing to metamorphosize into a beautiful butterfly. Sadly he suffocated and died.*
Kent: *His Japanese parents did not attend his funeral. But White Ninja did. From that moment on he vowed to honor the dead caterpillar by living each day to the maximum amount of awesome possible.*

The reason that these stories seem so incompatible is because, well, they are total lies. Lies, lies, all of it lies. But here, right now, we want to set the record straight and give the absolute honest truth about the origin of White Ninja. Everything you hear after this, even if it comes from our own mouths, is lies. So here we go, the really, totally, super-real origin of White Ninja:

Origin story #infinity
It was the Great Depression and times were hard. Life was especially difficult for a newlywed immigrant couple on the Canadian prairies, Jacob and Rebecca McDonald. They moved to the dust bowl from Ireland a mere eight months before the stock market crashed, and they and their infant twins, Matthew and Joseph, were starving – starving for food to eat.

And then, just when the starving family had lost all hope, there was a knock at the door of their quaint prairie house. It was an evil wizard who had come to kill them! A ferocious battle took place, and though the couple perished, they were able to save small Matthew and Joseph by their amazing powers of love. Their love surrounded the infants in the form of a neon force field which the wizard could not penetrate. He retreated to the dark shadows of the night, and young Matthew and Joseph were left all alone.

Days later, the unhappy infants' cries were heard by a hungry wolf. The wolf lunged at the boys, but the force field of love had not yet worn off, and the wolf was repelled with a painful zap! Intimi-

Arrrr!

dated, the wolf swore an oath of allegiance to Matthew and Joseph, vowing to protect them at all costs.

Four years later, in a moment of weakness, the wolf again tried to eat the boys. Again the wolf was repelled by an electric shock. This time, though, the shock was much less powerful than before. The twins' force field was wearing off! Surely the wolf would succeed in eating them in a future attack. They cast the wolf away from their presence and went into hiding.

Their hiding spot was a poor one – a pair of white bed sheets. Matthew got the top sheet, Joseph the fitted bottom one. As their force field diminished in strength, the boys imagined their white bed sheets to be their new force field. In reality, the sheets held no powers and were no more protective than a child's security blanket. Subconsciously they must have known this since they began training to defend themselves, just in case.

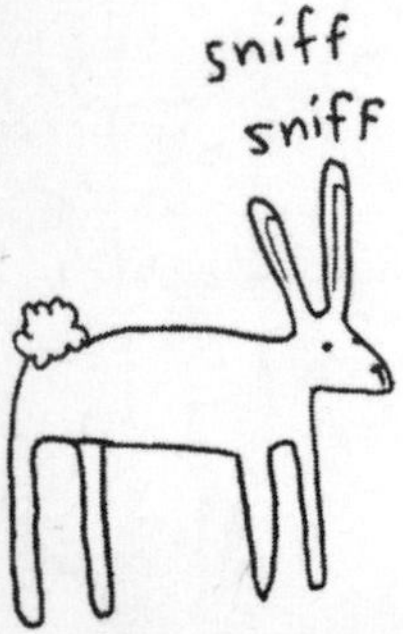
sniff
sniff

As Matthew and Joseph grew older, towns sprung up all around them, with churches and schools. Still adorning their white disguises, the boys attended school, not to learn to read and write, but to practice their surprise attacks on unsuspecting children. It was at this time that they became known as the White Ninjas.

And then Joseph died. He had a peanut allergy, and the school they often raided was not a peanut-free environment. Matthew suspected foul play from the wizard. He also suspected, based on clues and things, that the wolf that had tormented them was actually the wizard in a transformed state. Terrified, he continued hiding.

This is where the White Ninja adventures begin. Each new adventure, each daily wandering, is the result of Matthew McDonald's stealthy avoidance of his enemy, the "Wolfzard."

-Scott